New Essays on Religious Language

New Essays on Religious Language

EDITED BY
DALLAS M. HIGH

New York
OXFORD UNIVERSITY PRESS
1969

Copyright © 1969 by Oxford University Press, Inc.
Library of Congress Catalogue Card Number: 73-75116
Printed in the United States of America

Foreword

This book is designed to bring into direct company of one another essays by significant scholars who have contributed to the great and growing interest in the philosophical-theological discussion of religious language. More importantly, these essays represent the dialogue between philosophers and theologians as it has entered a second but new phase in twentieth-century discussion of religion. This new phase has moved beyond the narrow confines of verifiability and/or falsifiability theories of meaning and the cognitive-emotive compartmentalizing tactic with attending restrictures on religion. Instead, what has begun to emerge is a focus on and an exploration of actual uses of religious discourse, a constructive analysis, resulting in an enriched understanding of the life forms of religion. A primary reason for a new phase in philosophical-theological discussion is that the later works of Ludwig Wittgenstein, already philosophically efficacious, are creating an expanding but revolutionary impact on our first as well as second thoughts about religion.

Accordingly it seems important and needful to provide students in philosophy and religion, for classroom or private use, and non-specialist readers with a ready source of readings in the new phase. The volume contains two essays with extraordinary insight into Wittgenstein and his relevance to our cultural time and its theological thinking. All the other essays were selected for the reason that they show how the methods of empirical-linguistic analysis can provide fresh and clear discernment of religious issues and doctrines. Yet like most works under the tacit impact of Wittgenstein, they go on with little invocation of his name. Consequently, they have the advantage of standing on their own. All the essays can be read independently following the order presented or the reader can pick his own way through. However, for someone who is just beginning an inquiry into Wittgenstein and religious discourse, the sequence offered may be helpful.

D. M. H.

Hiram, Ohio
January 1969

Acknowledgments

Grateful acknowledgment is hereby made to the authors, editors, and publishers for permission to reprint the essays in this book.

"Ludwig Wittgenstein: Unphilosophical Notes" is reprinted from *The Artist's Journey into the Interior* (1965) (previously appearing in *Encounter*). © Copyright 1959, 1965 by Erich Heller. Reprinted by permission of Random House, Inc., Martin Secker & Warburg, and Erich Heller.

"Wittgenstein and Theology" is reprinted from *Reflection* (65, no. 4, 1968) by permission of the editor and Paul L. Holmer.

"Religion and Science: A Philosopher's Approach" is reprinted from *The Church Quarterly Review* (vol. 162, 1961) by permission of the editor and I. T. Ramsey.

"Mapping the Logic of Models in Science and Theology" is reprinted from *The Christian Scholar* (XLVI, 1963) by permission of the National Council of the Churches of Christ and Frederick Ferré.

vii

"Metaphysics and the Limits of Language" is reprinted from *Prospect for Metaphysics,* edited by Ian Ramsey (1961) by permission of George Allen & Unwin Ltd. and C. B. Daly.

"God and the 'Private-I'" is reprinted from *Philosophy and Phenomenological Research* (XX, 1960) by permission of the editor and William H. Poteat.

"Paradox in Religion" is reprinted from *Proceedings of the Aristotelian Society* (supplementary vol. XXXIII, 1959), Copyright 1959, The Aristotelian Society, by permission of the editor and I. T. Ramsey.

"Birth, Suicide, and the Doctrine of Creation: An Exploration of Analogies" is from *Mind* (LXVIII, 1959); republished in *Religion and Understanding,* edited by D. Z. Phillips (Oxford: Basil Blackwell, 1967). Reprinted here by permission of Gilbert Ryle, editor of *Mind,* and William H. Poteat.

"The Justification of Religious Belief" is reprinted from *The Philosophical Quarterly* (vol. 11, 1961) by permission of G. P. Henderson, editor, and Basil Mitchell.

"Assertion and Analogy" is from *Proceedings of the Aristotelian Society* (LX, 1959–60), Copyright 1960, The Aristotelian Society; republished in *The Philosophy of Religion* by Thomas McPherson (London: D. Van Nostrand, 1965). Reprinted here by permission of the editor of The Aristotelian Society, D. Van Nostrand Co. and Thomas McPherson.

"A Neglected Use of Theological Language" is reprinted from *Mind* (LXXII, 1963) by permission of Gilbert Ryle, editor, and Robert C. Coburn.

Contents

Introduction

The question of the meaning of religious language has presented
one of the most pervasive challenges to contemporary philosophical-theological activity. The challenge is not one that has
simply yielded a negative result—an attack on religion—although
that too has occurred, largely as a consequence of the principles,
and often "ghosts" of the principles, of "logical positivism." The
challenge has yielded and continues to yield a constructive result.
With the philosophical dominance of what is called (perhaps,
misleadingly) "linguistic analysis" in the English-speaking world
and the incomparable influence of Ludwig Wittgenstein on
philosophical activity, the widespread interest in and the constructive contributions to the linguistic puzzles of religion are
beginning to take more definite form. This fresh approach to
philosophical-theological knots may after all provide some un-
paralleled help in untying those knots. The basic ones, it is increasingly admitted in various circles, are "linguistic" and/or
"conceptual." What does the term or concept "God" mean? Do
science and religion employ incompatible conceptual models? Is
"paradox" a useful concept? Is "creation-talk" meaningful? Are

religious utterances reasonable and justifiable? These questions, and others like them today exert a good deal of pressure on religious claims, or better, because people today are prone to raise these questions of religion, pressure is exerted. The "linguistic key" is struck not merely by a vogue in philosophy but as much by the kinds of questions we ask or feel constrained to ask in a particular cultural time.

The challenge presents itself still further in a correlative way. Ludwig Wittgenstein himself was preoccupied with the concept of meaning; yet his references to the meaning of religious language, theology, etc., occupy a very small proportion of his published writings. However, ever since his later teachings (principally in *Philosophical Investigations*) have taken root as a new way of thinking, it has been largely agreed that religious uses of language are "somehow" meaningful. Since it is also true that Logical Positivists' critiques of religion and restrictive theories of meaning no longer have an essential cash-value, the way seems open and the tools appear at hand to provide a constructive and novel inroad into problems besetting religion. Yet, this in no way lessens the urgency of the question of the meaning of religious language. Once that much is seen, or even said and done, school is *not* out. What is not said is how specifically and in what circumstances religious discourse means or what jobs are performed by religious uses of language. The essayists in this volume share at least the concern to "get on" to display constructively various features of religious language as it is used and lived—all seen in a contemporary culture well mirrored and set in particular relief, perhaps, by the influence of Wittgenstein.

The distinctive feature of these essays is that rather than prescribing limits for the meaning of religious language or arguing over preconceived categories for religious talk, something done a decade or so ago, the authors, without saying so, have taken seriously the later Wittgenstein's lesson to "look and see" or as he puts it in another way "don't think, but look!" [1] This does not mean that the essayists agree in all their efforts at analysis nor

1. PI, §66.

that they should be expected to agree. Rather the essays represent an expanding new phase in philosophical-theological discussion by providing constructive analyses, looking at the uses and learning from that, instead of making philosophical-theological pronouncements of how things "must" be. The essays are not cure-alls nor should the book be taken as a programmatic set of systematic answers. The book's chief purpose is to encourage discussion, not stifle it; to stimulate further careful and sensitive investigation of the meaning of religious language, not prevent it.

The reader should not mistake that this volume is intended as some corporate forerunner to a Wittgensteinian or linguistic theology (natural or unnatural). Professor Holmer, in his essay, rightly warns against that. Moreover, this is not to say that systematic theology or full-scale philosophical theology may not again have essential cash-value; rather, it is to say that the contributors to this volume have sensed the need, which contemporary sensibility has pressed upon us, to explore positively and in piecemeal fashion what is "more fundamental" to the possibility of religion, theology, or whatever—the meaning of the language. In this sense, the volume represents an editorial effort to bring together some of the most careful and fruitful contributions of scholarship, previously scattered about and sometimes hidden, in "getting some religious concepts clear."

Although talk about some things as "more fundamental" is dangerous, and on the whole un-Wittgensteinian, talk about the piecemeal work of "getting some concepts clear" is not. Paul Engelmann, a close friend of Wittgenstein, has written of Wittgenstein, Karl Kraus, and Adolf Loos that their common concern was "their insistence on truth and clarity." He goes on to say, ". . . and this seems to me precisely what is missing in the cultural efforts of our age, and which, therefore, it should be the first and foremost task of all men dedicated to culture to emphasize in all spheres of intellectual and artistic activity." [2]

While it may be true that "clarity is not enough," it is also

2. Paul Engelmann. *Letters from Ludwig Wittgenstein, With a Memoir*, translated by L. Furtmüller (Oxford: Basil Blackwell, 1967), p. 132.

true that no colossal-size philosophizing or theologizing will en-
liven or understand the religious sense of a culture unless the
conceptual underpinnings are "unpacked" and shown to have
some common market value. Otherwise such talk may, after all,
be gibberish or, at least, systematized and invented jargon. Very
often the breakdown in belief, including religious belief, can be
traced to a breakdown or credit-rating decline or simple disregard
of the concepts ever before us. This tracer is one that leads directly to a serious and careful look at the language and its meaning and may call for a changed mode of thought and life. Matters
so deep and complex as these are not settled by individual invention and salesmanship of new vocabularies, for very often, too,
the changed mode of thought and life concerning language has
not been invoked. In a place which, at first glance, appears as an
unlikely source of stimulation about religious problems, Wittgenstein wrote in *The Remarks on the Foundations of Mathematics*
that "The sickness of a time is cured by an alternation in the
mode of life of human beings, and it was possible for the sickness
of philosophical problems to get cured only through a changed
mode of thought and of life, not through a medicine invented by
an individual." [3] We can, I believe, without injury to the original statement, substitute the words "religious problems" for
"philosophical problems."

The sustained attacks on what F. Waismann has called the
"clarity neurosis" are, I think, correct. Clarity that seeks to reduce
logic and meaning to deduction and induction (verification or
falsification) or to mathematics and science is not what I or the
contributors ever had in mind. Nor do we have in mind induce-
ment of clarity by invention of new but lifeless forms. Rather it
is clarity by the appeal to the diversity of the ways in which
things are and can be said and by patient probing into the roots
of religious discourse.

Much of philosophy and analysis of religious discourse following the later Wittgenstein has been concerned to show how and
in what situations speech does its job. Religious assertions, as

3. P. 57e.

claimed by I. T. Ramsey in another place, "are *not* strangled in the grip of some tight, deductive metaphysics, nor made to conform to a supposed ideal of descriptive picture assertions." [4] The essays in this volume represent an effort of making use not only of an "opened-up" empirical analysis and its "open-textured" account of language (and its logic) but seek the "depth grammar" in which one "meets" the meaning as distinguished from the "surface grammar" of words and sentences "taken in by the ear." This again is Wittgenstein's distinction. This distinction, of course, calls attention to two equally possible dangers: (1) we can listen to a sequence of apparent words only to discover that what we heard is meaningless or (2) declare what we hear as meaningless without attending to its meaning in the meeting of its depth grammar. Theological "thinking" and system building as well as philosophical critiques of religion have not escaped either of these dangers. And often much of this can be attributed to mistakes about language and meaning, especially where religious sensibility appears. It is as if we have had a lot of "thinking" going on about religion but very little "looking and seeing." "The confusions which occupy us arise when language is like an engine idling, not when it is doing work." [5]

I am not so insular as to suppose that there are no other constructive contributions to the discernment of religion. Indeed, contributors to this volume make use of Existentialists, Phenomenologists, Thomists, and others. Yet, if piecemeal operations at conceptual elucidation, whatever their philosophical-theological brand names, teach the writer and the reader more humility and induce profound frustration over claims for final success, so much the better.   D. M. H.

4. "Contemporary Philosophy and the Christian Faith," *Religious Studies*, I (1965), p. 61.
5. PI, §132.

New Essays on Religious Language

I

Wittgenstein:
Unphilosophical Notes[1]

ERICH HELLER

1

What manner of man was Ludwig Wittgenstein? One answer which is easy to come by, vague, large, and true, is: a man of rarest genius. Of all words that defy definition—which may be, simply, all words—genius is the most defiant. But how else de-

1. The original occasion of this essay was the appearance of Ludwig Wittgenstein's *The Blue and Brown Books* (Oxford: Basil Blackwell, 1958; New York: Harper, 1958), and Norman Malcolm's *Ludwig Wittgenstein, A Memoir,* with a biographical sketch by Georg Henrik von Wright (London and New York: Oxford University Press, 1958). *The Blue and Brown Books,* prefaced by Mr. Rush Rhees, were dictated by Wittgenstein to some of his pupils between 1933 and 1935. They are indispensable for any study of the intellectual history that led, within the lifetime of the mature generation of Anglo-Saxon philosophers, to a change in philosophical opinion—a break outwardly less dramatic but probably more significant than that which occurred when Bertrand Russell and G. E. Moore banished the very much post-Hegelian metaphysics of F. H. Bradley and Bernard Bosanquet from the academic scene; and it was the most strange characteristic of that new "revolution" that it was the same man, Ludwig Wittgenstein, who both perfected the "old system" (in the *Tractatus Logico-Philosophicus,* finished by 1918, first published in 1921) *and* initiated its destruction (with *Philosophical Investigations,* completed by 1949, post-

3

scribe a man who was a logician of the first order; a writer of
German prose abundant in intellectual passion and disciplined
clarity (perhaps only talent is needed for writing such prose in
any other language, but certainly genius for writing it in German); an engineer of great promise and some achievement; the
achitect of a modern mansion; a gifted sculptor; a musician who
very probably would have become, had he chosen this career, a
remarkable conductor; a hermit capable of enduring for long
periods the utmost rigors of mind and loneliness; a rich man
who chose poverty; a Cambridge professor who thought and
taught but neither lectured nor dined?

He was also an Austrian who conquered British philosophy;
but this, as befits Austrian conquests, was due to a misunderstanding. At least he himself believed that it was so. When the
pages of the journal *Mind* were filled with variations on his
philosophical themes, he praised a certain American magazine
of detective stories, and wondered how, with the offer of such
reading matter, "anyone can read *Mind* with all its impotence
and bankruptcy";[2] and when his influence at Oxford was at its
height, he referred to the place as "a philosophical desert" and
as "the influenza area." [3] These were ironical exaggerations, but
undoubtedly serious expressions of Wittgenstein's discontent.

Why should he have been so displeased with the role his
thought played in contemporary philosophical circles? What was
the source of his suspicion that a misunderstanding was viciously
at work in the proliferation of his views and methods throughout
the departments of philosophy? And if it was a misunderstanding, was it avoidable? These questions raise a bigger one: What
is the nature of philosophical opinion?

There are philosophies which, however difficult they may be,

---

humously published in 1953). Mr. Malcolm's *Memoir,* greatly assisted by Professor Wright's informative sketch, is a noble biographical document, the more
moving by virtue of its simplicity and affectionate restraint. It is from this book
that the biographical references of my notes are taken.
2. Norman Malcolm, *Ludwig Wittgenstein, A Memoir* (London and New
York, 1958), p. 35 f.
3. *Ibid.,* p. 98.

are in principle easy to teach and to learn. Of course, not everyone can teach or learn philosophy—any more than higher mathematics; but the philosophies of certain philosophers have this
in common with higher mathematics: they present the simple
alternative of being either understood or not understood. It is,
in the last analysis, impossible to *mis*understand them. This is
true of Aristotle, or St. Thomas Aquinas, or Descartes, or Locke,
or Kant. Such philosophies are like mountains: you climb to
their tops or you give up; or like weights: you lift them or they
are too heavy for you. In either case you will know what has
happened and "where you are." But this is not so with the
thought of Plato, or St. Augustine, or Pascal, or Kierkegaard,
or Nietzsche. Their philosophies are like human faces on the
features of which are inscribed, disquietingly, the destinies of
souls; or like cities rich in history. "Do you understand Kant?"
is like asking "Have you been to the summit of Mont Blanc?"
The answer is *yes* or *no*. "Do you understand Nietzsche?" is like
asking "Do you know Rome?" The answer is simple only if you
have never been there. The trouble with Wittgenstein's thinking
is that it sometimes looks like Descartes': you believe you can
learn it as you learn logic or mathematics; but it almost always
is more like Pascal's: you may be quite sure you cannot. For to
understand it on its own level is as much a matter of imagination
and character as it is one of "thinking." Its temperature is of its
essence, in its passion lies its seriousness, the rhythm of the sentences that express it is as telling as is that which they tell, and
sometimes a semicolon marks the frontier between a thought and
a triviality. How can this be? Are we speaking of an artist or a
philosopher? We are speaking of Ludwig Wittgenstein. *"Der
Philosoph behandelt eine Frage; wie eine Krankheit."* It is a
profound semicolon, and not even a philosophically initiated
translator could save the profundity: "The philosopher's treatment of a question is like the treatment of an illness" is, by
comparison, a flat *aperçu*.[4]

4. Ludwig Wittgenstein, *Philosophical Investigations*, tr. by G. E. M. Anscombe (Oxford, 1953), §255.

Philosophy, for Wittgenstein, was not a profession; it was a consuming passion; and not just "a" passion, but the only possible form of his existence: the thought of losing his gift for philosophy made him feel suicidal. He could not but have contempt for philosophers who "did" philosophy and, having done it, thought of other things: money, lists of publications, academic advancements, university intrigues, love affairs, or the Athenaeum—and thought of these things in a manner which showed even more clearly than the products of their philosophical thought that they had philosophized with much less than their whole person. Wittgenstein had no difficulty in detecting in their style of thinking, debating, or writing the corruption of the divided life, the painless jugglery with words and meanings, the shallow flirtation with depth, and the ear deaf to the command of authenticity. Thinking for him was as much a moral as an intellectual concern. In this lay his affinity with Otto Weininger, for whom he had great respect. The sight of a thought that was detachable from a man filled him with loathing and with an anger very much like that with which Rilke in the Fourth of the *Duino Elegies* denounced, through the image of the dancer, the cursed non-identity between performer and performance:

> . . . How gracefully he moves!
> And yet he is disguised, a dressed-up philistine,
> Who will come home soon, entering through the kitchen.
> I cannot bear these masks, half-filled with life.

Had Wittgenstein ever cared to write about himself, this apparently most "intellectual" of philosophers might have said:

> I have at all times thought with my whole body and my whole life. I do not know what purely intellectual problems are. . . . You know these things by way of thinking, yet your thought is not your experience by the reverberation of the experience of others; as your room trembles when a carriage passes. I am sitting in that carriage, and often am the carriage itself.

This, however, was written by Nietzsche.[5] And it was Nietzsche whom he resembled in many other ways: in his homelessness, his restless wanderings, his perpetual search for the exactly right conditions in which to work, his loneliness, his asceticism, his need for affection and his shyness in giving it, his intellectual extremism which drove thought to the border of insanity, the elasticity of his style, and (as we shall see) in one philosophically most important respect. Like Nietzsche, then, he knew that philosophical opinion was not merely a matter of logically demonstrable right or wrong. This most rigorous logician was convinced that it was above all a matter of authenticity—and thus, in a sense, not at all of negotiable opinions. What assumed with him so often the semblance of intolerable intellectual pride, was the demand, which he made upon himself still more than upon others, that all utterances should be absolutely authentic. The question was not only "Is this opinion right or wrong?" but also "Is this or that person *entitled* to this or that opinion?" At times this lent to his manner of debating the harsh tone of the Old Testament prophets: he would suddenly be seized by an uncontrollable desire to mete out intellectual punishment. He reacted to errors of judgment as if they were sins of the heart, and violently rejected opinions, which in themselves—if this distinction were possible—might have been harmless enough or even "correct," and rejected them because they were untrue in the self that uttered them: they lacked the sanction of the moral and intellectual pain suffered on behalf of truth.

Wittgenstein once said, using a comparison with swimming, that "just as one's body has a natural tendency towards the surface and one has to make an exertion to get to the bottom— so it is with thinking." And in talking about the stature of a philosopher, he remarked "that the measure of a man's greatness would be in terms of what his work *cost* him." [6] This is Kantian

5. Nietzsche, *Gesammelte Werke*, Musarion-Ausgabe (Munich, 1926–29), Vol. XXI, p. 81.
6. Malcolm, *op. cit.*, p. 55.

ethics applied to the realm of thought: true moral goodness was
for Kant a victory over natural inclination, the costlier the better. By character and insight, Nietzsche too was such a Kantian
moralist of the intellectual life. Yet he, who was never more
ingenious than in producing the devastating argument against
himself, could also say this:

> The labor involved in climbing a mountain is no measure of its
> height. But where knowledge is concerned, it is to be different;
> at least this is what we are told by some who consider themselves
> initiates: the effort which a truth costs, is to decide its value! This
> crazy morality is founded upon the idea that "truths" are like the
> installations in a Swedish gymnasium, designed to tire one out—a
> morality of the mind's athletics and gymnastic displays.[7]

Perhaps it is a pity that Wittgenstein was not the man to say
also things of this kind. It might have lightened the burden of
earnest irritability carried by many a contemporary philosophical
debate.

2

The appreciation of Wittgenstein as a person and thinker (and
how misleading is this "and"!) is bedeviled by a persistent optical
delusion: the high moral pathos of his life (in which his "legend"
has already taken firm roots) *seems* at first glance to be uncon-
nected with the drift and trend, the content and method of his
philosophical thought. Every page of Pascal, or Kierkegaard, or
Nietzsche, at once conveys, however impersonal may be the
subject matter, a sense of urgent personal involvement; but it is
possible for anyone but the most sensitively predisposed to read
many pages of Wittgenstein's without suspecting that the ruth-
less precision and often apparently eccentric virtuosity of this
thinking, which has neither models nor parallels in the history
of philosophy, is anything but the result of the utmost intellectual detachment. Its first emotional effect upon the reader

7. Nietzsche, *op. cit.*, Vol. IX, p. 183.

may well be one of exasperation or melancholia—the effect which Robert Musil (not for nothing an Austrian contemporary of Wittgenstein's) ascribes in *The Man without Qualities* to a certain thinker:

> He had drawn the curtains and worked in the subdued light of his room like an acrobat who, in an only half-illuminated circus tent and before the public is admitted, shows to a select audience of experts his latest break-neck leaps.[8]

Yet Wittgenstein's work is none the less suffused with authentic pathos, and it will one day be seen as an integral part of the tragically self-destructive design of European thought.

If by some miracle both European history and thought continue, then the future historians of thought will be not a little puzzled by Wittgenstein. For nothing could be less predictable than that a work which more deeply than any other affected contemporary Anglo-Saxon philosophy, Wittgenstein's *Philosophical Investigations,* should have as its motto a sentence from the classical comic playwright of Austria, Nestroy, or that its philosophical author should have experienced a kind of religious awakening thanks to a performance of *Die Kreuzelscheiber* by Anzengruber, a considerably lesser Austrian dramatist.[9] However, these will be minor surprises, less important, certainly, than the discovery of the affinities between Wittgenstein's manner of thinking and writing and that of the great eighteenth-century German aphorist Lichtenberg.[10] But of greater weight still would be the realization that the name of Wittgenstein marks the historical point at which, most unexpectedly, the cool analytical intellect of British philosophy meets with those passions of mind and imagination which we associate first with Nietzsche and then, in manifold crystallizations, with such Aus-

8. Robert Musil, *Der Mann ohne Eigenschaften* (Hamburg, 1952), p. 114.
9. Malcolm, *op. cit.,* p. 70.
10. Professor Wright was, to my knowledge, the first to draw attention to this; a fuller discussion of this intellectual kinship can be found in J. P. Stern's book on Lichtenberg, *A Doctrine of Scattered Occasions* (Bloomington, Ind., 1959).

trians as Otto Weininger, Adolf Loos, Karl Kraus, Franz Kafka, and Robert Musil.

Like Otto Weininger, Wittgenstein believed in the surpassing ethical significance of thinking, and in thought as both a deeply personal and almost religiously supra-personal dedication; with Adolf Loos he shared the rejection of all ornamental comforts and decorative relaxations of the mind, and the concentration on the purest lines of intellectual architecture; with Karl Kraus, he had in common the conviction that there is an inescapable bond between the forms of living, thinking, feeling, and the forms of language (Wittgenstein's dictum "Ethics and aesthetics are one and the same" [11] may serve as a perfect characterization of Karl Kraus's artistic *credo*). As far as Kafka and Musil are concerned, a comparison between their styles of writing (and therefore their modes of perception) and Wittgenstein's would certainly be as fruitful as that between his and Lichtenberg's, and the more revealing because there can be no question of influence beyond the anonymous and peculiarly Austrian dispensations of the *Zeitgeist*. There even is a family resemblance between the logical structures, motives, and intentions of Wittgenstein's *Tractatus* and those of Schönberg's musical theory: for Schönberg too is guided by the conviction that the "language" of his medium, music, has to be raised to that level of logical necessity which would eliminate all subjective accidents. It is in such a constellation of minds that Wittgenstein is truly at home, whereas in the history of British philosophy he may merely "hold an important position." This, at least, is one way of accounting for the discomforts he suffered from the British philosophical climate and from a philosophical company which so deceptively appeared to consist largely of his own disciples.

What are the motives and intentions behind Wittgenstein's philosophy? What is, beyond and above its own philosophical declarations, the historical meaning of that "revolution" which changed the face of Anglo-Saxon philosophy in the course of

11. Ludwig Wittgenstein, *Tractatus Logico-Philosophicus,* tr. by D. F. Pears and B. F. McGuiness (London and New York, 1961), §6.421.

Wittgenstein's gradual modification and final abandonment of some of the principles laid down in his *Tractatus Logico-Philosophicus?*

In his book *My Philosophical Development*, Bertrand Russell engages in a bitter attack on the author of *Philosophical Investigations*, a broadside which, if it is not damaging, is yet illuminating. The man who was one of the first to recognize Wittgenstein's *Tractatus* as a work of philosophical genius (even if he interpreted it too exclusively as the culmination of his own doctrine of Logical Atomism) says of the *Philosophical Investigations* that he has not found in it "anything interesting"—"I cannot understand why a whole school finds important wisdom in its pages." He abhors the suggestion, which he believes to be implied in Wittgenstein's later work, "that the world of language can be quite divorced from the world of fact," and suspects that such a view must render philosophical activity trivial ("at best, a slight help to lexicographers, and at worst, an idle tea-table amusement") by insidiously giving to "language an untrammelled freedom which it has never hitherto enjoyed." He disagrees most emphatically with the disciples of Wittgenstein when they tend to regard "as an outdated folly the desire to understand the world"—a desire, it would seem, very different from their own to understand the workings of language. If incomprehension can ever be significant, then this can be said of Lord Russell's estimate of *Philosophical Investigations*. For he certainly knew what he attacked when once upon a time he victoriously fought the domineering influence of Bradley's Idealism, and also knew what he welcomed when Wittgenstein first sent him the *Tractatus;* but the later Wittgenstein is to him, he confesses, "completely unintelligible." [12] This might clearly show which of the two recent changes in philosophical outlook—Russell's dislodging of Bradley, or Wittgenstein's superseding of Wittgenstein—is the more profound.

Bertrand Russell was at ease intellectually with Bradley as

12. Bertrand Russell, *My Philosophical Development* (New York, 1959), p. 216 ff.

well as with the Wittgenstein of the *Tractatus* because both
were, like himself, philosophers thinking *within* the metaphysical
tradition of European philosophy. This goes without saying in
the case of Bradley; in the case of the *Tractatus* it may sound
alarming. But it is true to say that in its own way—and an exceedingly subtle way it is!—the *Tractatus* participates in a pre-
Kantian metaphysical faith: there is, in however small an area
of human understanding, a pre-established correspondence between the cognitive faculties of man and the nature of the world.
In other words: what man thinks and feels—and therefore *says*
—about the world, has a chance of being true in a *metaphysical*
sense. At a time when philosophers were still on intimate terms
with God, this metaphysical faith found its luminously comprehensive dogma: God is no deceiver; He has created the world
and planted in man the desire to understand it; He has also
endowed him with perception and rationality, faculties which
man cannot help taking for the servants of this desire. Could it
have been God's intention to frustrate it from the outset by
giving man nothing but the *illusion* of understanding? Is the
creature made in His own image to be the eternal dupe of the
universe? The simple faith that this cannot be lies at the heart
of the complex metaphysical systems of the seventeenth century
that have profoundly affected European thought. This faith is
discernible behind the scholastic apparatus of Leibniz's Pre-established Harmony and Descartes' *Cogito ergo sum,* those grandiose
attempts to demonstrate logically the integral accord between
human thought and the true nature of Being. And it is the same
faith in reason's power to "comprehend the wondrous architecture of the world," which inspires the great cosmic discoveries
of that age; or as Kepler puts it at the end of the ninth chapter
of the fifth book of his *Harmonices mundi:* "Thanks be unto
you, my Lord Creator! . . . To those men who will read my
demonstrations, I have revealed the glory of your creation. . . ."

It is a far cry from Descartes to Wittgenstein's *Tractatus;* and
yet there is an angle of vision from which the *Tractatus* looks like
a last victory of the traditional metaphysical faith: a Pyrrhic vic-

tory. Compared to the vast dominions that metaphysical thought had claimed in the past for its settlements of truth, there is now hardly more than a little province of "significant" speech in a vast area of silence. But within this catastrophically narrowed space, man can still confidently assert some truths about the world, utter words whose meanings are not imprisoned within themselves, and speak sentences whose significance is not wholly embedded within the flux of linguistic commerce and convention. No, there are still words and sentences which are true in an absolute sense, reflect what "is the case" and *picture Reality*. Of course, this ideal correspondence between picture and model, thought and world, language and reality, is not easily attained. Its condition is the observance of the strictest logical rules. Thus it will hardly ever occur in the actuality of human speech. Yet it is realized, nevertheless, in the *essence* of language: indeed, it is its *real meaning*. True, in order to speak "essentially" and "significantly," we must leave much unsaid; but once we respond to the "atomic facts"—the bricks of the intelligible world—with "atomic propositions" or their "truth-functional compounds"— concepts which Wittgenstein, considerably modifying and refining them, took over from Russell—our speech, and therefore our thought, is perfectly attuned to Reality: for "Logic is not a body of doctrine, but a mirror-image of the world." [13] And although Wittgenstein courageously insisted that in proposing this relationship between language and fact he himself broke the law governing meaningful propositions,[14] his *Tractatus* is yet built upon a site salvaged from the metaphysical estate of the Pre-established Harmony. The ground, however, was soon to give; and as it gave, Bertrand Russell, for one, saw nothing but total collapse. And it is true to say that from the *Blue Book* onward Wittgenstein immersed himself in a philosophical enterprise which, if set up against the traditional hopes of philosophers, looks desperate indeed. For its intention is to cure

13. *Tractatus*, §6.13.
14. *Ibid.*, §6.54.

philosophers of a sickness the name of which may well be—
philosophy. His aphorism of the philosopher's treating questions
as if they were patients has more than epigrammatic relevance.

3

The break between *Tratactus* and *Philosophical Investigations*
is of the same kind as that between Nietzsche's *The Birth of
Tragedy* (1871) and his *Human, All-too-Human* (1879). In both
cases it was brought about by the abnegation of metaphysics,
the loss of faith in any pre-established correspondence between,
on the one hand, the logic of our thought and language, and,
on the other hand, the "logic" of Reality. In the course of those
eight years stretching from *The Birth of Tragedy* to *Human,
All-too-Human,* Nietzsche came to believe that he had freed himself of this "philosophical prejudice"—which he diagnosed as
the prejudice vitiating the whole history of thought—by turning
(to use Wittgenstein's obviously autobiographical words from
Investigations) his "whole examination round. (One might say:
the axis of reference of our examination must be rotated, but
about the fixed point of our real need.)" [15] It is no exaggeration
to say that Nietzsche could have written this. Indeed, it might
serve as an exact description of what he claimed as his great
achievement: to have turned our whole horizon 180 degrees
around the point of our "real need," which was radically different from that

> which had been satisfied in forming the . . . [traditional] catego-
> ries of thought; namely the need not to "recognize" but to subsume,
> to schematize, and, for the sake of communication and calcula-
> tion, to manipulate and fabricate similarities and samenesses. . . .
> No, this was not the work of a pre-existent "Idea"; it happened
> under the persuasion of usefulness: it was profitable to coarsen
> and level down things; for only then were they calculable and
> comfortable. . . . Our categories are "truths" only in so far as
> they make life possible for us: Euclidean space is also such a

15. *Investigations,* §108.

purposeful "truth." . . . The inner compulsion not to contradict these "truths," the instinct to reach our kind of useful conclusions is inbred in us, we almost *are* this instinct. But how naive to take this as proof of a "truth *per se*." Our inability to contradict proves impotence and not "truth." [16]

It was Nietzsche's declared intention not to follow any longer this "instinct" and thus to cure the philosophical sickness of centuries, just as it was Wittgenstein's to "solve the philosophical problems" by recognizing their source in "the functioning of our language"—"*in spite* of an instinct to misunderstand it." [17] For Nietzsche the truth about man was that he must live without Truth. This was the "real need." The creature that would satisfy it Nietzsche called Superman—and never mind the offensive word, poetically begotten in a great mind by a Darwinian age. In his letters he often used less grandiose, if not less ambitious, words in speaking of his philosophical goal, words to the effect that "he felt as though he were writing for people who would think in a quite different way, breathe a different air of life from that of present-day men: for people of a different culture. . . ." But this is reported by Professor von Wright as a saying of Wittgenstein's.[18]

It would of course be absurd to represent Wittgenstein as a latter-day Nietzsche, and the comparison is certainly not meant to "manipulate and fabricate similarities and samenesses." The two philosophers could hardly be more different in the scope and object, the approach and humor, the key and tempo of their thought; and yet they have in common something which is of the greatest importance: the creative distrust of *all* those categorical certainties that, as if they were an inherited anatomy, have been allowed to determine the body of traditional thought. Nietzsche and Wittgenstein share a genius for directing doubt into the most unsuspected hiding places of error and fallacy:

16. Nietzsche, *op. cit.*, Vol. XIX, p. 27 f.
17. *Investigations*, §109.
18. Malcolm, *op. cit.*, p. 2.

namely where, as Wittgenstein puts it, "everything lies open to view," where everything is simple and familiar, where, day in day out, man takes things for granted—until suddenly one day the fact that he has habitually ignored the most important aspects of things, strikes him as the "most striking and most powerful." [19] This may happen on the day when suspicion reaches the notion of "meaning," that is, the idea, held however vaguely, that through some kind of cosmic arrangement, made by God, or logic, or the spirit of language, a definite meaning had become attached to the world, to life, to facts, or to words. When Nietzsche discovered the "death of God," the universe of meanings collapsed—everything, that is, that was founded upon the transcendent faith, or was leaning against it, or was intertwined with it: in fact, *everything*, as Nietzsche believed; and henceforward everything was in need of re-valuation.

With Wittgenstein the decisive change of vision, which occurred between *Tractatus* and *Investigations*, seemed centered upon an event less dramatic than the death of God; namely, the vanishing of the belief in a categorical logic of language, and hence in a categorically harmonious relationship between words and world. But the event behind the event was of the same magnitude as the Nietzchean demise of the divinity; it entailed the same crisis of metaphysical confidence that, through the metaphysical audacity of certain German and French thinkers, led to the great perversion of metaphysics: the loss of the belief in any metaphysically dependable dealings with Reality was made up by the notion that a Pre-established Absurdity determined the relationship between the intellectual constitution of man and the true constitution of the world. Nietzsche was the first to conceive of such a possibility, and after him European art and literature excelled in showing man and world laboring under the tragic, or melancholy, or grotesque, or hilarious compulsion to make nonsense of one another. And there is a historical sense in which the two extremes of contemporary philosophizing,

19. *Investigations*, §§126, 129.

Heidegger's tortuous metaphysical probings into language and Wittgenstein's absorption in language-games (and some of the examples he chooses reveal an almost Thurber-like talent for absurd and grotesque inventions) can be seen as two aspects of the same intention: to track down to their source in language, and there to correct, the absurdities resulting from the human endeavor to speak the truth. It is an intention which was by no means alien to Nietzsche. Certainly his universal suspicion did not spare language, and some of his utterances on the subject are virtually indistinguishable from those of Wittgenstein.

Very early in his philosophical life, Nietzsche knew that he "who finds language interesting in itself has a mind different from him who only regards it as a medium of thought," and he left no doubt which of the two he regarded as the more *philosophical* mind: "Language is something all-too-familiar to us; therefore it needs a philosopher to be struck by it." [20] This is Nietzsche's way of saying what Wittgenstein said when he discovered that "the most important aspects of things are hidden from us by virtue of their simplicity and familiarity." [21] And when Nietzsche said that "the philosopher is caught in the net of *language*," [22] he meant much the same as Wittgenstein when, referring to his own *Tractatus,* he wrote: "A *picture* held us captive. And we could not get outside it, for it lay in our language and language seemed to repeat it to us inexorably." [23] Indeed, Nietzsche sounds as if he had in mind the metaphysics of the *Tractatus* when he speaks of the conclusion of a primitive metaphysical peace which once upon a time fixed "what henceforward is to be called truth": "A universally valid and compelling notation of facts is invented and the legislation of language fixes the principal rules for truth." This would seem to come close to what Wittgenstein attempted in the *Tractatus:* "To give the essence of a proposition means to give the essence of all descrip-

20. Nietzsche, *op. cit.,* Vol. II, p. 29.
21. *Investigations,* §129.
22. Nietzsche, *op. cit.,* Vol. VI, p. 45.
23. *Investigations,* §115.

tion, and thus the essence of the world." [24] *But*, Nietzsche asked, "is language the adequate expression for all realities?" [25] And soon he was to be quite sure that it was not. On the contrary, the grammatical and syntactical order of language, its subjects, predicates, objects, causal and conditional connections, were "the petrified fallacies of reason" which continued to exercise their "seductive spell" upon our intelligence.[26]

> Philosophy is a battle against the bewitchment of our intelligence by means of language.

This last aphorism is by Wittgenstein;[27] but it would be impossible to guess where Nietzsche ends and Wittgenstein begins.

4

One of Wittgenstein's aphorisms runs as follows:

> Philosophy results in the discovery of one or another piece of simple nonsense, and in bruises which the understanding has suffered by bumping its head against the limits of language. They, the bruises, make us see the value of that discovery.[28]

And in one of the jottings of his late years Nietzsche wrote under the heading "Fundamental solution":

> Language is founded upon the most naive prejudices. . . . We read contradictions and problems into everything because we *think only* within the forms of language. . . . *We have to cease to think if we refuse to do it in the prisonhouse of language;* for we cannot reach further than the doubt which asks whether the limit we see is really a limit. . . . *All rational thought is interpretation in accordance with a scheme which we cannot throw off.*[29]

24. *Tractatus*, §5.4711.
25. Nietzsche, *op. cit.*, Vol. VI, p. 78.
26. *Ibid.*, Vol. XV, p. 304 f.
27. *Investigations*, §109.
28. *Ibid.*, §119. This is one of Karl Kraus's aphorisms on language: "If I cannot get further, this is because I have banged my head against the wall of language. Then, with my head bleeding, I withdraw. And want to go on." (*Beim Wort genommen* [Munich, 1955], 326.)
29. Nietzsche, *op. cit.*, Vol. XIX, p. 34.

Yet neither Nietzsche nor Wittgenstein "ceased to think." In Nietzsche's thought, the persistent misgiving that the established conventions of philosophical language did not cater for our "real" intellectual needs was only one facet of his central thesis: With the death of God, with the silencing of that Word which was at the beginning, *all* certainties of faith, belief, metaphysics, morality, and knowledge had come to an end, and henceforward man was under the terrible compulsion of absolute freedom. His choice was that of either creating, with the surpassing creativity of the Creator, his own world, or of spiritually perishing. For the world *as it is* has neither meaning nor value. Meaning and value must be *given* to it: by God or by man himself. If God is dead and man fails, then nothing in this world has any value and our own language deceives us with all its ancient intimations of higher meanings.

> In the world everything is as it is, and everything happens as it does happen: *in* it no value exists—and if it did, it would have no value.

These sentences from Wittgenstein's *Tractatus*[30] might have been invented by Nietzsche—and many like these were in fact invented by him in *The Will to Power*, where, as an inspired actor, indeed as an initiate, he defined the mind of European nihilism which he so urgently desired to overcome.

Wittgenstein's *Investigations* would be as trivial as Bertrand Russell thinks they are, were they not, in their infinite intellectual patience, informed with a sense of urgency not altogether unlike that which inspired Nietzsche's prophetic impetuosity. To bring some light into "the darkness of this time"—this was the hesitant hope of the author of *Philosophical Investigations*. This hope, like all true hope, was founded upon the paradox of faith: faith despite doubt. It was, for Wittgenstein, a faith in language; and language remained all-important for him even after it had ceased to be the mirror of Reality. Having exposed all its dangers, shown how our minds are held captive by its metaphors, denounced the

30. *Tractatus*, §6.41.

witchcraft with which it assails our intelligence, he was still left with the ineradicable trust in its ultimate wisdom and its power to heal our disease.

Nothing in Wittgenstein's work is more vulnerable to further questioning than this trust; indeed, its very intellectual vulnerability confirms it as his faith. Often he speaks of language with utmost vagueness:

> When philosophers use a word—"knowledge," "being," "object," "I," "proposition," "name,"—and try to grasp the *essence* of the thing, one must always ask oneself: is the word ever actually used in this way in the language in which it has its home? [31]

One may well ask: who, with language speaking in a hundred tongues through our literatures, dialects, social classes, journals, and newspapers, establishes this actual use? Shakespeare? Donne? James Joyce? the *Oxford English Dictionary*? the College Porter? the habitual reader of *The News of the World*? And when Wittgenstein says, "What *we* do is to bring words back from their metaphysical to their everyday usage," [32] or "When I talk about language, . . . I must speak the language of every day," [33] one is struck by the homely imprecision of this program and wonders why he does not wish to bring language back to Lichtenberg's or Gottfried Keller's usage, or speak the language of Karl Kraus, which is in fact much closer to Wittgenstein's than is the speech of a Vienna or London "every day"?

Wittgenstein said:

> Philosophy may in no way interfere with the actual use of language; it can in the end only describe it. . . . It leaves everything as it is. [34]

> We must do away with all explanation, and description alone must take its place. [35]

31. *Investigations*, §116. Was it the vagueness of this which induced the translator to use "language-game" where the German has simply *"Sprache"*?
32. *Ibid.*
33. *Ibid.*, §120.
34. *Ibid.*, §124.
35. *Ibid.*, §109.

But might we not be "held captive" by a picture "actually used" in language, and can we be sure that "actual usage" will never "bewitch our intelligence"? And if it does, how are we to loosen its grip without "explaining" its nature? (And I am using "explain" here as it is "actually used.") Or is Schopenhauer, who so indignantly "interfered" with the corrupt use made of language by those who thoughtlessly speak or print it day in day out, guilty of errors of judgment *because* he wrote a prose inspired by a literary tradition which indeed he believed was being more and more betrayed by the everyday traffic in words? And what is the "everything" that philosophy "leaves as it is"? Not, surely, the manner of thinking and uttering thoughts. Many philosophers, like all great poets, have deeply affected our perception, and therefore our language, and thus have changed our world: Plato, for instance, or Descartes, or Rousseau, or Kant, or Nietzsche, or indeed Wittgenstein.

When Wittgenstein speaks of the language of every day, he does not mean what "actual usage" suggests he means. In fact, he means Language—means something that is of surpassing importance as the repository of our common humanity, of understanding, knowledge, and wisdom. Why then does he describe what he means with the words "actual usage" or "the language of every day"? Is this merely an uneasy concession made by a believer to an empiricist? Or a way of denouncing the violations of language of which many a philosopher has been guilty in his pursuit of spurious heights and depths? This may be so. But he may have been prompted even more by a Tolstoyan belief in the virtue of the simple life, a belief that he applied to the life of language. Tolstoy indeed was one of the very few writers of the nineteenth century who deeply interested him; and thus it was perhaps a kind of linguistic Rousseauism that led Wittgenstein to insist upon "natural" language, a language unspoiled by the dubious refinements of a philosophical "civilization" which, having uprooted words from the ground of their origin, had made them serve "unnatural" demands.

In *Investigations* there are, above all, two aphorisms that allow the reader to observe how Wittgenstein avoids, in the manner of an empiricist fighting shy of metaphysics, the open declaration of his all-but-metaphysical faith in Language. This is the first:

> The problems arising through a misinterpretation of our forms of language have the character of *depth*. They are deep disquietudes; their roots are as deep in us as the forms of our language, and their significance is as great as the importance of our language.[36]

How true! And yet how disquieting is the word "misinterpretation"! It seems to suggest that there is, or can be, an absolutely reliable "rule" for deciding, philosophically or philologically, what is a correct and what is a wrong "interpretation" of every particular "form of language." But no such standard can apply. For to a higher degree than is dreamt of in linguistic philosophy, language has in common with other forms of human expression that it often evades unambiguous "interpretation": it can be as purely allusive as are dance and gesture, as evanescent in meaning as is music, as ungrammatically extravagant as is life itself. No sooner have we left the field of logic, grammar, and syntax, than we have entered the sphere of aesthetics where we do not ask whether a writer "interprets" [37] words correctly, but whether he uses them well or badly: and whether or not he uses them well, depends not upon his ability to "interpret" them, but upon something more adequately described as a feeling for language, as sensibility, or as genius. However original such genius may be, tradition has helped to form it—tradition or, to use Wittgenstein's words, the particular "form of life" within which alone, according to him, language has its meaning: "to imagine a language means to imagine a form of life." [38] That this is so, is one of Wittgenstein's most striking realizations; and indeed it not only renders the "rules of language," as he well knew, logically unmanageable but also makes their "description," which he hoped for, a task that could not be fulfilled by even a legion of

36. *Ibid.*, §111.
37. *Ibid.*, §§106, 107.
38. *Ibid.*, §19.

Prousts and Wittgensteins: for what is *the* "form of life" which, in one language, is shared by Goethe and Hitler, or, in another, by Keats and the *Daily News*?

With the "deep disquietudes" caused by a "misinterpretation of our forms of language," the quoted aphorism suggests something even more misleading than is the word "misinterpretation" itself. For the suggestion is that depth is a by-product of error. But if words like "depth" or "truth" or "error" are meaningful at all, then truth is deeper than falsehood; and indeed the suggestion is, as it were, withdrawn by the aphorism's very form and rhythm, which unmistakably intimate that language itself, not only its misinterpretation, has the character of depth, and that the disquietudes which arise from it are as deep as is the peace it may bring: through a great writer and even, rarely, through a philosopher whose thought is rooted in the mystery of words—or, to use the terms of the second aphorism we have had in mind, "in the ground of language." This second aphorism does indeed come close to revealing Wittgenstein's metaphysical secret. "What is it that gives to our investigation its importance," he asks with the voice of an imaginary interlocutor, "since it seems only to destroy everything interesting? (As it were all the buildings, leaving behind only bits of stone and rubble.)" And he replies: "What we are destroying is nothing but houses of cards and we are clearing up the ground of language on which they stand." [39] The ground of language—it is a transparent metaphor; and what shines through it is a mystical light, even if there is nothing left for it to illuminate but a philosophical landscape most thoughtfully cleared of all the fragile and disfiguring edifices built throughout the ages by the victims of linguistic delusion, such as Plato, St. Thomas Aquinas, Spinoza, or Immanuel Kant, those "ancient thinkers" who, wherever they "placed a word," believed

they had made a discovery. Yet the truth about it is quite different!—they had touched upon a problem and, deluding them-

39. *Ibid.*, §118.

selves that they had solved it, put up an obstacle to its solution.—
To come to know means now to stumble over petrified words that
are as hard as stone, and to break one's leg rather than a word.

Wittgenstein? No, Nietzsche.[40]

It is an ending a little like that of Goethe's *Tasso* where a man,
a poet, with all his certainties shattered, holds fast to his last
possession: language. And it has remained an open question of
literary interpretation whether that ending promises an ultimately
happy consummation or a tragedy. Be this as it may, Wittgenstein
was not a poet but a philosopher. And philosophy enters with
Wittgenstein the stage which has been reached by many another
creative activity of the human mind—by poetry, for instance, or by
painting: the stage where every act of creation is inseparable from
the critique of its medium, and every work, intensely reflecting
upon itself, looks like the embodied doubt of its own possibility.
It is a predicament which Nietzsche uncannily anticipated in a
sketch entitled "A Fragment from the History of Posterity." Its
subject is "The Last Philosopher." Having lost faith in a commu-
nicable world, he is imprisoned within his own self-consciousness.
Nothing speaks to him any more—except his own speech; and,
deprived of any authority from a divinely ordered universe, it is
only about his speech that his speech can speak with a measure
of philosophical assurance.[41]

In *Philosophical Investigations* Wittgenstein said: "What is
your aim in philosophy?—To show the fly the way out of the fly-
bottle." [42] But who asks? Who answers? And who is the fly? It is
an unholy trinity; the three are one. This way lies no way out.
This way lie only fly-bottles, and more and more fly-bottles.

40. Nietzsche, *op. cit.*, Vol. X, p. 49.
41. *Ibid.*, Vol. VI, p. 36.
42. *Investigations*, §309.

II

Wittgenstein and Theology

PAUL L. HOLMER

I

Ludwig Wittgenstein's thought is not easily summarized. I shall not attempt it. But its thrust can be exploited without it being summed up. Consider, for example, the following lovely passage from his pen:

> Why is philosophy so complicated? It ought to be altogether simple. Philosophy unties those knots in our thinking which we have unwittingly put there; however, this requires movements as complicated as the knots. Though philosophy's result is simple, its method, if it is to arrive at that result, cannot be. The complexity of philosophy is not in its subject matter but rather in our knotted understanding.[1]

Wittgenstein wrote that passage when he was a relatively young man. He had already published a very complicated book with a very complicated title, TRACTATUS LOGICO-PHILOSOPHICUS (1921). Ten years thereafter he was still doing philosophy and still in a

1. *Philosophische Bemerkungen.* Oxford, 1964. p. 52. Translation my own. This passage was penned between January, 1929, and September, 1930.

difficult way, but he was aiming not so much at the big topics, reality, truth, and being, as at the knots in his understanding. As he went on, teaching and writing for the next twenty years (he died in Cambridge, England, in 1951), he increasingly strove to untie the knots or, to use another metaphor, to dissolve the problems. Philosophical problems can be considered in a variety of ways. Despite Wittgenstein's negative demeanor, he gave great dignity both to the problems and to philosophical activity by showing how deep they were, how complicated the knots, and how strenuous and technical one had to be to get rid of them. His criticisms were not cheap strictures nor easy dismissals.

Right here was one of Wittgenstein's biggest points, namely, that philosophical problems were like knots, also like "bewitchments" of our intelligence. Most of them were like . . . "deep disquietudes; their roots are as deep in us as the forms of our language and their significance is as great as the importance of our language." [2] Instead of crediting the problems with a kind of face value and then seeking still another answer to them, Wittgenstein tried to describe how we got into such confounding problems. He did not seek any new information nor advance any kind of theory; but he looked very concertedly at the workings of our language—concepts, names, forms, rules, grammar, beliefs enshrined in familiar expressions (meaning, sensation, thought, intend, feel, know, etc.)—in order to see how knots in our understanding developed. Most of Wittgenstein's literature bears him out: "The problems are solved, not by giving new information, but by arranging what we have always known." [3] And, in part, philosophy becomes also a treatment, sometimes even a therapy, often a technique, not for resolving the problems as much as setting the man straight.[4]

Philosophical problems always seem to be foundational, ulti-

2. *Philosophical Investigations.* Transl. by G. E. M. Anscombe. Oxford, 1953. no. 111.
3. *Ibid.* no. 109. Also, 119, 126 and 127. "The work of the philosopher consists in assembling reminders for a particular purpose."
4. *Ibid.* nos. 254–55, p. 208; also note *The Blue Book,* pp. 58–59.

mate, and inescapable. They are invariably talked about as if their subject matter were extremely subtle phenomena, terribly hard to get hold of. Or, like theologians talking about God, it seems that, of course, there is a God, but our experience is too gross, or our language is too crude, or we are finite and He is infinite, or something of this kind.[5]

Then the problems of philosophy—and theology—seem to root in this fantastic incommensurability, where we get only a myriad of answers and somehow have to content ourselves therewith. We are tempted to think that philosophers and theologians have to be more subtle and refined in thought because there is also a more subtle knowledge of the fact still awaiting our discovery.[6]

II

But our concern here is with theology. There are many ways to relate philosophies and philosophers to theology. We have all read about "idealistic," "Platonistic," "Aristotelian," and other kinds of theology, made into "kinds" by philosophies. We can suppose, too, that there might be "Wittgensteinian" theology some day. But I neither wish that nor need it, and I can only urge something more modest. But even that modest attempt would be a failure if it only gets theology up to date or if we think the latest is sure to be best. If there is any point to reading Wittgenstein with the hope that he might help in one's theological difficulties, it might be because one could paraphrase him like this:

> Why is theology so complicated? It ought to be completely simple. Theology also unties those knots in our thinking which we have so unwisely put there; but its ways in untying must be as complicated as the knots are in tying. . . . The complexity of theology is not in its subject matter but rather in our knotted understanding and personality.

If anyone has tried to understand Christianity in our day he

5. *Philosophical Investigations.* no. 436.
6. In *The Blue Book,* W. says: "There is no common sense answer to a philosophical problem." (p. 58) But he argues that one can be cured of the temptation to attack common sense.

finds himself led down a very difficult path indeed. For as soon as he starts to think hard, he is led to theology. Kierkegaard told about the man who saw the sign, "Pants Pressed Here," in a window. He rushed in, stripping off his trousers, only to be told that the sign was for sale. Kierkegaard thought it was like that with the philosophers and reality. Sick of sham and make-believe, a man hears about philosophers and reality; but all that there is, is one more system for sale, highly recommended to be sure. And about God, is there any knowledge about Him anywhere to be had?

Of course, there are all kinds of theologians, and they are quite smart fellows. They do all kinds of respectable things, like lay bare presuppositions, relay the last word from here and there, explore implications, make inferences, historicize, synthesize, and analyze. And one seems churlish, boggling over such endeavors. Besides, theologians have good reasons for arguing that their subject is difficult. It has a long history, there are built-in complications—myths, history, "truth," spiritual stuff in flesh, necessity, contingency, finite and infinite. In addition, it has all been kneaded into a tough dough that can be fashioned into a thousand loaves! Besides, considering that God's ways are not man's, there is an even deeper reason for the uncertain shape of the loaf. The point I want to make is that often theology, like philosophy, is most disappointing when it is most obviously prosperous—when there is not only one theology but dozens of them. All one seems to get is points of view and not knowledge of God. Everything seems well until one tries to make up his mind between Christologies, theologies, and theological anthropologies. In virtue of what does one decide?

Instead of knowing about God, via the theology, one gets a new kind of problem, namely, trying to understand theology and theologies. One began trying to understand God and hoping that theology could help; one ends up trying to understand the theologies. If it were clear that the difficulties were only due to the simple ignorance of the learner, that would be, however uncomfortable, at least tolerable. But it is not quite that, either. For precisely in those respects where philosophy and theology blend and pool resources, there too Wittgenstein's animadversions about philosophy seem to fit also theology.

Therefore, the thought that Wittgenstein brings to all of this is not the possibility of a more subtle theology—one which will hold the field for a generation or two. Neither does he say such stupid and sweeping things as "all theology is nonsense" or "thinking does not pay." He gives no consolation to the thoughtless or to the impatient. He is not against thinking, but he also thought about the problems and how we got ourselves into such morasses, where disagreements proliferate and confusions multiply. Instead of yielding to an easy skepticism, it seems to me that Wittgenstein's work urges more concern with details and closer scrutiny of the source of the theologian's puzzlement.

One way to put this is simply that most of us are dissatisfied with the way the Bible and hymnody and catechetical teachings—let us call this a kind of notation—talks about Jesus, God, and the world. For the moment, let us admit that this notation is rather pervasive and common. It may hold us in its grasp. Yet we are inclined to think that certain facts are not taken into account, that some of our experience is omitted, that this system of notation is old-fashioned and inadequate. We want a new notation, a new scheme, a new set of concepts, and a new language by which to say everything that was said in the old notation, plus taking cognizance of the differences. So, theology begins to lure us. And it is no answer to anyone to say that "the Bible says . . . ," or "my church teaches . . . ," or "in the words of an ancient hymn. . . ." The old notation is precisely what is inadequate (so we think), and we cannot satisfy the quest by clever restatements.

So, theologians, like philosophers, begin to write out notational systems, some of them plain, some of them subtle. All of them seem dependent upon the earlier, but most of them are not simple restatements. Of course, some of them are that, but these often seem no better than the originals. Theologies which are existentialist, phenomenological, neo-metaphysical, idealistic, etc., often look as if they are getting at more subtle matters. Furthermore, they seem to be giving one the "minima," the foundational fact or concept, upon which the rest depends. But the difficulty is that there is no agreement. Nowhere is skepticism so learned and disagreement so profound. Yet we all are inclined to think that there must be something there to be discovered, that the "minima" have not yet been properly described.

Wittgenstein thought that the source of such conviction lay very deep indeed. I have no doubt that some Christian factors feed this source in additional ways. For one thing, Christians are inclined to put God among the invisibles, the intangibles, the really "real" behind appearances, etc. And God must be a fact, ultimate and final. So, whatever the sources that Wittgenstein thought drove intelligent people to disparage their working speech in favor of a more subtle and refined one (I am not talking here about the scientists' preference for a language alien to the man on the street), these seem to be compounded by impulses throbbing among the religious!

I have no cure-all. But Wittgenstein said in a letter to a friend (1917): "I am working reasonably hard and wish I were a better man and had a better mind. These two things are really one and the same—God help me!" [7] Maybe only some things in theology are a public craft. Theology, too, has become a business, and its integrity is often vouchsafed for it by public criteria. Wittgenstein had to break with obvious public criteria in order to philosophize about "knots in understanding." Perhaps it is appropriate to say that "knots in understanding" also pervade theology. If so, this will make theology harder work rather than easier. It will ask for more passion rather than less. Such work will not make it a "game" in an invidious sense, but it will demand greater congruence between our thoughts and our form of life.

7. Paul Engelmann, *Letters from Ludwig Wittgenstein*. Transl. by L. Furtmüller. New York, 1968. p. 5.

III

We are strongly inclined to think that: "God's truth is independent of whether men believe it or not." So, we might also want to say: "God is in Christ" and "Christians believe that God is in Christ." If one says the former, then we say something that is theological. The second, about what Christians believe, is more like saying that a certain group of people have come to a theological view.

Those two statements have quite different uses. If one asks about the truth of the second, we do quite distinctive things to ascertain what is what. Our measures and rules are different when we discuss whether or not there is "believing" than when we discuss whether God is in Christ. If someone said: "I'm going to find out whether Christians believe that," his statement, on the face of it, at least, would not be absurd. But if he were going to find out whether God was in Christ, we might think him a little odd. Can one do research on that? Can one examine documents to find out? Has some testimony been overlooked? Does testimony count?

Still, people have said: "God is in Christ." Maybe one wants to say that such a saying is only one man's point of view, or that the original speaker was trying to say something else, or that the being of God is somehow being addressed with those words, or that the words are only an expression! If we say any of the latter things, it might well be that we have a theory that all we ever have on such matters is a point of view, or that what is before a speaker's mind is always imperfect when made public, or that "being" (or "God") is always supposed by any descriptive language, or even that words are also like a cry or a grin or smirk— speaking inadvertent volumes!

But I note these because all of us are prone to accept a strong view like: "God's truth is independent of whether men believe it or not," as if that surely must obtain. However, when we mention a particular case, "God is in Christ," we begin to see that there is no expert judgment to which we can repair. It is not testimony that proves it, for proof is not quite what we can have. If I said: "2 times 2 is 4," then I say something mathematical. Again there is no expert on "twos" and "fours" who assuages doubts and establishes the case. Instead this business called mathematics is both an activity, such that men have made it, and a branch of learning, and hence not arbitrary. Most things false in mathematics are like abrogations and exceptions. And about these particular issues Wittgenstein has said a great deal.[8] However, if one said, "Mathematical truth is independent of whether men believe it or not," the view is quite without a context. Does it make any kind of sense to say it? Always? What are the measures for its truth? We do not know whether the view makes any sense at all.

If everybody believed that God was not in Christ, would God still be in Christ? Now we may be inclined to say "yes." What is wrong with that? Well, for one thing, we have probably coasted on some analogies. Two and two make four whether Johnny believes it or not, but that does not say that mathematics is independent of all belief whatsoever. No, mathematics was constituted by the activity of mathematicians—it is now a game with rules. Is theology only a game? Not quite like mathematics: "The mathematician is an inventor, not a discoverer." [9] The Apostles were not inventors of the Gospel the way mathematicians invented numerals and the rest of mathematics. Or, were they? Is theology a kind of knowledge of God that can be stated independently of being believed?

I suspect that Christian beliefs seem dismaying to most persons—at least in hymns, Bible, and simple teaching forms—also because so much seems to depend upon "believing." We feel thwarted and confined by having to believe. In mathematics, "believing" seems rather trivial (except when we consider that without mathematicians doing it, there would not be any). In

8. *Remarks on the Foundations of Mathematics.* Transl. by G. E. M. Anscombe. Oxford, 1956. Part I, nos. 163 ff.
9. *Ibid.* no. 167.

a Christian context, whether one believes or not is a religious test par excellence. And there are peculiarities. God is like a judge or even a teacher, whose examination is not meant to inform others about the subject matter but about the person examined (whether he believes or does not). Right here, we seem, nonetheless, constrained to say that our theological interests are higher and more refined. We want to know whether God is in Christ or not. To say, "I believe that God is in Christ, but it is not so," is a blatant contradiction. Why, in heaven's name, and on simple logical counts, too, does it not make sense to ask: "Isn't it so?"

Theology, in one of its forms, gives expression to the conviction that there ought to be knowledge of God, independent of belief. Most "belief" looks like a transition into knowing, a temporary mind-state, vanquished by knowledge. We have a kind of standard forced upon us by the notion of being rational, namely, that we first find out whether it is so, then we, too, will believe. And our theologies tend in the direction of feeding this conception of rationality. However, this may well be the biggest knot in our understanding, the cramp in our thought, that produces some of the theologies and our misgivings about them when we get them. For they do not satisfy us, nor do they untie the knot. Nothing quite fills the bill.

But just why there might be a difference in "belief" in respect to Christian teachings as over against other kinds of "beliefs" (e.g., Goldbach's theorem, or "that the chair will hold me") is lost to us by a very learned way of speaking.[10] We say that we believe in propositions and that propositions have to be true, etc. The words "belief," "proposition," "true," already have put our considerations into a mold. It seems to make no difference what we deal with so long as propositions are involved. "Belief is belief," we are inclined to say, "all that matters is 'what' you believe." With such elegant simplicities the web of thought is spun around us. To break out takes an enormous effort indeed. Breaking out means that one looks at the teachings again, at the very homely details.

10. *Philosophical Investigations*. nos. 574 ff.

There is something about Christian believing that makes it a constant struggle. One has to hold fast, almost in spite of the way the world is. One is tempted to say, in spite of the way that theology is, too. But surely something is wrong. It must be that part of the theological task is to free us from misleading analogies and the making of ideologies in Jesus' name. Maybe theologians also have to describe, not invent, and get clear the limits of language for us once more.

Wittgenstein was once mildly chided by a friend for his lack of faith. Typical of him, he did not blame it on to the age or the rise of science or modern culture. With a perspicuity that was almost alarmingly honest, he clearly saw that the lack of faith and belief was not a fault of life and society as they are. And this is what is so moving about the man, this is what makes him a teacher who gets one into the Christian arena despite his professed lack of faith. He never blamed the world. He saw that the issue here was himself, and he never let go of that, as far as I can tell from his pages. But in response to that friend's inquiry, Wittgenstein said:

> I am clear about one thing: I am far too bad to be able to theorize about myself; in fact, I shall either remain a swine or else I shall improve, and that's that! Only let's cut out the transcendental twaddle when the whole thing is as plain as a sock on the jaw.[11]

There seems to me to be something moving and right about that remark. Furthermore, it puts us in the right frame of mind for thinking about Christianity. It might even help us to keep our theology directed against everything that clouds the simplicities and destroys both our confidence in thinking and our faith in God.

But Wittgenstein's work is also safeguarded by his fine irony. Kierkegaard said that some readers of his literature would complain that it was too scientific to be edifying and too edifying to be scientific. About Wittgenstein's works we can say confidently

11. Engelmann, *Letters from Wittgenstein*. p. 11.

that its technicalities are aimed at making us think right, but to think right requires that we live right. Few thinkers have been so technical and so disinterested as he was, but few thinkers have forced us to such honesty and such scrupulous self-understanding. It just might be that one can be edified in such a context too. Maybe these are the requisites of theology as well as philosophy.

III

Religion and Science: A Philosopher's Approach[1]

I. T. RAMSEY

In recent days there has been a variety of attempts by very diverse people, and not always for the same reasons, to stress not so much, or even at all, the conflict between religion and science, as their radical difference and independence. Professor John Wisdom, for example, began a notable essay on *Gods*[2] by saying: "The existence of God is not an experimental issue in the way it was"—looking back, rightly or wrongly, to the time when Elijah proved his case before the prophets of Baal. Professor A. G. N. Flew broadened the point by arguing, again rightly or wrongly, that while the believer in God can allow nothing to count against his belief, everyone knows that scientific generalizations on the other hand can always be falsified and will be set aside if events so demand.[3] But it is not only unbelieving philosophers who insist on differences of this kind between science and religion. In his book *Mystery and Philosophy* the late Michael Foster emphasized the way in which he thought that scientific method came dangerously near to being irreligious. "The aim of modern sci-

1. Based on a lecture given at Sion College, London, 30 November 1959.
2. *Proceedings of the Aristotelian Society*, 1944–5, pp. 185–206.
3. See e.g. *New Essays in Philosophical Theology*, Ch. VI.

ence is man's mastery over nature" [4] (he says) and nothing is more typical of these masterful intentions than "the experimental method" which "is a method of commanding nature to answer man's questions." [5] It is a "putting of nature to the question." [6] But if theology put God to the question and tested its theories by results, it would be, Mr. Foster would say, "to tempt the Lord God in the way prohibited," [7] i.e. in the Temptation narratives. These various quotations make two points:

1. that modern science encourages man to develop his own mastery and subjects nature to an Inquisition, and

2. that scientific method has to be set entirely aside when we turn to religion and theology. Indeed, to investigate God by the methods which natural science uses, would be to yield to a temptation of the devil, which the religious man must renounce. There is a methodological incompatibility between religion and science.

Now let me make it clear from the outset that it is not the purpose of this paper to assert the logical identity of scientific and religious discourse. That view belongs to a past age. Differences, and important differences, of methodology there certainly are. Yet I wish to show how the two approaches, *despite* their differences, are not incompatible. On the contrary, they have their meeting places. Nay, more, they may be and must be united.

Further, at the outset, let me emphasize that for the most part this paper will be concerned with scientific *method*. Science is not the name for some logically homogeneous group of assertions. It is rather a *method* in the development of which several kinds of logically distinguishable assertions are made, some, though not all of which, have theological associations of the kind we must explore. Let us turn then to scientific method and look at some of its logical features with a view to answering the question: how far is the approach, the attitude, the methods, of the scientist compatible with a religious attitude? For this is the question which spotlights for the philosopher the crucial

4. Loc. cit., p. 61.
5. Loc. cit., p. 61.
6. Loc. cit., pp. 56, 58.
7. Loc. cit., p. 62.

point of present day discussion about science and religion. The debate is not about conclusions, but about methodology.

For our purpose we shall distinguish five features in scientific method; five stages as the scientist proceeds from his simplest generalization to the most complex hypothesis:

1. *The Start*

Science starts with ordinary commonsense assertions about what can be seen, heard, touched, tasted, or smelt. For example, the following assertions would be among those of interest to the scientist: "There is a stone falling"; "See the planet moving"; "The water is boiling"; "These vegetables are decomposing"; "Those rabbits are reproducing."

2. *Simple Generalizations*

The scientist's next move is to formulate invariants within such ostensible diversity. To illustrate this second stage of scientific method let us take the simplest kind of scientific situation: Tom, Dick, and Harry, who are all boiling water. The scientist links these situations not merely because the phrase "boiling water" would be used by each of them—for this is a very vague phrase with a very open texture—but because a thread of mercury in a glass tube—a thermometer—measures in each calorimeter or beaker more or less what is called 100° Centigrade. Here, very roughly described, is the background to the simplest kind of scientific generalization: "Water boils at 100° Centigrade." Here is a phrase—"100° Centigrade"—which, as an invariant, not only brings precision and clarity into the assertions of Tom, Dick, and Harry, but unites all the Toms, Dicks, and Harrys boiling water in the kingdom. Yet already we must make two points which are often forgotten by those who make too superficial generalizations about scientific method. The first point is that even this simple generalization is not bound rigidly to the facts. It is suggested by them, yes. But in the end it is an option, which goes beyond them. How many thermometers measure accurately 100° Centigrade? Or would continue to register this temperature if peered at through lenses, and so on? The simple generalization is (as I have said) very closely associated with the facts, but it is reached in a disclosure which occurs when we survey the different thermometers, whereupon a certain figure "100° C" suggests itself, forces itself on our attention. The generalization depends on the "facts," but does not, in any science worthy of the name, merely report them in close detail.

The second point of importance is to recognize the important part which the appeal to "experimental error" can play. Here is a trump card which will safeguard most simple generalizations which are grounded in disclosures occurring around a group of closely similar spatio-temporal events. It can for so long, and in so many ways, feather-bed useful and simple generalizations which the scientist wishes to keep.

3. Development of Simple Generalizations

But let us not be unfair. Refuge will not always be taken in experimental error. Provided we are only boiling water in the cellar or in the attic, as well as in the kitchen, all will be well. But suppose we go to the top of Ben Nevis. We shall say that water "is boiling," but our thermometer will not read 100° C at the top of Ben Nevis. It will read somewhat less (say) 99.8° C. For some time we may talk about experimental error, but when a vast company of climbers, armed with thermometers, has boiled water at the top of Ben Nevis, and when all of their thermometers have significantly measured less than 100° C the earlier generalization will be modified. It would not so much be shown to be wrong, for the situations to which it gave precision and unity before would still be given precision and unity by it. It would still, over a certain area, be a reputable invariant. But its inadequacy has now been indicated. The simple invariant needs to be further extended, and we now say, "Water boils at 100° C at normal pressure." Or (still more accurately and typically) "Water boils at a temperature t when the pressure is p" and where for some function of t and p, $f(t, p) = 0$. Further, when p is "normal," $t = 100°$ C. With this more complicated phrase everyone's kettle is now covered, whether in laboratory, kitchen, attic, or cellar, or even on Ben Nevis. We have now produced a much more resistant generalization, a much better invariant arising in a disclosure which encloses many more spatio-temporal data than did its predecessors.

Further, we could now deduce that down a Lancashire coal mine, or a French limestone cavern, water will boil at a temperature greater than 100° C. Notice, that we can *deduce* such an assertion from our generalization, and further, that this assertion can be subsequently *verified*. Here is a crucial element in scientific method—verifiable deductions, and it is an element which (as we shall see) theology cannot and must not provide.

4. *Large-scale Hypotheses*

But the scientist's interest will not stop here. The better the scientist the more comprehensive, extensive, and powerful, must be his invariant. To illustrate the high generalizations at which the scientist aims, let us take a very mixed group of common-sense assertions such as the following, and for our purpose it does not matter whether they are true or false:

"An apple is falling to the ground."

"A planet is moving to an ellipse."

"That bullet will score a bulls-eye."

"A Britannia locomotive with twelve carriages will slip on certain inclines."

"The road must have a better camber at that corner if buses are not to turn over."

"High water at Greenwich yesterday was 10 p.m."

"A partial eclipse of the sun, visible in England, occurred in November 1959."

Now what the physicist does when searching for newer and more far-reaching theories is to bring together such diverse situations as these assertions describe, hoping that some common feature or other will strike him, will (in other words) evoke a disclosure. It is in this way that scientific "insight" is associated

with what we have called invariants, features (hitherto un-
noticed) which the diverse situations have in common; and the
more diverse the situations that an invariant unites when it becomes the occasion of a disclosure, the more original and distinguished the scientist. For example, in the case of the apple
falling and the planet moving, these two situations, hitherto
regarded as wholly disparate (as disparate indeed as earth and
heaven) may suddenly connect—as they once did presumably
for Newton. A moment of vision occurred around a common
feature: in this case, "force producing movement."

At this point we need to make an important complication to
the story. When the events are sufficiently similar (as in the cases
of boiling water) and the common feature is sufficiently simple
(as in the case of thermometers registering 100° C), the scientist
may well imagine that no currency beyond the mathematical
symbols (here: "100° C") is required to do justice to what is
disclosed.

But when invariants are associated with vastly diverse situations, two possibilities arise:

(i) As in the simpler case, so in this, mathematical symbols
may still be invaluable as currency for the invariant.

(ii) At the same time the disclosure which embraces so much
spatio-temporal diversity may well also suggest some word of a
metaphysical brand, especially if a similar disclosure embracing
a similar diversity has been in the past the basis for such a metaphysical word. For instance, a certain invariant arising in a disclosure which embraces great diversity (such diversity as is indicated, for instance, by the assertions at the start in this section)
may be expressed in terms of the symbols for a mathematical
point (x, y, z). But since this invariant arises in the same sort of
context in which metaphysicians have spoken of "particle" or
"atom"—when a disclosure likewise embraces various "things"
of maximum diversity—the invariant may be given a metaphysical interpretation as well. We may thus call the invariant
(mathematically) (x, y, z), or (metaphysically) "a particle."

Now in the old days the mathematical symbols and the meta-physical concept were virtually equated. Here were the days when mathematics was thought to describe "reality," which was neither more nor less than mathematics talked about. But to-day the question arises: Is "mass," for example, merely short-hand for something measurable, a mere label for the symbol "m," or does it tell us of some metaphysical secret of the Universe vouch-safed in a disclosure? Or again, in the case of "force": here is a word which may be taken as merely labelling what can be symbolized mathematically as "rate of charge of momentum" $\left(\dfrac{d}{dt}(mv)\right)$ or it may be a concept from metaphysics, when it is assimilated to "power" and "activity."

Those same two possibilities can arise not only about mass and force, but, for Newton, they also arise about absolute space and absolute time. They also arise around an atom for Dalton, natural selection for Darwin, periodicity for a theory of the ele-ments, the electron when used as a basis for an electronic theory of valency or of co-ordination compounds, and so on; and with continuous creation for Hoyle. All these words might work meta-physically or not. Let us look a little more closely at this ambi-guity which such key-words display.

Let it be granted that, so far as physics and chemistry go, we might take words like "Force" or "Absolute Space" in Newton's hypothesis, or "Periodicity" in the case of the elements, as no more than convenient co-ordinating words or classificatory de-vices which have neither meaning nor function other than the heuristic use they are thus given. On this view dominating ideas rounding off a scientific theory of high generality would be just jingles whose use is assimilated to the appropriate mathematical symbolism, or spatio-temporal pattern of scientific interest. With such a status they would resemble very closely Kant's Ideas of Reason as used "regulatively," and it is interesting to remember that Kant himself compared this regulative use of an Idea of Reason with the physicists' use of the concept of "image," under whose unifying power various haphazard generalizations became a theory of reflection, from which could be deduced countless easy deductions which are subsequently verified.[8] But are the key-ideas of large scale scientific theories no more than jingles?

Certainly most scientists in theory, and all scientists in practice, have behaved as though the key-words of a scientific theory were more than jingles. Newton's hypothesis, as we have seen, was linked with a "metaphysical" background (however uneasy or otherwise the relationship between them both in his own mind). Dalton's Atomic theory had its ancestry in the more or less vague atomic "meta"-"physics" of Democritus, Boyle, and Newton. Even though the Periodic Table may seem to be exceptional and a plain case of nothing but a classificatory idea, I think it is quite clear that someone like Mendeleeff, who elaborated it for the first time, thought he had somehow been taken nearer to what he would have called the "Truth": a full insight into the universe.

At any rate it is certainly the case that as scientific hypotheses increase in scope and importance, embracing a whole variety of generalizations, scientific method sponsors increasingly scientific invariants or absolutes which happen to have an ambiguous status. Now one possibility of science being different from, yet united with, theology, depends precisely on the possibility of these key-words, which arise in relation to disclosure situations, being capable of more than a mathematical interpretation. Does science itself rule out that possibility? Or, on the contrary, does it even hint at it? This question leads us at once to two important if rather difficult topics.

(a) The first topic is known as *operationalism*, which for our present purpose can be seen as a method of giving these scientific absolutes a wholly scientific placing. Certainly we must allow that at least since Einstein, many scientific concepts, some of which in earlier days seemed highly metaphysical, e.g. Absolute Space, have been given an "operational" definition, referring

8. *Critique of Pure Reason.* Appendix to the Transcendental Didactic. "The Regulative Employment of the Ideas of Pure Reason." N. Kemp Smith (abridged translation), p. 301.

more or less directly to what can be measured and calculated. So Absolute Space is given a relativistic setting. Here are concepts which Bridgman calls "instrumental," [9] and which Dingle[10] would suggest can be derived from an analysis of what measurement involves. So far it looks as if scientific procedure could get rid of all hang-overs from earlier metaphysics.

But it is significant that when one sort of metaphysics has thus been expelled by this empirical rigour, the need for other concepts with a curious logical status, has immediately shown itself. We have needed other correlating concepts—key-ideas, dominating analogies—not altogether unlike what Bridgman calls "paper and pencil" concepts; not unlike the correlating concepts to which Dingle would give a pictorial use, where such pictures are associated with flights of the imagination, and (let us remember) talk of imagination is never very far from talk about disclosures.

So, as scientific hypotheses increase in scope and become wider generalizations, it is true that operationalism often purifies these hypotheses from crude metaphysical speculations which have hung around from the beginning as man's vision is extended, as he seeks a theory of the Universe. But, as the second type of concept suggests, it is a mistake to suppose that in consequence hypotheses at some time might dispense with "queer ideas" altogether. Certainly the ideas may get fewer, but if anything, they get queerer. The further operationalism goes, the more the need for correlating unifying concepts. So we do not seem able to avoid the conclusion that scientific method, when it reaches this fourth stage, demands metaphysics. One sort of metaphysics is expelled, only to make room for another. Nor is this surprising. For if our account is correct it suggests that the key-words derive from, and witness to, the scientist being more than a detached observer; that they may arise from that kind of transaction with —even rapport with—the Universe we have called a disclosure.

9. *Nature* 166. 1950. p. 91. See also the discussion by M. B. Hesse, *Science and the Human Imagination*, Ch. VII.
10. *The British Journal for the Philosophy of Science*, I. 1950.

Operational concepts are thus founded in what the scientist does, and the theory of operationalism brings the observer centrally and actively into the scientific situation. This means that our earlier question—about the double interpretation of key-words—is now transformed and becomes: Can an account ever be given *by* the scientist himself, *of* the scientist himself, in wholly scientific, i.e. "object," terms? Here is a question which is surely to be given a negative answer: otherwise, we would objectify the subject.[11] So room is left for metaphysical key-words.

(b) The same conclusion is reached by considering the development in physics known as *information theory,* which would analyse scientific knowledge in terms of the acquisitioning of information. We have seen already, from our independent approach, that scientific conclusions always witness to the language tool being used to extract them. Information theory likewise emphasizes that scientific answers are always relative to the particular scientific questions that are being asked at a given time, and to the features of situations being thus examined.[12]

But the further claim is now made that typical scientific concepts like entropy, and generalizations such as the Uncertainty Principle, are nothing more than indicators which register and exhibit the kind of questions being asked. In other words they reveal nothing more than the character—the logical structure—of the scientific language being used. Once again scientific method, with empirical rigour, may be brushing away subsistent entities by the dozen. At the same time, however, the scientist is becoming essentially involved in his science. Scientific procedure becomes more and more akin to a question-answer game, with its language resembling the logic of a dialogue. Key-words now relate to large-scale options made by the scientist in his interchange with the universe, and scientific theory expresses a

11. For a further discussion see: *Proceedings of the Aristotelian Society,* Suppl. Vol. XXXIII, 1959, I. T. Ramsey, "Paradox in Religion," esp. pp. 214–15 [reprinted in the present volume, see pp. 158–59. Ed.] and I. T. Ramsey, *Freedom and Immortality,* esp. Ch. I and II.

12. Once again we can see why scientific hypotheses, if any use at all, are never wholly outmoded.

scientist's attempt at conversation with the universe. There is no suggestion that the scientist is a Grand Inquisitor.

It looks, then, as if science cannot exclude metaphysical words. Though it may try to lay less and less weight on them within scientific method, scientific method itself involves the scientist as an active subject who cannot himself be objectified and restricted to observables. Scientific Method then points to a metaphysical supplement. But does it ever positively *need* these words? Does scientific method ever call explicitly for metaphysics? So we come to 5.

5. *The Conversion of Hypotheses:*
the Demand for a Total Map

It is now time to see what happens when a hypothesis, no matter how previously convincing or comprehensive, is modified or converted, and (as we shall see) this will in the end afford us an answer to the question we have just raised. In the conversion of hypotheses certain key-words, around which cluster on the one hand mathematical equations and techniques, and which on the other hand are associated with disclosures, these key-words are replaced by others allowing of more powerful generalizations. One of the best known examples is the progressive modification of the phlogiston theory of combustion and its ultimate replacement by the oxygen theory. Another example is the Newtonian hypothesis which with all its glorious generalizations and dominating concepts, had in the end to give place to others. Experimental data in heat, light, and electro-magnetics led respectively to the concept of entropy, the theory of relativity and to the quantum theory, for none of which a straightforward Newtonian treatment could be given. Thus arose Einstein with the idea of relative space; and nearer our own time, Eddington with his cosmical number and so on.

Notice that a scientific hypothesis may be modified or there may be a conversion, but a scientific hypothesis is never given a knockdown falsification. There is no comparison with a betting game; no scientific hypothesis is ever "dead right" or "dead wrong." It is merely that one scientific absolute from a certain point of view produces a more powerful synthesis than another. But the usefulness of the old absolute remains. A scientific hypothesis, if it is ever any use at all, will always continue to have that use.

When people speak, as they once did, of a scientific hypothesis being completely falsified, the idea was that facts and language were both homogeneous. So H_1 was said to be a good approximation for an area of facts A_1. But when, for some reason or another, A_1, became A_2, an area which included A_1 and something else, whereupon another hypothesis, H_2 was demanded, it was said either that H_1 was somehow or other "in" H_2, or that H_2 was a hypothesis which showed that H_1, which had once been supposed valid, was now false. But what we have come to see is that there is only the most remote logical kinship between H_1 and H_2. Here are two distinct logical areas. But the point was only seen when scientific method demanded and profitably used both the hypotheses H_1 and H_2 at the same time.

Not long ago the scientist was puzzled by this demand and possibility, and to recall a hackneyed example we may mention the two theories of light—the corpuscular theory and the wave theory—both of which were demanded for scientific inquiry. Here were phenomena demanding on the one hand treatment in such mathematics as suggested wave pictures, continuous wave motions; on the other hand treatment was also demanded in terms of mathematics whose pictures were discontinuous corpuscles or particles. At first, with the old picture of scientific method and hypothesis in mind, scientists tried somehow to make the two hypotheses one. But by this time the attempt has been seen for what it is—a wild goose chase, and scientists must be content to use at one and the same time, languages of different logical structure about similar situations. Here, briefly and crudely expressed, is the theory of complementarity.[13] The pic-

13. The example may stand even though claims have been made that in this case fragmentation has been overcome. This claim I would counter on logical grounds, but in any case fragmentation in general remains simply because

ture of scientific language, far from being homogeneous as was at one time supposed, has rather to be pictured as a hierarchy of logically diversified languages.

Nor let us suppose that this outlook is all that modern. Let us notice a footnote which is to be found in a quite elementary book published some twenty-five years ago: F. B. Finter's *Introduction to Physical Chemistry*. He says, in connection with the atomic theory (p. 15), "Even if we attempt to 'explain' chemical reactions in terms of electrons instead of atoms, the validity and the use of the atomic hypothesis remains unchanged. We are only superimposing an additional 'electronic hypothesis,' in an attempt to get still nearer the truth." Finter spoke of Dalton's atomic theory, but the same could be said for the Newtonian hypothesis and, I would dare to say, the phlogiston theory.

Where now is this leading us? For the moment it seems as though we are left with what is often now called the fragmentation of science. Ask "why" questions in one way and we get a question-answer game played in the language H_1; ask "why" questions in another way and we get a question-answer game played in the language H_2.

Yet we must recall that scientific method never gives up its fifth feature, its hope of sponsoring some one overall scheme, one total language map, for the whole universe. But how is this going to be reached from a multiplicity of logically variegated languages? Has the old idea of science to be abandoned? Can scientific method never again give us one theory of the Universe? Are we committed to a scientific Tower of Babel? That is the problem which contemporary science by its increasing fragmentation sets us. We shall see presently that it is precisely at this point that science can profitably and properly call again on those metaphysical words which for the first four stages of its method it had rather cold-shouldered. But before continuing our argument, let us summarize our position so far in four points to see how far

no scientific theory of any real use is ever "falsified." Nor do more comprehensive scientific theories say *everything* which was said by the more restricted theories they often replaced. Cf. the preceding paragraphs and the next two paragraphs.

and where this scientific methodology is compatible with a religious attitude.

1. The scientist, as we have seen, does not keep all that close to "the facts." What he needs besides and more than the facts, is insight, intuition, some sort of disclosure. To that degree the scientist is not particularly "humble" before "the facts." At the same time, he has generalizations from which deductions can be made which can be verifiably tested. Now here is a divergence between the hypotheses of science and religion, if religion be allowed hypotheses at all. The scientist has options which are always just a little far-fetched, but they can find currency in, e.g. mathematics, which permits of deductions, verifiable or falsifiable as the case may be.

2. Yet the scientist does not put the universe to the test; he tests rather his generalizations, the invariants which have been disclosed to him, which have been grasped by his insight, an insight correlative with a disclosure. The scientist does not put the universe to the question. He rather puts his questions— about his provisional invariants—to the universe and lets the universe decide for him. All he puts to the question are his theories. He sponsors some invariant and follows it through till the universe gives him an answer, tells him whether his faith has been well-founded, or not; whether his insight has or has not been reliable, whether or not he is a false prophet. Here is something potentially religious.

3. Further, the scientist is always willing to revise his beliefs and to sponsor alternative absolutes. In this sense he is humble, and again potentially religious.

4. At the same time the scientist searches for an overall scheme and to this extent his whole aim might be said to be to control everything by scientific techniques.[14] Here, it might be

14. Some might think that the technologist was of all scientists the most "dangerous" to religion, the one whose methods and practices reflect nothing but a striving for mastery, and that Michael Foster might well have had the technologist in mind rather than the pure scientific thinker. Now it is true that the technologist will have little time for disclosures. Rule of thumb methods; the slide-rule and so on represent best his habits and practices. At

said, and here especially, is Michael Foster's strong point. But can the languages of science give us a completely exhaustive map? The brief answer is, logically, no. For what exceeds the language of science are the very disclosures which scientific method itself demands, and which become the more prominent, and their logical status the clearer, as scientific method proceeds.

On what conditions, then, shall we ever possess one adequate language-map of the Universe—a map embracing not only the diverse languages of science, but also the supplement which those languages seem to need? The question has brought us back to the point where we paused in the discussion, and it is time to take up the matter again. Fragmentation, we noticed, is logically inescapable if we are to be mere scientists. As a scientist, a man is doomed to disappointment if his aim is an overall scheme. Each generalization, each theory, has its significance which is never wholly taken over by another. The scientist has a diversity of options. But now the vital question recurs: Can we, and on what conditions can we, recapture the old ideal of science as providing us with one language-map of the universe? Where can words be found to unite the diverse languages of science? Where can science find its hopes justified? What does conversation and dialogue with the universe imply?

Here at the end I venture to outline a possible answer. I would like to argue that it is at this point that science and religion become supplementary in a way which helps both, yet humbles both.

There is no space to do more than give a mere outline. But let us approach that outline with such reflections as these.

If a word (or words) is to unite the diverse languages of science, it must occur in phrases which are entailed by all kinds of scientific assertions. Yet it must not of itself be native to any one of the logically diverse languages of science, or fragmentation will remain. But because the key-word is *not* native to the

the same time, his scientific progress raises moral problems of the highest magnitude: and it may be that here he finds his disclosures—moral disclosures—which can supply him with the "compensation" he needs. In short, the salvation of technology may well have to be found in the moral issues to which it stirs the technologist.

language of science, it now follows that key-assertions will never entail verifiable deductions. How can this be? Have we any paradigm for such words or phrases?

Let us begin by taking the assertion "I exist." This certainly is entailed by all kinds of scientific assertions. "He has a heart beating," "He has a blood count of X," "He has a digestive system characterized by all that the bio-chemistry of fats, proteins, carbohydrates, and enzymes can teach us," "He has such and such reflex actions," "He has such and such brain potentials": "I exist," is entailed by all these, when said of me. But "I exist" entails none of these. We cannot necessarily *deduce* from "I exist" any of these *particular* assertions. Yet the affirmation of my existence is that which gives all these varied assertions their concrete reference; is that which unites them all.

Now what I suggest is that the word "God" must be seen as a logical kinsman of "I" in having, at least in these two respects, a similar logical behaviour. "God exists" entails no particular verifiable assertions. Theology can provide no verifiable deductions. But this does not mean that it has no empirical relevance. On the contrary, like "I exist," "God exists" is a phrase which is in fact entailed by and so linked with verifiable language, while entailing none of it. The latter point used to be expressed in old-fashioned language by people who said "The world is not necessary to God." As to the earlier point, namely: that scientific assertions entail "God exists" as some entail "I exist": this used to be expressed as "God is necessary to the world." Further, the basis for "God exists" is an affirmation which arises around the universe in a moment of disclosure, in a moment of worship, indeed in prayer. It is thus like the basis for "I exist." [15] Here, in worship, scientific assertions are integrated with, yet distinguished from, the theological assertion of God's existence.

Let us go back for a moment to Professor Wisdom and Elijah. Not even here had we an experimental issue. The fire did not test a hypothesis. No assertion about fire coming down can be

15. Cf. I. T. Ramsey, loc. cit. and *Religious Language,* esp. pp. 61-5; also *The Philosophical Quarterly,* July 1955, pp. 193-204.

deduced from "God exists" or from anything Elijah said. When the fire came down it did something very different from providing the verifiable criteria for a hypothesis, something very different which Wisdom (and, it may be said, others) does not sufficiently distinguish. It answered a prayer. Indeed we may, with due deference, suggest that in many ways the story would have been religiously more enlightening if the fire had not come down. For it would have shown us better how the religious man can keep his affirmation but modify and develop his theology. As it was, the verifiable success might have tempted Elijah or his opponents to think that God could always be tested, would always provide verifiable criteria and then God would have become a scientific concept. Here I entirely agree with the protests that Mr. Foster makes.

Yet if religion and science are not identical, I want to emphasize that they are complementary. Religion can give to science that affirmation of the universe which it needs. It can give to science the basis of fact presupposed by operationalism and information theory; it can supply a suitable key-word to organize the logical diversification of large-scale scientific theory. Religion can give all this to the scientist. But the scientist must then, *in the end,* give up his verifiable hopes. For this key-word "God" has not a scientific logic so that "God exists" entails no verifiable conclusions; besides "I," its kinsmen are rather those "metaphysical" words which science has from time to time sponsored, and which (as we saw) were currency for disclosures, even though the scientist for most of his working day might find a mathematical understanding of the disclosure quite adequate.

Science can satisfy religion in its venture after fuller and fuller relevance, after more and more adequate discursive expression. But theology must then share in the tentative character of science, and be prepared to lose any verbal and verifiable guarantees for which it might once have yearned. We can regain the old ideal, alike of science and metaphysical theology, for one map, only when that map loses in the end its purely scientific character; only when it sponsors some metaphysical words of

which "mass," "force," "evolution" were once favourites, though
I have outlined a means of substituting "God" for them all. I
have suggested that the scientist can only secure his wildest
dreams when he becomes religious. At the same time the theologian can only secure his wildest dreams when he becomes
scientific.

Science and religion may find a synthesis in their methods.
But the cost to each is great. The theologian must admit a
tentative theology; the scientist must admit key-words which
cannot (and it is a logical *cannot*) be given straight scientific
verification. Yet theologian and scientist meet where all meet—
in the affirmation of the universe which is wonder and worship
at what the universe discloses.

IV

Mapping the Logic of Models in Science and Theology

FREDERICK FERRÉ

My purpose in this paper is to show that the notion of the "model," which has received considerable attention and stimulated much controversy among scientists and philosophers of science, should be recognized as of central importance to theologians and philosophers of religion. In order to reach my goal I shall have to survey and attempt to make at least roughly intelligible a domain for which there exist few charts and within which there is as yet little agreement on boundaries, trail markings, or compass directions. To do a really comprehensive job, such as is urgently needed, will not be possible within the limitations of an essay; but if the existence and fertility of the territory can be established and if a few major landmarks can be plotted with reasonable accuracy, even a large scale logical map may prove useful.

I

Models and Theories

The term "model" has one fairly common use, found most frequently among social scientists and psychologists, that is more or less equivalent to "theory." One word becomes a virtual synonym for the other. Such a rough and ready way with language, however, will not satisfy our present needs. It not only conflates what can usefully be distinguished but also may subtly beg important questions by leading us precritically into what will later be seen as a particular view of models and their logical role. Some preliminary formal analysis of "model" is required to set off models from theories without prejudicing later material analyses.

One such formal descripion of "model" and "theory" is offered by Ernest Nagel, who distinguishes between (1) the "abstract calculus" which provides the logical skeleton of a theory, (2) the "rules of correspondence" which connect the implicitly defined statement-forms of the theory with experience, and (3) the "model" which serves to *provide an interpretation for the abstract theory*.[1] Equipped with these distinctions, Nagel proceeds to use "model" and "interpretation" interchangeably:[2] the statement-forms of a theory's abstract calculus remain devoid of intelligibility until provided with a sense, and that which provides this sense for the theory is its "model." (Nagel should not be misunderstood to be speaking *temporally*. The theory does not necessarily stand first a naked skeleton of statement-forms, later fleshed out by a model. These are stages of analysis, not of development.) But useful as this proposal for the use of "model" and "theory" can be shown to be in many respects, Nagel's analysis has the unfortunate consequence of making every theory separated from a "model" (in his sense) merely a theory-*form;* and once again substantial questions are obscured by making a "model" (i.e. "interpretation") of *some* kind necessary, by definition, for every "theory" that is fully to be a theory.

R. B. Braithwaite avoids this danger by maintaining that the distinction between a model and a theory is properly located in the relative epistemological priority of those higher-level

1. Ernest Nagel, *The Structure of Science: Problems in the Logic of Scientific Explanation* (New York: Harcourt, Brace & World, 1961), Ch. 5.
2. Cf. *ibid.*, pp. 90, 95, 96, 107, etc.

formulae of the calculus that contain theoretical terms.[3] A model and a theory, for Braithwaite as for Nagel, utilize the same formal calculus-skeleton; but for the model it is the *initial* formulae of the calculus that are epistemologically prior (i.e. intuitively clear to us) whereas for the theory it is the *derived* formulae of the calculus that possess this priority, the initial formulae gaining interpretation in reverse order from the order of logical dependence.[4] Given Braithwaite's terminology it is logically possible that a theory may stand in full independence from any model, since it is not a logical necessity, *prima facie* at least, that epistemological and logical priority must parallel one another for the provision of an adequate interpretation for the statement-forms of a theory's calculus. But, on the other hand, it is also perfectly conceivable that operating with the same terminology one might discover reasons for insisting (as Braithwaite does not) that models and theories are somehow essentially linked together by logical, epistemological, or psychological bonds.

Because of the initial neutrality of this formal analysis of the relation of models to theories, I shall make use of it in what follows. A model, let me repeat, is not itself a theory but fits to some extent, or is believed to fit, the same abstract calculus as does the theory; the difference between them resides in the fact that a theory draws the meaning of its initial (or "abstract" or "theoretical") formulae from the meanings of the lower level formulae that have been deduced from those logically prior but epistemologically secondary initial formulae, whereas a model presents the meaning of its high level formulae somehow directly.

Views of Models

Just what it is that makes for this "direct presentation" of meaning—what "models" are, not formally and abstractly but concretely and "in the flesh"—has been the subject of sharp debate

---

3. R. B. Braithwaite, *Scientific Explanation: A Study of the Function of Theory, Probability and Law in Science* (London: Cambridge University Press, 1953), Chapter IV.
4. Cf. *ibid.*, pp. 89–90.

and, I am afraid, of much needless misunderstanding. I shall now offer, as data which will have to be drawn together into some kind of order, a sampling of substantive views on this subject.

One familiar and frequently influential view of models has taken them to be essentially mechanical contrivances designed to illuminate, by their working, the meaning of a scientific theory. Lord Kelvin, it is said, complained that he could not frankly consider himself to "understand" a physical theory unless he could build some such mechanical model to illustrate it.[5]

Another view considers models as primarily scale reproductions (larger or smaller) of an object or type of object being studied. The relation between the planets, their sizes, satellites, relative orbits and orbital speeds, and so on, are often shown by a scale model at a planetarium. If it is a working scale model, the theory (for instance) explaining apparent planetary retrograde motion can be made vividly intelligible; but whether or not a scale model also "works" (à la Kelvin), much of value may be learned from it.[6]

Others may mean by "model" only a mental picture of some kind. The late Arthur Pap, for example, comments: "It is a natural tendency of the human mind to think of physical reality as something that can be pictured, on the analogy of the objects of common-sense experience. As a result, physical theories are intuitively satisfactory only if they gain pictorial content through models."[7] Supporting Pap's view that models are something essentially picturable are such men as Sir James Jeans, to whose views we shall need to return before long, and the great physicist P. A. M. Dirac who is quoted by Schrödinger as having said in conversation: "Beware of forming models or pictures at all."[8]

5. For a specific case, cf. Nagel, op. cit., p. 114.
6. Cf. Max Black's discussion of scale models in his Models and Metaphors (Ithaca: Cornell University Press, 1962), pp. 220–221.
7. Arthur Pap, An Introduction to the Philosophy of Science (Glencoe: The Free Press, 1962), p. 355.
8. Erwin Schrödinger, Science and the Human Temperament (translated by J. Murphy and W. H. Johnston), (New York: W. W. Norton Co., 1935), p. 160.

A fourth view, cited by physicist and philosopher Henry Margenau, is that models are best understood as "auxiliary concepts" [9] which are more useful for the purposes of theory-construction than of description. This position, Margenau says, holds "that science, released from the bondage of sensory experience, no longer describes reality but makes 'models' of reality which serve only the purpose of explanation and calculation." [10] Such a view, premised on "release" from sensory experience, would seem to involve the "*un*picturability" of models and thus to depart sharply from Pap, Dirac, and Jeans.

Margenau is not alone, however, in recognizing a use of the term "model" for referring to what cannot be pictured. A fifth usage finds "model" equivalent to "analogue," and thus applicable to wholly formal and unpicturable domains of thought. The British philosopher Mary B. Hesse, for example, notes that Riemann's non-Euclidean geometry functioned as an important model for Einstein's general theory of relativity. In light of this and many other similar cases the term "model" may even mislead: "Sometimes the models used in physics are purely mathematical in character, and this is why the word *analogue* is generally preferable to *model,* because the latter may seem to imply something mechanical or at least picturable." [11] With this position[12] we have moved far from Kelvin or Dirac, for whom "model" (for better or for worse) *should* "imply something mechanical or at least picturable."

A sixth conception of "model" finds the essential question not in the issue of picturability or non-picturability but in the capacity of a model to focus language drawn from one domain of discourse onto another and less familiar domain. Max Black supports this view of what he calls "theoretical models" and

9. Henry Margenau, *The Nature of Physical Reality. A Philosophy of Modern Physics* (New York: McGraw-Hill Book Co., Inc., 1950), pp. 44–46.
10. *Ibid.,* p. 45.
11. Mary B. Hesse, *Science and the Human Imagination* (London: SCM Press, Ltd., 1954), p. 138.
12. Cf. also Max Black's excellent discussion of analogue models and mathematical models in Black, *op. cit.,* pp. 222–226.

declares: "the heart of the method consists in *talking* in a certain way." [13] It is this general sort of model with which we shall be largely—but not exclusively—concerned in the present essay.

Let us, finally, bring to a close this sampling of views on the meaning of "model"—that elusive companion to a theory that somehow brings epistemological familiarity (for good or ill) to the abstract logical structure of pure theory—by noticing a striking use of the term by Stephen Toulmin. Toulmin, in his latest book on the philosophy of science, discusses those broadest understandings that men may have concerning the natural order. In any such view, Toulmin says, we find some elements that are taken as simply self-explanatory, basic truths that simply "stand to reason" and on which all other explanations are based. "Such models and ideals, principles of regularity and explanatory paradigms, are not always recognized for what they are; differences of opinion about them give rise to some of the profoundest scientific disputes, and changes in them to some of the most important transformations of scientific theory . . ." [14] "Model," here, has obviously come to mean something vastly different from Lord Kelvin's "rude mechanical models," [15] Margenau's "auxiliary concept," or Hesse's mathematical isomorphism.

Has this brief excursion revealed nothing but ambiguity and equivocation? Or can we, as map-makers, hope to lay hold of some principles of projection with the help of which we may discover form and intelligibility within the logical terrain we have now surveyed? Our next task must be to develop, if possible, such cartographic tools as may be applicable to this pursuit.

II

The differences of opinion and usage which we have noted may on inspection be seen to fall into three classes. First, there is a

13. *Ibid.*, p. 229.
14. Stephen Toulmin, *Foresight and Understanding: An Enquiry into the Aims of Science* (Bloomington: Indiana University Press, 1961), pp. 42–43.
15. Sir William Thompson, quoted in Black, *op. cit.*, p. 229.

class of questions concerning a model's degree of concreteness—whether a model must be of a sort to be actually built or may only be pictured or, perhaps, merely be conceived. This class of questions is directed at discovering what I shall call the *type* of a model. Second, there is a class of questions concerning a model's degree of inclusiveness—how much a model may be supposed to represent: a single entity, a general species of thing or event, or still wider domains of thought. Here the questions revolve around what I shall name the *scope* of a model. A model's scope, it will be noted, does not necessarily depend on its type or *vice versa*. Third, there is a class of questions concerning a model's degree of importance—how highly valued should models be: are they indispensable, dangerous, or may they "be taken or left alone"? This sort of query is concerned with what I shall label the *status* of a model. Judgments of status may, or may not, vary with different attributions of type and scope. Let us now put these distinctions to use in an attempt to sketch in an orderly way the major features of the landscape before us.

Mapping Models in Terms of Type

Some models, as we have seen, may be of a type that permits their being built in the laboratory or the shop. Mechanical models and scale models have already been mentioned. Some scale models are supposed to work, as certain models of steam or gasoline engines; some scale models fortunately do not, as, for instance, the huge model of a locust used in zoölogy lectures. Working models, likewise, may or may not be true to scale. The logically important function of the scale model is to permit spatial relationships to be read off in true proportion; the logically significant function of the working model is to illustrate a process and to permit temporal elements to be read off in true succession. In those cases where one has a scale model that also works, one is given a representation of both spatial and temporal relations. In other, commoner, cases when one has a model either built to scale or built to function mechanically, but not both, the temporal and the spatial proportions of the model, respectively, are logically irrelevant. This notion of "relevance" and "irrelevance," as we shall see throughout the present study, is of critical importance for any logical analysis of models.

Still another kind of model of the type that permits construction may be neither a working model nor a scale model. We are all familiar with the models constructed out of little balls and dowel to illustrate various sorts of molecules and their structure. These models are neither expected to "work" (as in a model steam engine) nor to be true to scale. At the same time, however, they "work" *logically* by offering an epistemological immediacy to the theoretical term "molecule" which, as a term appearing only in the higher level formulae of the calculus-skeleton of the molecular theory, would apart from a model of this or of some other kind have needed to have had its meaning derived much more indirectly.

At this point we find ourselves approaching a type of model which fulfills its function of offering epistemological vividness to that which it represents merely through mental images. It is clear that any model which can be built may also be pictured. The reverse, however, is not so obviously true. Some picturable models may defy construction. Cosmologist Fred Hoyle's "steady-state universe," for example, may with a stretch of imagination be crudely pictured in the "mind's eye": a spheroid blob surrounded by absolutely nothing, in which hydrogen endlessly pops into existence in the center at the same rate at which constantly accelerating galaxies around the edges twinkle out of existence. But such a model could not even conceivably be built in the laboratory shop!

There may, indeed, be some difference of opinion as to whether Hoyle's model can even be a mental picture. Sidestepping this controversy, which is not really important to the typology or to the thesis being presented in this paper, I am brought directly to the most inclusive type of model, within which all previously mentioned types must fall. Here we permit the term "model" to apply to anything that manifests the formal characteristics of a model and *can merely be conceived*. It goes without saying that all models that can be built or pictured must be conceivable; it is not the case that all conceivable models can be pictured or built. It is no doubt on some such ground as this that there are those[16] who warn against taking "picturability" as a defining characteristic of models. That warning is well taken.

Within this most inclusive model-type we find a contrast between "substantive" and "formal" models.[17] The latter group will contain, for example, such models as are drawn from pure mathematics, where, as has frequently been the case in mathematical physics,[18] "the mathematical formalism of one theory can serve as a model for another theory with a more inclusive scope of application than the original one." [19] Here, too, we may find many of Black's "theoretical models," in which a "way of speaking" is of the essence. But theoretical models will not fall exclusively or even for the most part within the class of "formal models." Many of the ways of speaking which serve as models for one domain will be drawn from other, familiar, domains of life and discourse. And all these "substantive models," in contrast to formal models, will be such *because* they have been drawn from domains of familiar "filled" experience rather than formal relationship. All constructable or visualizable models are, of course, of the substantive variety, and it is argued by some that all substantive models are at least visualizable.[20] Is this the case? *Most* substantive models will, indeed, be picturable, but an interesting issue is raised by the question whether this is true for *all*. Erwin Schrödinger, for example, urged (some years ago) that irrelevant details simply be eliminated from substantive models of science, and he asserted that this process of selective elimination could be accomplished "without leading to the consequence, that no visualizable scheme of the physical universe whatever will prove feasible." [21] But he went on immediately to acknowledge that one of

16. Cf. pp. 57–58 above.
17. Nagel, *op. cit.,* p. 110.
18. Cf. *ibid.,* p. 111.
19. Nagel, *op. cit.,* p. 111.
20. Cf. *ibid.,* p. 110.
21. Schrödinger, *op. cit.,* p. 165.

the first "irrelevancies" to such important theoretical entities as electrons will be "the property of possessing this or that definite color, though common to all perceptible objects . . ." [22] Can the electron be "visualized" as colorless? We can hardly understand the question and still answer affirmatively, but if our answer is negative we shall be forced to admit that at least some substantive models defy our *imagining* if not (*pace* Berkeley) our *conceiving*.

This, however, is a puzzling conclusion, if a model's logical function is somehow to represent something with an epistemological vividness greater than that possessed by the theory! To what extent are we any longer "using a model" when we merely conceive the unimaginable? Is Schrödinger supposing that the *model* of the electron is without color (and thus unvisualizable), or, as seems more likely in context, does he take the model qua model to be fully equipped with some color but "read" or interpreted in such a way that the color aspect of the imagined model is deliberately ignored or suppressed as logically irrelevant? Once again we note the importance of our conventions of interpreting what is relevant, an importance that is underscored by Schrödinger who warns us that "it will be necessary to acquire a definite sense of what is *irrelevant* in our new models and schemes, before we can trust to their guidance with more equanimity and confidence." [23]

The understandings of "model" encountered in our initial sampling have proved to be far from mutually exclusive, at least with respect to type. Instead of spending our energies arguing with Kelvin against Hesse or with Black against Pap, we have discovered certain logical relations of inclusion and subordination among different concepts of model. In place of sheer diversity we have found some degree, at least, of underlying order. Whenever we encounter some use of "model" we shall do well to locate it as precisely as we can within the framework of types we have begun to construct.

22. *Ibid.*
23. *Ibid.*

Mapping Models in Terms of Scope

A second framework which may be provided our growing logical map of models deals with the extent of a given model's field of application.

At one extreme we find models with scope limited to a single entity like the city of ancient Troy, or the *Friendship Seven,* or the projected North Campus. In these cases the model may serve the function—when correctly interpreted with respect to its logically relevant features—of permitting measurements or manipulations, as well as an immediate mental grasp of the subject matter, which would be difficult or impossible to obtain from the original. It is noteworthy that models of this restricted scope usually have the highest proportion of logically relevant features. A model that represents the *Queen Elizabeth,* for example, will properly be interpreted as offering a great many more "relevant" details than a model representing, say, Cunard liners or twentieth century steamships in general.

In this way we move from models with scope limited to simple entities to models with a scope that is representative of a general class of entities. It is worth noticing that models with general rather than particular scope may in fact also be models of a single entity. A model of the *De Witt Clinton,* for example, may—depending on the context of its "reading," that is, the conventions of its interpretation—stand for the whole class of early steam railroad trains rather than the *Clinton* alone. But, on the other hand, a model with general scope may deliberately be fashioned so as to be unlike any particular member of the class of entities modeled, like the composite airplane appearing on some air mail postage stamps. This practice has the logical effect of emphasizing that the model is not to be interpreted as representing uniquely any single entity of the class within its scope—and thus that a large number of particular features of the model (e.g. the exact angle of slope of the rudder, the position of the cockpit windows, the length of fuselage relative to wingspan, and the like) are logically irrelevant.

It will be evident that my examples, although not drawn from science, have a bearing on the use of models in scientific inquiry. An astronomer may find a model of the moon useful as a model of particular scope, but he may in another context use the same model as representing simply "satellite"—in which case many features of the model that were logically relevant in the first use will become irrelevant in the new "reading." Even more obviously, an astrophysicist who utilizes Bohr's model of the sodium atom to help in his explanation of certain absorption lines in a spectrogram will not "read" his model as having unique reference to a particular atom. He will, instead, consider a great many features of his model as logically irrelevant—including not only (as Schrödinger mentioned) the color he may imagine the electrons to have, but also (as quantum theory insists) the fact that his model's electrons in their "orbits" all may have simultaneously determinable velocity and position.

Widest of all scope, at least for scientific models, is possessed by those models mentioned by Schrödinger as visualizable schemes "of the physical universe" or distinguished earlier by Toulmin as explanatory paradigms for the whole natural order. Models of this breadth of scope are no longer interpreted as representatives of limited classes of entities or events but as "conceptual archetypes" [24 and 25] for the synthetic organization and the synoptic "seeing" of all that is within the purview of the natural sciences. Once again, however, very simple and particular (as well as esoteric or abstract) phenomena may be chosen to function as models of this most comprehensive sort. Aristotle's model for a "self-explanatory" dynamic principle, drawn from particular common-sense experiences of objects "naturally" at rest when not being pushed or pulled,[26] undergirded much of his thought and, significantly, even spread its influence as far in time, space, and subject matter as to the first two of St. Thomas Aquinas' Five Ways of proving the existence of God! [27]

24. Stephen C. Pepper, *World Hypotheses* (Berkeley: University of California Press, 1942).
25. Black, *op. cit.*, p. 241.
26. Toulmin, *op. cit.*, for a fascinating treatment of this subject.
27. *Summa Theologica*, Q. II, Art. 3.

Mapping Models in Terms of Status

Any model, such as Aristotle's, that can function in dynamical explanation and in theological speculation is bound to stir philosophical controversy. Controversy, however, surrounds the entire territory we have been engaged in charting. There are those who insist that models are dangerous, others who consider them helpful but inessential, and still others who defend their employment as both rational and crucially important. A final set of conceptual guidelines will be provided for our logical map by an examination of the arguments stated by various sides of this dispute and by our own evaluation of the merits of the cases presented.

The physicist Dirac, we remember, warned Schrödinger against "forming models or pictures at all." And Sir James Jeans advances a case against models which would support that warning. It is perfectly possible, if a model is formally defined as an epistemologically familiar interpretation of a theory's abstract system of logical relations, for *more than one* such model to be found that would perfectly "fit" a single theory. But then, Jeans says, it would be impossible to choose between these models since, *ex hypothesi,* each is unable to be faulted "in the only property by which it could be tested, namely the power of predicting phenomena." [28] The models, however, may be mutually incompatible, though each fits the formal structure of the theory being interpreted. "Neither model could, then, claim to represent reality," Jeans concludes, "whence it follows that we must never associate any model with reality, since even if it accounted for all the phenomena, a second model might appear at any moment with exactly the same qualifications to represent reality." [29]

Why, if models are thus deceptive, have many physicists sought them and worked with them? Jeans explains that pictorial representations come more naturally to human minds than abstract mathematical formulae because "our mental faculties have come

28. Sir James Jeans, *Physics and Philosophy* (New York: The Macmillan Co., 1943), p. 10.
29. *Ibid.*

to us . . . from fishes and apes." [30] The pressures of survival would have naturally selected for mental traits "more suited to deal with concrete facts than with abstract concepts, with particulars rather than with universals; minds which are more at home in thinking of material objects, rest and motion, pushes, pulls and impacts, than in trying to digest symbols and formulae." [31] Our simian heritage must be overcome, however, for the sake of progress. Physicists may make use of many cognitive techniques: "but the final harvest will always be a sheaf of mathematical formulae." [32] To suppose otherwise is to be deceived by the Neanderthal in modern man. "Beware of forming models or pictures at all!"

Taken together with this case against models and this description of human mentality, it is especially revealing to note Jeans' repeated warnings that "knowledge of reality" or "understanding" of the "loom of things" is impossible for human beings. Apart from the concrete pictures and ideas drawn from sense, he seems to be saying, cognitive satisfaction is not to be had. The "sheaves of mathematical formulae" will be of use in describing our past observations and in predicting future observations, but they are of little use in *understanding*. "We see," Jeans says, "that we can never understand the true nature of reality." [33] Try as we may "to replace unintelligible universals by intelligible particulars," [34] we shall always fail. Intelligibility tantalizes but always escapes us. Models would serve to provide understanding and intelligibility if only they could be trusted, but—alas!—this is forever beyond our reach.

But is it? Jeans' case against models, though a powerful warning against an uncritical abuse of models, is nevertheless an overstatement in need of modification. The first assumption—that the only way of choosing between models is in terms of their

30. *Ibid.*, p. 9.
31. *Ibid.*
32. *Ibid.*, p. 15.
33. *Ibid.*
34. *Ibid.*, pp. 174–175.

predictive power—is open to serious question.[35] Even if this assumption were established, however, it would not follow that *just-because* more than one model could be formulated for a theory, *neither* model could "claim to represent reality." One of these models might still be supposed to "represent reality" to the exclusion of its rivals, just as an honest man at a Liar's Convention might continue to tell the truth though every one of his assertions is countered by a host of incompatible ones. Jeans himself later modifies his stand when he comes to recapitulate his argument. Instead of denying models the logical right even to *claim* to represent reality because of the possible plurality of predictively indistinguishable models, Jeans merely notes that in this situation: ". . . we should have at least one perfect model which did not correspond to reality. Thus we *could never be sure* that any model corresponded to reality." [36] From the outright denial that a model can represent reality to a warning against undue confidence in the representative power of models is a significant step. It is in this connection interesting to note that Jeans' earlier conclusion, "whence it follows that we must never associate any model with reality . . . ," is not repeated in his later statement of the argument, whence it would *not* any longer follow. Instead, a more moderate conclusion is drawn: "In brief, we can never have certain knowledge as to the nature of reality." [37]

With this more temperate view, Jeans very nearly approximates the position of those who, like R. B. Braithwaite, argue that models may have their uses but that they had better be used cautiously and with the steady awareness that a model, like alcohol, is a potentially dangerous luxury. Braithwaite acknowledges that "to think in terms of [a] model is . . . frequently the most convenient way of thinking about the structure of [a] theory . . ." [38] But this convenience consists primarily in permitting us to think about a theory without at the same time having to

35. Stephen Toulmin argues to good effect on this question in Toulmin, *op. cit., passim.*
36. Jeans, *op. cit.*, p. 175, italics supplied.
37. *Ibid.*
38. Braithwaite, *op. cit.*, p. 92.

expend the effort of thinking explicitly about the symbolic structure in which the theory is expressed. Since the theory's formal structure is "given" immediately and easily along with the concrete structure of any model that "fits" it, "the use of models allows of a philosophically unsophisticated approach to an understanding of the structure of a scientific deductive system." [39]

The perils of unsophistication, however, lurk close at hand. Braithwaite is quick to distinguish two such perils which may be serious enough under some conditions to militate against the use of models at all. They are, first, that "the theory will be identified with a model for it . . . ," [40] and, second, that someone will be misled into "transferring the logical necessity of some of the features of the chosen model on to the theory, and thus of supposing, wrongly, that the theory, or parts of the theory, have a logical necessity which is in fact fictitious." [41] Both dangers, if I may express them in terms that I have introduced earlier, reduce to forgetting that the model is a model and thus to taking certain of the model's "logically irrelevant" features (empirical or logical) as "logically relevant." "Thinking of scientific theories by means of models is always *as-if* thinking," as Braithwaite says. But as long as this is kept in mind, even Jeans is ready to accept some limited use of "pictorial representation." "Although we can never devise a pictorial representation which shall be both true to nature and intelligible to our minds, we may still be able to make partial aspects of the truth comprehensible through pictorial representations or parables. As the whole truth does not admit of intelligible representation, every such pictorial representation or parable must fail somewhere." [42] The main trouble with nineteenth century physics, it turns out, is not (as we might earlier have gathered from Jeans) that models were used *at all* but that the mistake was made "of treating the half-truths of pictorial representations and parables as literal truths." [43]

39. *Ibid.*, pp. 92–93.
40. Braithwaite, *op. cit.*, p. 93.
41. *Ibid.*, p. 94.
42. Jeans, *op. cit.*, pp. 15–16.
43. *Ibid.*, p. 16.

Even half-truths, however, are better than no-truths—if we can decide which "half" is which! Granting, as Braithwaite says, that "the price of the employment of models is eternal vigilance," [44] what in general shall we look for to help us exploit the value of models without falling prey to their irrelevancies? There is little use in ordering us to keep our eyes peeled without at the same time describing the colors of friend and foe. Here Jeans, in a far mellower mood than before, becomes explicit. Models can be compared with maps, he says; and just as two-dimensional projections can never tell the *whole* truth about a three-dimensional object, so models are limited to telling partial truths. But maps can be faithful to *aspects* of reality (even though distorting other aspects) and we can, if we are careful, *use a map only for the purposes suited to it,* avoiding the misleading consequences which would follow from taking its logically irrelevant features as logically relevant.

The model of "light as a wave" and the model of "light as a particle" each contains partial aspects of truth, Jeans says. "Neither of these can of course tell the whole truth. In the same way, an atlas may contain two maps of North America drawn on different projections: neither of them will represent the whole truth, but each will represent some aspect of it. An equal area projection, for instance, represents the relative areas of any two regions accurately, but their shapes wrongly, while a Mercator projection represents the shapes rightly, but the areas wrongly. So long as we can only draw our maps on flat pieces of paper, such imperfections are inevitable; they are the price we pay for limiting our maps to the kind that can be bound up in an atlas. The pictures we draw of nature show similar limitations; these are the price we pay for limiting our pictures of nature to the kinds that can be understood by our minds." [45] The important thing, then, is to be aware of which features of a model are functioning, in context, as relevant and which are not; we need to keep in mind, that is, what *kind* of map we are using. It may

44. Braithwaite, *op. cit.,* p. 93.
45. Jeans, *op. cit.,* p. 176.

be that many features will be relevant; it may be that they will be few. In any case we are warned that no sweeping *a priori* assumption that reality must resemble our models will be permitted. Resemblances of many kinds there may be between model and the reality modeled, but "the only resemblance required is that of formal structure." [46]

If a model can be depended upon for no more than formal or structural resemblances, and if a theory, unaccompanied by model, can provide this structural resemblance without raising the danger of subtly introducing irrelevancies and falsehoods into our conceptions of things, might we not be better off without models, despite their limited usefulness as intellectual conveniences? If there were no further logical considerations, this "take them or leave them alone" attitude toward models might be the most rational one to adopt. But there are further points of considerable importance to take into account before drawing any final conclusions about the proper status of models.

A model may be regarded not only as a labor-saving device, with Braithwaite, but also as a heuristic tool of no mean value. One must not overlook the usefulness of models at every stage of the theoretical enterprise. First, models may be of incalculable help in the original process of *suggesting* and *formulating theories*. As Ernest Nagel points out, offering copious historical backing for his claim, "a number of outstanding scientists have been quite explicit about the important role models play in the construction of new theories." [47] But this is only the start of the model's heuristic usefulness. Once a theory has been formulated and its main assumptions clarified with the aid of a model, it still remains for these *assumptions to be explored*, and the model may in this connection *suggest new questions* to be asked about the theory and hint at *new domains* for the theory's application. Nagel offers a good example of this process: "In the historical development of the kinetic theory of gases . . . the model for the theory suggested questions about the ratios of molecular diameters to the

46. Braithwaite, *op. cit.*, p. 91.
47. Nagel, *op. cit.*, p. 108.

distances between the molecules, about various kinds of forces between the molecules, about the elastic properties of moiecules, about the distribution of the velocities of the molecules, and so on. Such questions would perhaps never have been raised had the theory been formulated as an uninterpreted set of postulates. But in any case, these questions led to the deduction of a variety of consequences for the theory, some of which served as hints for reformulating experimental gas laws and for recognizing new ones." [48] More even than thus suggesting ways of extending the power of the theories "embedded in them," models may also be useful in offering ideas for *relating theoretical concepts to empirical ones.* Another example or two will help to illustrate this function: "Again, the interpretation of optical theory in terms of waves propagated in a medium invites the association of theoretical expressions referring to the amplitude of waves in the model with the intensity of the illumination; the wave interpretation also suggests the linking of theoretical expressions referring to the interference of waves with the dark lines (or absence of illumination) observed in certain experimentally generated patterns of light and shadow." [49]

But these heuristic functions, important as they are, do not exhaust the logical usefulness of models. There is no longer, I hope, the danger that the employment of models will be contemptuously considered merely "a prop for feeble minds . . . or a convenient short cut to the consideration of deductive systems . . . ," [50] but it still may not be fully recognized that models sometimes, as Max Black says, are "not epiphenomena of research, but play a distinctive and irreplaceable part in scientific investigation. . . ." [51] In what way can this claim be defended?

First, beyond its purely heuristic functions, a model may "contribute to inclusive systems of explanation" [52] not merely in terms of the limited domain of a single theory but in terms of its power

48. Nagel, *op. cit.,* p. 113.
49. *Ibid.,* pp. 113–114.
50. Black, *op. cit.,* pp. 235–236.
51. *Ibid.,* p. 236.
52. Nagel, *op. cit.,* p. 114.

to relate that theory plausibly to our whole conceptual account of reality. In this way a well chosen model may link *widely divergent domains of understanding* in a freshly intelligible way, substituting coherence and unity for fragmented and partial explanatory systems. Another way of putting this would be to say that a good model, as a "speculative instrument," [53] has the function of helping us "to notice what otherwise would be overlooked, to shift the relative emphasis attached to details—in short to see new connections." [54]

Second, can this function be shown really to be an "irreplaceable" part of scientific investigation? Our answer to this will depend on our view of the essential purposes of science itself. If, with Jeans, we conclude that "we can never understand what events are, but must limit ourselves to describing the pattern of events in mathematical terms . . . ," [55] and that "the study of physics has driven us to the positivist conception of physics," [56] in which the functions of science are reducible to prediction of phenomena, then the importance of models beyond their heuristic powers will be minimized. But if, as I believe, the aim of science is not merely prediction but also *understanding,* then it will turn out that "science progresses, not by recognizing the truth of new observations alone, but by making sense of them." [57] For this, models are needed to supplement theories serving as bare techniques for predicting. Even Jeans recognizes the presence of this wish for "making sense" of observations—while denying any possibility of its fulfillment—when he notes: ". . . we not only wish to predict phenomena, but also to understand them. Thus it is not surprising that philosophy and science alike have found this [predictionist] mathematical description unsatisfying . . ." [58] Grant science the function of making sense of phenomena, illuminating data, searching for understanding of reality, and models

53. I. A. Richards, cited by Black, *op. cit.,* p. 237.
54. *Ibid.*
55. Jeans, *op. cit.,* p. 15.
56. Jeans, *op. cit.,* p. 15.
57. Toulmin, *op. cit.,* p. 81.
58. Jeans, *op. cit.,* p. 174.

achieve a cognitive status of their own which defies replacement by the abstract calculi of theoretical constructs. Only at the price of shrinking science from what it is—a humane and imaginative attempt at rigorous understanding of wide domains of being— into a cramped technique for anticipating impacts on the senses, can one suppose that models are "disreputable understudies for mathematical formulas." [59]

We are well warned, by those who consider the status of the model to be primarily a dangerous incitement to metaphorical thinking, against approaching the use of a model literally, expecting the wrong things from it; we are also well warned, by those who look at models as primarily convenient luxuries, against adopting models uncritically being lured off into pseudo questions by logical irrelevancies. But we are now prepared to proceed, vigilantly but aware that models can add great power to our cognitive pursuits, with the knowledge that, risky or not, models put a tool in our hand for understanding what, without models, may remain opaque. And for the sake of understanding as best we can—within all our human limitations—we should perhaps be willing to take even serious risks.

III

I shall assume for the purposes of this essay that theology, like science, is interested in understanding—as far as may be humanly possible—the reality in which men find themselves. This is not, of course, an uncontroversial assumption; there are those who deny that theology is even *concerned* with cognitive questions, quite apart from her success or lack of it in answering them. Against this point of view, whether resting on philosophical or theological grounds, I have elsewhere[60] argued at some length, but I shall not repeat those arguments here. Instead, let me simply note that a faith unconcerned with cognitive issues is emascu-

59. Black, *op. cit.*, p. 236.
60. Cf. my *Language, Logic and God* (New York: Harper & Brothers, 1961), Chap. 12; also K. Bendall and F. Ferré, *Exploring the Logic of Faith* (New York: Association Press, 1962), Chs. 2 and 4.

lated. It is well for theologians to remind their critics (and their churches) that faith is not reducible without vastly important residue to cognitive assent given various propositional elements; but this salutary warning against the *reduction* of faith to "mere belief" must not be confused with an *elimination* of belief from faith. Without the retention of some element of belief, the theologian is required to abandon any pretense to interest in truth or falsity; he is forced to give up any chance of giving point or justification to his attitudes, emotions, utterances, or behavior; and he is condemned, as a purveyor of one more item of personal taste, to isolation from the determinative issues of life—toward which, ironically, his faith prompts him to speak with "the wisdom of serpents"—an isolation no less complete for its being self-imposed.

Assuming, then, that theology is not indifferent to truth about reality, it becomes relevant to ask whether there are models in theology as well as in science and, if so, how they should be related to other models on our logical map.

Finding the Models of Theology

If we continue to understand by "model" that which provides epistemological vividness or immediacy to a theory by offering as an interpretation of the abstract or unfamiliar theory-structure something that both fits the logical form of the theory and is well known, we shall find models in abundance within theology. In a very straightforward sense, every parable (as Jeans hinted in quite a different connection) is a model: " 'Listen! A sower went out to sow. And as he sowed, some seed fell along the path, and the birds came and devoured it. Other seed fell on rocky ground . . .' And he said to them, 'Do you not understand the parable? How then will you understand all the parables? The sower sows the word. And these are the ones along the path, where the word is sown; when they hear, Satan immediately comes and takes away the word which is sown in them. And these in like manner are the ones sown upon rocky ground . . .' " [61] Here

61. Mark 4:3 ff. (Revised Standard Version).

is an epistemological vividness offered by imagery drawn from common experience, but imagery which is deemed appropriate because it shares a common logical structure with a theory that can be duly stated, independent of the model, to a few initiated disciples. "Here is how you may *think* about it, if you like . . . ; but here is how it *really* is . . . ," is a frequently repeated pattern, and not only in Western religions. The open and abundant use of models, analogues, similitudes, seems to be an entrenched part of the religious mentality.

But clearly labeled uses, as in parables, are not exhaustive of the uses of models within theology. Within Christian thought, for example, there has been a long established practice of searching the scriptures for covert models of theologically significant figures or events. The many "types of Christ," for example, allegedly found by fundamentalist and pre-critical—or, interestingly, by some of the very newest and most sophisticated [62]—biblical scholarship are noteworthy here. Jonah's "three days and three nights in the belly of the fish," to choose but one crude example, has been taken as a model of Jesus' three days in the tomb. And in this sort of searching for significant models we may be discovering the quest for a unity and coherence in the biblical account as a whole which can bring together into a simple focus what might otherwise seem a sheer, vast multiplicity. Looking at one thing, and without in any way failing to see it in itself, many other things are seen as well. Finding or forming models in this sense of underlying patterns of structure within his religious tradition may help the believer see new connections within his data. And such "seeing" through models, by giving his theological beliefs increased internal coherence, may strengthen the believer's sense of the intelligiblity of his faith.

That this sense of intelligibility is illusory, however, apart from additional external relations of coherence between the cognitive context of faith and all established knowledge was one of

---

62. Cf. Ronald W. Hepburn's critiques of this form of theological interest in models in "Demythologizing and the Problem of Validity," *New Essays in Philosophical Theology* (New York: Macmillan & Co., 1955) , and "Poetry and Religious Belief" in *Metaphysical Beliefs* (London: SCM Press, 1957).

the most important emphases of the liberal theological movement of the nineteenth and early twentieth centuries; and it remains the one permanently valid contribution of all "rational
theologies," despite their many notorious defects. It is with
respect to this domain of theological interest—interest in cognitive ties with all knowledge and in beliefs about reality that
can be simply *true* or *false,* rather than "true within a certain
'language game' "—that we discover another sort of employment
of theological models, most conveniently called the metaphysical
use of models or, for short, "metaphysical models." When the
Judeo-Christian scriptures set about representing the nature of
ultimate reality, this enterprise is not approached through abstract theory but through epistemologically vivid stories and
anthropomorphically immediate images. Ideas drawn from one
area of experience are put to work in another area—an area in
which, we are explicitly warned, these ideas have no proper place.
The keystone of the biblical ontological scheme, the concept of
God, is beyond human conception: "His ways are not our ways,
nor His thoughts our thoughts." But in spite of such reminders,
the theoretical term "God" is constantly interpreted in terms
of epistemologically vivid personal models. The very warnings
against supposing our concepts of God to be literally representative are themselves couched in the language of the model: the
personal *His,* the anthropomorphic attribution of *thoughts* to
God. Even when, in the second of the Ten Commandments, the
people of Israel are warned against making themselves *graven*
images of God ("He Who Is," beyond images), or of forming
"any likeness of anything that is in heaven above, or that is in
the earth beneath, or that is in the water under the earth," [63] the
same commandment relies on forming *verbal* images of God and
offering the epistemological "likeness" of human passions as a
justification for this prohibition: ". . . for I the Lord your God
am a jealous God, visiting the iniquity of the fathers upon the
children to the third and fourth generation of those who hate
me, but showing steadfast love to thousands of those who love

63. Exodus 20:4.

me and keep my commandments." [64] Models, and warnings that
what we have to think with *are* models; epistemological vividness,
coupled with vehement affirmations of human ignorance before
ultimate reality as it is in and for itself—this is the ambivalent
approach of biblical religion.[65]

The dominant attitude of biblical faith is not nescience, however, but a sense of understanding. The models are *trusted* even
when recognized as images and likenesses of a reality that stands
beyond human powers of imagining or comparing. And for
Christians, of course, the models of the Old Testament—however
helpful or even essential—all take second place to what they
believe to be the one supremely reliable model for God, Jesus of
Nazareth. In looking at one thing, a human life of a certain
quality and with certain specifiable empirical characteristics, they
are given a concrete interpretation of the abstract concept, "God,"
that is totally without the epistemological immediacy of the
model. One of the tasks of the church, we may note, has been
the difficult one of distinguishing between what are properly
to be taken as "logically relevant" and "logically irrelevant"
features of this supreme personal image of ultimate reality. Their
problem has been how rigorously to interpret the key epistemological statement of the New Testament: "He who has seen me
has seen the Father; how can you say, 'show me the Father'?" [66]
Every christological formulation that takes that statement seriously is, whether consciously or not, a study in epistemology and
an exercise in model-reading.

Christian faith does not abandon the Old Testament, however,
and because of this it has avoided the temptation to reduce the
meaning of "God" to any single one of its models, including its
supreme model. Instead, the great numbers of epistemologically
immediate images, stories, and anthropomorphic conceptions
of scripture are blended together into a panoramic mosaic picture

64. *Ibid.*
65. Analogous things could be said, I believe, about other major religious
traditions of the world, but defense of such a thesis must remain beyond the
scope of this paper.
66. John 14:9 (Revised Standard Version).

of reality including God, man, and nature. This is a picture shot through, as we have seen, with unifying strands based on master models; it is a picture with a definite place for everything under the supreme sovereignty of a personal God; and it is a picture of the world which, if taken as literally descriptive either in terms of the mosaic-bits which make it up or in respect of its "three storey" world-picture as a whole, is unquestionably false—to the consternation of Rudolf Bultmann and his "demythologizing" followers. But if this composite picture, what we may call the biblical model of reality or the biblical metaphysical model, is properly taken *as a model,* it may be that the very *falsity* of its empirical pseudo claims falls into that "half" of all such "half-truths" which *should be read as logically irrelevant.* Perhaps, we may find, theological metaphysical models do not function as rivals to the models of empirical science.

Mapping the Models of Theology

How shall we locate the models, particularly the metaphysical models, of theology in terms of the triple conceptual framework we constructed earlier? It will help to sharpen our understanding of them to plot their position in terms of type, scope, and status.

First, as to type, it is clear that the models of theology are not of a sort that *must* be constructed. We have already noted an explicit Old Testament prohibition against such attempted constructions, and although this commandment is not felt by Christians to stand in the way of religious art, the fact remains that the Jews have shown that biblical models can function perfectly well without overt portrayal of this kind. At the same time, however, the very existence of artistic representations of biblical imagery in sculpture, painting, stained glass, and the like, proves that we are not dealing with that type of model—at least in all aspects—which logically defies pictorial representation. The vigorously anthropomorphic Father God in Michelangelo's great "Creation," for example, should not properly be an object of embarrassment to the theological purist; on the contrary, the rugged vitality of

Michelangelo's bearded patriarch is magnificently in keeping with a biblical logic which glories in anthropomorphism. The purist who squirms at anthropomorphism in his religious conceptions might well listen to Feuerbach's crusty truth: "He who dreads an existence that may give offence, who shrinks from the grossness of a positive predicate, may as well renounce existence altogether. A God who is injured by determinate qualities has not the courage and strength to exist." [67]

It might, however, be misleading to leave the impression that all "determinate" qualities are visualizable ones. "Picturing" language is sometimes rather loosely used. Sometimes it is said that one can "picture how Harry must have felt." But if more is meant by this than that one can visualize facial expressions, gestures, and the like, associated with certain feelings, the metaphor of the "mind's eye" is being stretched rather far. Theological models, likewise, may be considered of the essentially "picturable" type only by an extended metaphor. The emotions of jealousy or love cannot be pictured, strictly speaking, but they can be imagined. And in this sense we shall classify the bulk of biblical metaphysical models as substantive-conceptual in type.[68] Within this type, as we saw earlier, there may be models open to imagination but not to visualization, models open to visualization but not to construction, and models open to construction as well as to conception and visualization. All the important models of biblical religion are to be found here, from the clearly labeled parables of Jesus to the overarching composite biblical model of reality as a whole, despite the presence in the Bible of some models which may be considered "formal" (note the importance of the numbers "seven" or "three") but which are definitely subordinated within the substantive mosaic biblical model taken as a unity.

67. Ludwig Feuerbach, *The Essence of Christianity* (translated by George Eliot) (New York: Harper & Brothers, 1957), p. 15.
68. It should not be assumed that such a classification necessarily holds good for all metaphysical models. Aristotle's hylomorphic metaphysical system, for example, may utilize the formal-conceptual model of the grammatical relationship between subject and predicate. The application of my remarks to the whole field of metaphysical construction cannot, however, be made in this place.

Next, turning from type to scope, we see at once that although there may be models of different degrees of appropriate extension within theology, the key metaphysical model of reality possesses the widest possible degree of application and relevance. There is nothing in principle, beyond the scope of the biblical model of nature, man, and God. The function of this model, indeed, would seem to be that of laying down guidelines for what may be counted as being real! Therefore anything counted by Christians as real will—must, *a priori*—fall within the scope of this model.

A consequence of this unlimited scope of the biblical metaphysical model [69] is the notorious unfalsifiability of theological concepts.[70] It would take us too far afield from models to the workings of theological theory itself to explore this issue in detail, but it may quickly be seen that a model which is taken to include, in principle, all real or possible events, cannot be disproved by any real or possible event that comes to pass. It has already, in germ, *accounted for* anything that might occur, and accounted for it within an interpretative framework that cannot possibly be tested independently of the framework, since any test—and any outcome of that test—that is real or possible is already accounted for within the framework! The adequacy of the "fit" of theological models with respect to whatever structure reality as a whole may have, then, is not able to be tested through straightforward empirical criteria; and it is seriously questioned by many whether any tests at all are possible. Max Black, for example, warns that the widest models may become "permanently insulated from empirical disproof," and that the consequence of this development is the model's becoming "a self-certifying myth." [71] But it is not

69. In contrast to their multiplicity of types, all metaphysical models, theological or otherwise, share this characteristic of unlimited scope. I would, indeed, wish to argue that such scope is the key defining characteristic of metaphysical models, providing both the necessary and the sufficient condition of their metaphysicality.

70. Cf. Antony Flew's "Theology and Falsification" and subsequent discussion in *New Essays in Philosophical Theology, op. cit.*, or my treatment of this question in *Language, Logic and God*, Chap. 3.

71. Black, *op. cit.*, p. 242.

necessarily the case that "open to empirical disproof" or "self-certifying myth" are, as Black here assumes, the only viable alternatives. To explore this question further here is impossible, since any methods of testing models—including metaphysical models —are inseparable from the theories with which the models are associated, and this additional question must remain beyond the reach of the present study.[72]

Touching even briefly on this falsification controversy, however, brings us inevitably to the question of the status of theological models. What importance or value do they have?

Such a question always demands the counter-question: "Value *for what?*" To begin most narrowly, the biblical metaphysical model provides theology with the possibility of offering intelligible interpretations for its lesser parables and models. We have noted earlier that a parable is of the form: "Here is how you may think about it, if you like . . . ; but here is how it *really* is . . ." What is it, though, that the interpreter of the parable must put in place of his parabolic imagery? He is forced back upon more imagery, perhaps of wider scope and different emotional impact than before, but imagery none the less. Jesus' parables of "The Kingdom" substitute homely likenesses for more august ones, but *likenesses* of one sort or another are not avoided: certain characteristics drawn from a mustard tree or a pearl of great price are used to bring into vivid focus certain others drawn from the human experience of living in great societies under the reign of kings. Of course this divine "King" will be "ruler" of all creation who will be "just," "merciful," "slow to anger," "aware of and concerned about his lowliest subject," and so on—he will be far superior to any king actually experienced and his Kingdom will be far more wonderful than any earthly kingdom ever known— but the dependence on some form of the personal root model will remain vital to the interpretation of any lesser model or figure of speech. In terms of the intra-theological interpretation

---

72. But cf. *Language, Logic and God, op. cit.,* and *Exploring the Logic of Faith, op. cit.,* especially Section 10 of the latter, for a suggested method of testing a metaphysical model-cum-theory.

of theological parable, then, we discover that the metaphysical-theological model has an essential status.

This point must be generalized, however; for not only are the models of theology essential for interpretation of theological discourse within the language using community but—at least equally important—these models are necessary for the expression of religious beliefs to the world at large. Apart from concepts intelligible to human minds, theology remains empty of meaning to friend and foe—as well as to the theologian himself! And it is in the *models* of theological theory, not in abstract theory itself, that all intelligible theological ideas are rooted. Let us briefly, without plunging deeply into the nature of theological theory as distinct from models, consider why this must be.

First, it might be supposed that theology could rest content with giving its theoretical terms ("God," "Christ," "the world," and the like) merely *implicit* definitions, that is, definitions reflecting the logical relations of these terms within the abstract calculus of the theory. To this we may reply that implicit definitions of this kind can always be provided within an uninterpreted formal system, but such definitions remain purely formal. On the basis of implicit definitions it is possible to construct well-formed formulae of the system in question (e.g. "God was in Christ reconciling the world to Himself"), but this turns out to be no more than the manipulation of empty tokens. The apparent intelligibility of such formulae is due to the model by which we habitually interpret these terms. Shorn of its model-evoking terms, the resulting formula (e.g. "A was in B relating C asymmetrically to A") would more accurately reflect the emptiness of a theology attempting to depend on nothing but implicit or syntactical definitions.

But, second, the theoretical terms of a scientific theory may be given a meaning indirectly and without a model by the expedient of our working back from the theory's lower level experimental formulae to the higher level theoretical formulae of which the former are logical consequences. May this not be done in theology? No, it may not; and the reason for the theologian's inability to define his higher level formulae indirectly in terms of the particular observation-statements they entail and exclude is the fact, briefly noted above, that theological systems cannot be falsified by any observation-statement. If they cannot be thus falsified, they cannot be supposed to entail any particular observation-statements; for if they did so entail any particular observation-statements, the empirical discovery of such statements to be false would be tantamount, by *modus tollens,* to a falsification of the theological system. It may be argued that the theologian's difficulty is due to the fact that his system entails *every possible* observation-statement. But this, if so, would have the same net logical result, with respect to the present question, as if his system entailed *no* observation-statement, since no particular empirical meaning can be derived for the system in either case, and that which means nothing in particular is no better off than that which means nothing at all! Theological models provide the particularity of concept that would otherwise be missing from theology.

Even the theologian's technical vocabulary is not so independent of his model as he might think. Is "God's transcendence" under discussion? An analyst need not look far before he finds the thinly disguised spatial metaphor that underlies this term. Everywhere the model peeps through, and it is more difficult than many realize to be rid of it and still to *say the same thing* that was intended before. "Transcendent? That means above the universe. Above? Well, not really above, but *beyond.* Beyond? No, not in space—but simply not exclusively in the universe. *In . . . ?"*

Is this merely a difficulty, or is it a logical necessity that without his model the theologian simply cannot say what he wants to say without a change of meaning? That is, is it a logical necessity that the theologian must depend on the model? I have been trying to show that models are necessary in terms of the cognitive enterprise of the theologian, and I think the case is sound. But whether or not I have been correct in my argument so far, the injection of non-cognitive dimensions of meaning into the question should tip this balance quite independently of the previous logical considerations. For it is without doubt the imagery of the models in theology which evoke the communal adoration, obeisance, awe, devotion, ecstasy, courage—the emotive and conative dimensions of faith that constitute it *religious faith* rather than philosophical speculation or metaphysical system-building. I am not claiming that imagery alone can support such non-cognitive elements—courage without *belief* that courage is appropriate in the situation is something less than courage!—but it is precisely because the models of faith are taken as trustworthy, that is, believed to be in some sense true, that their non-cognitive functions are possible. Toward a theory without the vividness and immediacy provided by the biblical model, however, such responses could never be expected; and without the language of the model, having the power to bring together and to intertwine domains of personal value and of ontological plenitude in emotional as well as cognitive relation, distinctively religious dimensions of meaning could not be expressed by the believer.

The status of metaphysical models in theology, then, is essential, since it turns out that the presence of these models is a necessary condition[73] of theological meaning and belief. But to what extent, we may still ask, is theology itself essential? Models may be of the greatest importance to theology, but of what importance is theology to us?

There can be no simple answer to this question, and a full answer would be too much to undertake here. I shall make only two brief and unsupported points. First, theology is at least no worse off, in epistemological principle, than rival metaphysical

73. But not a sufficient condition, since a model must be provided with relations to other domains of interest and knowledge and must be explicitly affirmed before it can be considered to be functioning fully theologically. It is perfectly possible, for example, that an important biblical model—or even the key biblical model of reality itself—may be contemplated aesthetically or otherwise entertained in thought without being given a full theological employment. The missing element, in these cases, is the "theory" or "conceptual synthesis," concerning which space forbids me to deal in this monograph.

systems. Every metaphysic relies, no less than the theological metaphysic, on its own model; and in its long history the personal model of biblical faith has proved itself not only highly evocative, non-cognitively, but also an interpretative tool with claims to real cognitive power. Second, it must be acknowledged that metaphysical beliefs are indeed useless in connection with the scientific enterprise of solving empirical problems or with predicting and controlling the world. Thus, if human life can be lived to its full entirely with reference to the anticipation and the manipulation of one's environment, then metaphysics—and with it theology on its cognitive dimension—is without importance and the status of metaphysical models may be reckoned low. *If,* on the other hand, man is more than a tool-user and a problem-solver, *if* his yen for understanding first principles and his thirst for searching out the most nearly intelligible and the most nearly reliable notion of the ultimate nature of things is inexpungeable—*if* these characteristics are constitutive of man (and these are not questions invulnerable in principle to empirical testing, though the tests would be extremely difficult and time-consuming), then theology, as one candidate for metaphysical truth, is potentially of the greatest possible importance. And if there are those who find full contentment in tool-using and problem solving, for whom the vast speculations and unsettleable disputes of metaphysicians are only a waste of precious time, they are asked to be tolerant toward those others to whom these questions seem the very stuff of life. Grasshoppers, as well as ants, must live as best they can.

IV

We have now reached the point in this study where I can bring the models of science and theology into a single focus. In order to make this possible I have attempted to impose some definite form on the protean concept of "model" in general, with particular emphasis on the fields of science, wherein the notion is most often encountered; and I have attempted to chart the location and logical character of models for the field of theology, wherein they are seldom explicitly acknowledged at all. Now, taking readings from the conceptual map with which we have provided ourselves, let us attempt to determine the distances, relative positions, and topographical relations of these models, which, in both fields, we have discovered to be useful *instruments for understanding.*

Reading off Common Features of the Models in Science and Theology

There are certain features shared by scientific and theological models by virtue of their being models that no longer need detailed reviewing here: e.g. that any model *models something else* to better or worse effect, that any model is offered *within a context* and *for a purpose,* that these purposes even for the same model may not always be the same in different contexts, that different purposes lead to different characteristics of models being taken as "logically relevant" or "irrelevant," that models have heuristic value in formulating theories, that any use of models involves certain risks, and so on. More interesting now are certain particular consequences of these general constitutive characteristics of models as they make themselves analogously felt in the two fields.

James Clerk Maxwell, working scientist, made some perceptive comments on scientific models (he calls them "physical hypotheses") which, with certain significant exceptions, could almost be echoed in somewhat modified language by a working theologian. I shall reproduce his words, quoted by Max Black, as a basis for discussion. "The first process therefore in the effectual study of the science must be one of simplification and reduction of the results of previous investigation to a form in which the mind can grasp them. The results of this simplification may take the form of a purely mathematical formula or of a physical hypothesis. In the first case we entirely lose sight of the phenomena to be explained; and though we may trace out the consequences of given laws, we can never obtain more extended views of the connections of the subject. If, on the other hand, we adopt a physical hypothesis, we see the phenomena only through a medium, and are liable to that blindness to facts and rashness in assumption which a partial explanation encourages. We must therefore discover some method of investigation which allows the mind at every step to lay hold of a clear physical conception, without being committed to any theory founded on the physical science from which that conception is borrowed, so that it is neither drawn aside from the subject in pursuit of analytical subtleties, nor carried beyond the truth by a favorite hypothesis." [74]

First, then, a model *simplifies* the data at hand "to a form in which the mind can grasp them." And if this is important within a branch of science, how much more pressing still must be the importance of this possibility for a theology which hopes to bring meaning and order to the "scheme of things entire"—including not only all the data and all the conclusions of all the sciences but also all the realms of value, obligation and aspiration felt by men! The theologian, like the scientist, is justly grateful for his model.

But both, second, need to be wary since models permit this simplification by requiring their users to "see the phenomena only through a medium." A model may be useful—may even be indispensable for many purposes—but it is not the same thing as what it models. A model filters the facts. And the temptation to forget this because of the values of the model can become great, great enough to deprive the user of the model of appropriate humility before his own intellectual powers and before the realities mediated by his model. Both scientists and theologians frequently stress the virtues of humility and the serious consequences to those who become "wise in their own conceits." And it is interesting to note that the greatest among scientists and theologians have been more prone to take these warnings seriously in their own work than have their lesser followers or men in the street. The creative scientist is usually well aware of how

74. James Clerk Maxwell, quoted in Black, *op. cit.*, p. 226.

far his models fall short of exhausting his subject matter, and the sensitive theologian is sharply conscious of the truth in the ancient *via negativa* which stands over against all his affirmations, however needful and trustworthy they may be.

This means, third, that the reliance upon models in either of these fields demands that we learn how to employ an epistemologically immediate conception "without being committed to any theory founded on the [domain] from which that conception is borrowed." The physicist must not permit himself to become *committed* to the point by point relevance of the theory of wave-dynamics, when he is studying the behavior of light, even though the theory is fully established in its own domain. He must remember that the conception of the wave is still a borrowed conception and that however fruitful it may be in its new application it remains a model. Conversely the theologian needs to resist supposing that because elements in the models he uses have a domain in which they would properly be taken as empirical propositions (e.g. "the bush was burning, yet it was not consumed") he needs, *ipso facto,* to be committed to the primitive theories and physical conceptions reflected in that domain. A well confirmed theory in one domain may prove a very good— or a very poor—model in another domain; and, likewise a poorly confirmed or even a positively disconfirmed theory may find new life as a model in another domain. The logic of a conception used as a model must be distinguished from its logic—its usefulness, degree of confirmation, truth-value, and so on—when it is used in its own proper domain. Both theologians and scientists will gain maximum value from their models, then, when with the benefits of *simplification* from seeing their subject matter *through the medium* of a model, they combine a conscious *freedom from commitment to* any theory grounded in the model's original domain.

Lurking behind our use of models, whether as scientists or as theologians, there may be some question as to the degree of actual correspondence between our model and what it models. This is no less true for theologians than for scientists. Jeans, we have seen, discourages the scientist from expecting such correspondence; Braithwaite, agreeing, asserts that "thinking of scientific theories by means of models is always *as-if* thinking . . . ," [75] and Toulmin adds, "to think that A *is* B is one thing, to think of A *as* B is another. . . ." [76] The relation, as we have seen, between model and subject is not identity. Still, as Black points out: "we pin our hopes upon the existence of a common structure in both fields." [77] May the "structure" hoped for in common be more than *logical* structure alone? May scientists and theologians hope for some kind of imaginatively accurate representation of this subject matter through their models? In some cases the answer is plainly negative, when there are convincing grounds in principle that prevent even conceiving such a model without contradiction. A familiar case of this sort in science has to do with the theoretical impossibility of producing an imaginative model that can be supposed to correspond to the electron.[78] And a similar theological case would be with respect to the theoretical impossibility of "visualizing accurately" an *ex hypothesi* invisible God. In other cases, where there are no reasons to judge one way or the other, it would be foolhardy to make an assertion either way. Certainly one's sense of the explanatory power of a model is enhanced by one's supposition that it may be "quite a lot like" that which it models, but where there are no grounds there can be no cognitively relevant judgment.

In still other cases, however, it may be possible to test a scientific model against its original. Nothing stands in the way *in principle* of observing directly the molecules of gases that are now modeled as little elastic pellets like billiard balls. Perhaps more powerful electron microscopes will one day permit a point for point comparison of billiard balls and simple molecules. Then the scientist will know just how accurate or how inaccurate

75. Braithwaite, *op. cit.*, p. 93.
76. Stephen Toulmin, *The Philosophy of Science* (New York: Harper & Bros., 1960), p. 165.
77. Black, *op. cit.*, p. 238.
78. Cf. Norwood Russell Hanson, *Patterns of Discovery* (London: Cambridge University Press, 1958) , especially Chapter VI, "Elementary Particle Physics," for a clear discussion of the logical grounds of this impossibility.

his models have been. And he will need his billiard ball model far less than before. At this point, however, we take leave of the features shared by scientific and theological models and begin to notice points of divergence between them. These similarities have perhaps been instructive; the divergences may be no less so.

Reading off Divergent Features of the Models in Science and Theology

Previously, in examining the status of theological models, we noted the dependence of theology on its models—particularly on the key composite biblical model of ultimate reality—for the very statement of distinctively theological dimensions of meaning and belief. The model, we say, is a *necessary condition* of theological theory. This dependence, not shared by scientific theories, leads to a consequence which was not pursued earlier. Cognitive assent cannot be given to theological theories alone, stripped of their models, as can be done (in principle at least) for scientific theories which in Maxwell's earlier-quoted words "may take the form of a purely mathematical formula" rather than the form of a "physical hypothesis" or model. Any act of cognitive assent to theology's claims will have a necessary reference to theology's model of reality. But cognitive assent to a claim, P, incorporating P into one's scheme of things, is equivalent to affirming that P is *true*. Thus, since every theological truth-claim has a necessary involvement in the key theological model, the *model* in this sense must be judged true or false if any theological statements at all are judged true or false. This is not usually supposed to be the case with respect to scientific models, which are termed "fruitful" or "misleading," and the like, but not "true or false." Theological models, however, are of the essence for theology, and any attempt to withhold the notion of truth from these models is in effect a move to deny theology the right to deal in truth or falsity at all.

Theological models, however, cannot justly be judged with respect to truth or falsity apart from the theories that articulate them, interpret them, and relate them to other cognitive domains, i.e. that provide the conventions for "reading" them cognitively. Here we have moved out, once again, to the edge of the subject matter to be dealt with in the present study, but it will at least be noticed that if theories in theology are never intelligible or true *qua* theological theories without models, so theological models do not function (cognitively, at least) without some theory, however implicit or however crude.

A further difference which may be startling to those accustomed to the high rate of turn-over among the models of science is the remarkable resistance to change exhibited by theological models. The situation in this respect is reversed in the two fields. For science, models are altered, discarded, or replaced with relatively little compunction as knowledge increases and the demands of theory develop. The highest level theoretical constructions, however, are tampered with only when absolutely necessary—and then reluctantly, since altering the prime theories of a science can bring about a major scientific revolution that may sweep away the patient labors put in by many over long periods of time. For theology, theories on the interpretation and the linking up of models to other areas of thought are abandoned or replaced in the light of increasing knowledge far more readily than are the models themselves. And the highest level models, those at key positions within the overarching model of reality, are defended at all costs—defended most bitterly against the prophetic personalities who are usually the very ones who best succeed in altering the fundamental religious models—in the knowledge that a change in model signals a religious revolution that may sweep away that which has received the devotion of multitudes over the ages.

The logical characteristic which may account for this interesting reversal is the difference between the *scope* for scientific and theological models. Theological models, sharing the unlimited inclusiveness of all metaphysical models, are in a limited sense "above change." Their empirically unfalsifiable character makes of them not necessarily "self-certifying myths" in all respects (since theological models *do* change and religions *are* reformed—

and abandoned), but it does free them from the kind of forced change that is both the despair and the glory of the sciences.[79] Just as a mountain of experimental data cannot move a mustard-seed of faith, so scientific conclusions and models of limited scope cannot by themselves threaten or support theology. The science *versus* religion conflicts of yesteryear, on which we may now bring this study to a close, rested, most commentators now agree, on a mistake.

But what was the mistake and on whom did it rest? The answer to this question is not so simple or straightforward as is sometimes assumed, inasmuch as exclusive responsibility cannot be thrown onto either the scientist or the theologian and inasmuch as the mistake itself is less garish than are the colors in which it is sometimes painted.

Essentially, theologians and scientists both misinterpreted the logic of theological models, "reading" them as empirical assertions which could be (and were, on this interpretation, in fact being) disconfirmed in just the way appropriate to the assertions of astronomy, geology, or the like. Both must share responsibility for the error. But there are mitigating circumstances often unrecorded by modern analysts: the theories associated with theological models still tended to encourage just the error that was made, and it was only later, thanks largely, no doubt, to the way in which theological models refused to "stay falsified," but could endlessly bounce back from every scientific victory, that the logic of theological affirmations began to come clearer to all sides of the dispute.

79. My remarks about the *experimental* unfalsifiability of theological models should not obscure the requirement that the cognitive dimensions of theology eventually stand exposed to *some* forms of critical evaluation (that is, broadly speaking, to "verification" or "falsification"). These forms or methods will have the character of metaphysical testing in general, wherein the model-cum-theory's power to make coherent sense out of all empirical fact is one vastly important component. In this extended sense, then, even metaphysical world views are "falsifiable"; but this is "falsification" of a different kind than is being spoken about in most current discussion. The true "falsification" of a metaphysical position is more like an erosion than an explosion—a gradual process in which the inadequate metaphysical view is not disproved but, rather, is quietly abandoned.

To compound the situation, the logical status of the scientist's own assertions were also not altogether clear to either of the contending parties. Just as theologians needed to learn that their statements of universal scope were not designed to rival the function of the scientist's limited and empirically confirmable propositions, so scientists required a warning against supposing that their carefully controlled and empirically specific statements could be set to work as propositions having unlimited scope and in competition with theology's—*while remaining scientific statements*.[80] If a sentence bred in science's neatly fenced pasture wanders off to frolic in metaphysics' Elysian Fields, it had better expect to receive new brand-markings!

Here, then, is a more complex picture than is normally offered. Scientific models and theories can, it seems, be metamorphosed into world-hypotheses of unlimited scope and thus become genuine metaphysical rivals (or allies) of theological models and theories. And the latter, while not entailing any specific empirical consequences or permitting straightforward empirical falsification can never be indifferent to scientific conclusions, since they have as one of their most important cognitive functions the simplification and bringing into coherence of all knowledge.

It was a mistake for scientists and theologians to have battled so hard over, say, the theory of evolution. Yes, but it was a mistake with many levels to be untangled. Theologians were wrong to argue, *qua* theologians, for the immutability of biological species; but scientists were equally wrong to argue, *qua* scientists, that the evolutionary model, once scientifically established, could take the place of the God of theism.[81] Both these questions must be argued with appropriate tools and on appropriate grounds. The concept of fixed species may be better or worse biology than the concept of mutating species, but to determine which

80. Cf. Stephen Toulmin's excellent article, "Scientific Theories and Scientific Myths" in *Metaphysical Beliefs*, *op. cit.*, for a discussion of scientific propositions gone astray.
81. Cf. Julian Huxley's *Religion Without Revelation* (London: Max Parrish, 1957, revised), Ch. IX, for a book that is well written and thoughtful but none the less an excellent specimen of this mistake.

is the case biological and paleontological arguments, not metaphysical ones, are appropriate; the model of a personal deity may or may not be better metaphysics than the model of an evolutionary universe, but to guide our choice metaphysical arguments, not biological or paleontological ones, are required.

These points may help to place in logical focus the tensions which still may be found between science and religion—enlightened men in both fields knowing that they *ought* not to have any conflicts with the "other side," and yet finding grounds for anxiety or relief in pronouncements made or conclusions published. To a certain extent it is legitimate and even essential for theologians to be concerned about the models and theories of the sciences. Not only is it theology's job to offer (ideally) a conceptual synthesis containing all such models and theories but it may be that new models of great scope being developed by scientists may offer cognitive support or challenge. Where there is a challenge it will usually be found that the challenger is attempting to replace the theological model with the claim to do the cognitive job of the biblical picture of reality but to do it more adequately. And when there is support it will usually be found that the model taken by the theologian as promising support will do so by providing the theological model with new theoretical ties to other domains of established knowledge, these new semantical connections thus increasing the power of the biblical model to do its cognitive job more effectively than before. When a new model appears in field-theory, for example, the theologian may adopt it as part of the interpretative net surrounding his model and may draw upon it to help explicate that primary model and to draw coherent relations between it and other bodies of knowledge. "Perhaps *this* is what Christian faith means by 'man's freedom,' " a theologian might say, "man's behavior and choices determined by a *field* of forces responsibly controlled but not mechanically compelled. . . ." As such the scientific model (no longer used scientifically in any sense) becomes subordinate to the key biblical model itself, but it may thus function for theology with considerable importance. Unfortunately, it may acquire such importance to the theologian that when scientists, who have in the meantime hurried on, tell him that the model is "on the way out" or that it is being replaced or radically altered in its own domain, the theologian may feel threatened and thus be tempted to argue against the scientists—far over his depths and floundering, but properly subject more to compassion than to ridicule. And so the weary science-religion conflict goes on.

My paper, for want of existing maps to follow, has had to make its own way through the underbrush. I hope that this initial exploration has not distorted its subject matter any more horribly than did the quaint old maps of Greenland or Africa now resting, peacefully, in antique shops. But even they, for all their faults, once served a purpose, until other expeditions and other cartographers returned to correct their errors. Similarly, this venture will have served its main intended function if it can attract others to see—and to improve—for themselves. Maps, after all, are logically no more than models. And models, we have learned, are to be taken as sacred only in theology.

V

Metaphysics
and the
Limits of Language

C. B. DALY

I shall not begin by attempting to define what I mean by metaphysics; it has become clear in recent discussion that most of the difficulty about deciding whether or how metaphysics is possible comes from confusion or uncertainty about how to define metaphysics. In a sense, the whole point of this paper is a request for a definition of metaphysics; the definition cannot come at the beginning, but will, it is hoped, emerge in the course of the paper. I shall begin with some historical considerations.

I. METAPHYSICS IN RECENT BRITISH PHILOSOPHY

The most convenient point at which to begin a survey, which must here be brief and sketchy, of recent discussion on the possibility of metaphysics, is with the belligerent anti-metaphysical doctrine of the Logical Positivists, particularly as formulated in the first edition of Professor Ayer's *Language, Truth and Logic*. In assessing the value of any "elimination of metaphysics," it is important to find out what precisely is being marked down for elimination, as well as the reasons given for the elimination. A good deal of the discussion about metaphysics in the last twenty years has been vitiated by the unhistorical and question-begging descriptions given of metaphysics, and by the unfortunate habit of condemning metaphysicians on the basis of propositions torn from their context and understood out of all relation to the immediate argument and the ultimate intention of the author. For Ayer, in 1935, metaphysics seems to have been represented mainly by some of the more paradoxical sentences of Bradley or McTaggart and some of the more tortuous and obscure utterances of Heidegger; but it is not evident that he tried very hard to enter into the minds or discover the intentions of these philosophers.

Ayer left his readers in no doubt as to what metaphysics meant for him. It meant one or other of two things: either assertions about "a reality transcending the world of science and common sense"; or assertions purporting to describe empirical reality and yet not being statements of science or of common sense, and not being amenable to observational tests. Both types of metaphysics are excluded for the same reason, that they fail to conform to the conditions of empirical verification under which alone a factual statement can be meaningful. Philosophical analysis can, he claimed, uncover the grammatical blunders and logical errors which led philosophers into the illusion of metaphysics. But this is a work of supererogation: the verification principle, by itself, deprives metaphysics of all plausibility and all excuse. Whether it claim direct acquaintance with non-empirical "entities" like moral values, or immortal souls, or God; or whether it claim to know these indirectly by inference from experience; or whether it claim to deduce the nature of reality from rational principles, metaphysics is in all cases a tissue of pseudo-propositions.

This "elimination of metaphysics" amounts to the claim that only the empirical sciences can know objective reality or discover facts or utter meaningful sentences about facts; and that metaphysics, claiming to describe reality and to state objective truths is, necessarily, literally senseless. That logical positivism was itself a nest of metaphysical assumptions and fallacies is now generally agreed and a matter of history. But it had at least the effect of focusing the attention of philosophers upon the nature of metaphysics and its relationship to science and its claim to meaningfulness and truth. Discussion arising out of the logical positivists' monolithic doctrine of meaning have led philosophers to recognize the endless diversity of languages and of meanings. The monopoly of meaning is denied to "science and common sense"; and attention is paid to the persuasive, promissory, poetic, ethical and metaphysical uses of language and to their varieties of claim to meaning. The "Wittgenstein I" slogan, "The meaning of a proposition is the method of its verification," has been replaced by the "Wittgenstein II" slogans, "Don't ask for the meaning, ask for the use," and "Every kind of statement has its own kind of logic."

The dogmatic denial of meaning to metaphysics has thus been succeeded, in British philosophy, by a qualified tolerance which is prepared to concede that metaphysics has some sort of meaning and to enquire into what kind of meaning this can be. This marks a definite progress. It is, however, a limited progress. The first qualification of the new tolerance towards metaphysics is that it is still fairly universally assumed that, whatever validity metaphysics may have, it cannot make true statements about Reality. Hence, its validity can consist only in its power to call attention, by paradox, to neglected aspects of experience and to recommend new descriptions of familiar facts. It will be granted today that "a metaphysical system may have many virtues, such as elegance, simplicity, originality, comprehensiveness, depth, or the power to give psychological satisfaction; but," it is added, "the claim that any such system is exclusively true or uniquely faithful to Reality, is a claim which sets metaphysics on quite the wrong ground." [1] Metaphysics is often accorded respect today as a work of inventive or constructive imagination. Its role is acknowledged in breaking the tyranny of established linguistic habits and conventions and thereby stimulating scientific re-

1. G. J. Warnock in *The Revolution in Philosophy* (London, Macmillan, 1956), pp. 122-3.

search along new lines. Although its questions cannot be answered, they may challenge and spur science to discover answers
to questions that can be answered. Metaphysics may thus turn
into science.[2]

In the context of contemporary discussion, it is obvious that a
major problem for the metaphysician is to clarify the relationship between metaphysics and the empirical sciences, between
metaphysical statements and empirical facts. He must resume
Professor Wisdom's reflections (in the paper on "Gods") as to
how metaphysical disputes can be carried on when there is, in
one sense, "agreement about the facts" and, in another sense,
"in part a difference as to what is so and therefore as to the facts."

The second qualification attaching to the new open-minded-
ness about metaphysics is the persisting bias against general ideas,
against the posing of problems in general terms, or the attempt
to find general laws of thought or ultimate justifications of reasoning. It is still widely held that such terms of traditional metaphysics as "reality," "being," "existence," "universals," are, or
are derived from "systematically misleading expressions." Thus,
there is no such thing as Being; there are beings. There is no
such thing as Truth; there are true statements. There is no
problem of induction; there are enquiries into the validity of
particular inductive arguments. One of the, to my mind, baleful
legacies of "Wittgenstein II" (as he is commonly interpreted)
to contemporary philosophy is the convention that philosophical
problems are not to be solved but to be dissolved, by the process
of translating them from the plane of abstract generality to the
plane of concrete particularity. This bias against the generalized
problem or the generalizing mind, this convention of "take-
nothing-but-the-concrete-case," is one of the favourite means of
escape from metaphysics in contemporary philosophy. The metaphysician must, therefore, show that it is possible and inescapable

2. See F. Waismann, "How I see Philosophy" in *Contemporary British
Philosophy*, ed. H. D. Lewis (London, Allen & Unwin, 1956), pp. 463-4, 490;
R. von Mises, *Positivism* (Harvard, 1951), p. 9; John Wilson, *Language and
the Pursuit of Truth* (Cambridge, 1956), pp. 94-7; cp. J. W. N. Watkins in
The Listener, November 28, 1957, p. 886.

to pose problems in terms of utmost generality; that there is a problem of existence, of truth, of how science or any knowledge is possible, of the conditions of intelligibility of experience as a whole, of the grounds of existence of the world and of myself.

But it will have to be shown, at the same time, that this does not mean that, in doing metaphysics, the (language-) "machine is idling," to use the "Wittgenstein II" terms now so often used to disqualify metaphysics. It must be made clear that the metaphysical problem is posed by experience, arises within experience; that the metaphysical idea is "gripping" into empirical reality; to put it crudely, that the metaphysical wheel is being turned all the time by empirical cogs.

II. THE PROBLEM OF THE SELF

This can perhaps be best shown by discussing the problem of the self. This problem, so important for all discussion of the possibility of metaphysics, is one of the most maltreated problems in contemporary British philosophy. Not unnaturally, discussion of this question frequently takes Descartes' *cogito* for its text. I select Professor Ayer's treatment of the *cogito* because I think it is representative of the contemporary approach to the problem. I hope to show that it both misunderstands Descartes and misrepresents the problem of the self.

In *Language, Truth and Logic*,[3] we read: "What [Descartes] was really trying to do was to base all our knowledge on propositions which it would be self-contradictory to deny. He thought he had found such a proposition in '*cogito*,' which must not be here understood in its ordinary sense of 'I think' but rather as meaning 'there is a thought now.' . . . . But even if it were true that such a proposition as 'there is a thought now' was logically certain, it still would not serve Descartes' purpose. . . . . 'I exist' does not follow from 'there is a thought now.' The fact that a thought occurs at a given moment does not entail that any other thought has occurred at any other moment, still less that there

3. Pp. 46–7.

has occurred a series of thoughts sufficient to constitute a single self. As Hume conclusively showed, no one event intrinsically points to any other."

The main defect of this critique of the *"cogito"* is that it sees Descartes as exclusively concerned to make a logical point and uses to refute him a logic which, because of metaphysical preconceptions, excludes the phenomenological or existential point which Descartes regarded as the core of the argument. Ayer's Russellian logic had no symbol for "I" or for "exists." This logic rests on the convention that "I" is a logical construction out of the objective sense data which alone are before "my" consciousness. One can give "I" meaning in this logic only by analysing it into the object-language of "something," "some particular perception." Therefore "I think" must be translated into "something thinks," from which all that would follow would be the tautology, "something is a thinking thing." Now the important point about this logic is that its epistemological basis is Hume's empiricism. It is a translation into logical syntax of the words: "When I enter into *myself,* I always stumble on some particular perception or other. . . . I never catch myself at any time without a perception and never can observe anything but the perception. They are the successive perceptions only that constitute the mind."

In *The Problem of Knowledge* (1956), Ayer's view of Descartes remains unchanged. He argues that the *"cogito"* succeeds only in making the trivial logical point, that, "if I start with the fact that I am doubting, I can validly draw the conclusion that I think and that I exist. That is to say, if there is such a person as myself, then there is such a person as myself, and if I think, I think." It is, of course, a fact, he goes on, that I know that I am conscious and that I exist. But these facts are of no logical significance. "It is conceivable that I should not have been self-conscious, which is to say that I should not know that I existed; but it would not follow that I could not know many other statements to be true . . . my whole conception of knowledge would be impersonal." Hume's point about the self, he contends, is true, not as a matter of psychological fact, but as a matter of logic. "There is nothing that would count as having an experience of one's self; the expression, 'having an experience of one's self' is one for which there is no use. . . . The consciousness of one's self is not one experience among others, not even, as some have thought, a special experience which accompanies all the others." The sentence, "I exist," is a degenerate statement, one in which the verb is a sleeping partner, all the work being done by the demonstrative. "It approximates, therefore, to a gesture or to an ejaculation. To say 'I exist' . . . is like saying 'look!' or pointing without words. . . . To know that one exists is not, in this sense, to know anything about oneself, any more than knowing that *this* exists is knowing anything about *this*." [4] Professor F. Alquié remarked, in the course of lectures on Descartes at the Sorbonne in 1955, that, so far as he was aware, no one had ever entertained an idea so absurd as that *"cogito"* meant "I am René Descartes." He seems to have overlooked Lord Russell and Professor Ayer.[5]

I believe that there are important mistakes in Descartes' inferences from the *"cogito"* to the nature of the *res cogitans* and other metaphysical conclusions. But the mistakes are not those attributed to him by Ayer. Descartes would have thought it absurd to say "there is a thought now." He would have held that it is not merely psychologically false but logically self-contradictory to say that if I were not self-conscious, and therefore did not know that I existed, "I [sic] could still know many other things." [6] Descartes' *"cogito"*-experience is of "I thinking, 'there is a thought now' ", "I knowing or doubting that I know many

---

4. Pelican edition, pp. 44–52. Lord Russell's treatment of the *"cogito"* is very similar. Thus in *History of Western Philosophy* (London, Allen & Unwin, 1946), p. 589, he writes: "The word 'I' is really illegitimate; Descartes ought to state his ultimate premiss in the form, 'There are thoughts.' The word 'I' is grammatically convenient but does not describe a datum." Compare his essay "Mind and Matter," in *Portraits from Memory* (London, Allen & Unwin, 1956), pp. 137–8.

5. See F. Alquié, *Science et metaphysique chez Descartes*, "Les Cours de Sorbonne," Centre de Documentation Universitaire, Paris, p. 74.

6. Ayer, *op. cit.*, p. 47.

things"; "I who doubts, understands, affirms, denies, wills, re-fuses, imagines, perceives"; "I co-existing with and involved in every experience." The empiricists are looking for some per-ceptible thing or object of experience corresponding to "I." Obviously there is no such "thing" or "object." They conclude that there is "no such thing" as "I." Descartes' whole point is that there is an "I," but it is not an object of thought but a subject thinking, without which there could not be any objects of thought.

For Descartes, "I think, therefore I am" is not a logical truism, much less an ejaculation or a gesture: it is an act of reflection which reveals the nature of man and of his situation in the world. I know that I exist precisely in my knowing that I think about and seek to understand the world, that I demand certitude but encounter error and feel doubt, that I think beyond the limits of my knowledge and grasp the idea of perfection in and with my recognition of my own imperfection. From the *"cogito,"* Descartes proceeds to reflect "on the circumstances that I doubted and that consequently my being was not wholly perfect" and to enquire "whence I had learned to think of something more perfect than myself." He seeks a reason why he should not have "the whole re-mainder of perfection, of the want of which I was conscious." He asks, "how could I know that I doubt, desire, or that something is wanting to me that I am not wholly perfect, if I possessed no idea of a being more perfect than myself, by comparison of which I knew the deficiencies of my own nature?" He finds in his own lack of being, his own desire and need for being, his own aspi-ration after perfection of being, the necessity to affirm his de-pendence for being on a Perfect Being who is God.[7] In other words, Descartes' themes are those of self-knowledge and self-activity, aspiration towards ideals, immanence and transcendence. They are the themes which are central in the philosophy of Europe, past and present, but are too often excluded from con-temporary British philosophy because they do not fit in with preconceptions derived from scientific empiricism.

7. Meditation II.

The "*cogito*" of Descartes is not, therefore, a logical, but an existential starting point. The true point of departure of Cartesianism it not *cogito* but *sum*. His question is not the trivial one "Am I?", but the one which has linked the great metaphysical with the great humanist tradition, the question "What am I?" Descartes' real significance is to have inspired the humanistic metaphysics of the French spiritualists down to Le Senne and Gabriel Marcel. It is not an accident that philosophies which accuse Descartes' procedure of barrenness and pronounce the notion of the self to be a mistake, tend also to be atheistic philosophies. It would seem that to exclude discussion of the self from philosophy is to exclude discussion of God from philosophy too. Professor Ramsey has called attention to the logical relatedness of "I" and "God." [8] This is surely an aspect of the truth, so familiar to saints and mystics, that God is *intimior intimo meo*. It receives striking negative corroboration in modern positivism, for which both God and self are meaningless.

III. THE PROBLEM OF EXISTENCE

Traditional metaphysics saw itself as concerned with being-in-general. By far the most important single cause of the anti-metaphysical movement in recent British philosophy was Russell's logic, in so far as this forgot its proper character and mistook itself for an ontology. Russell's theory of descriptions was long thought to have disposed of the problem or problems of being which had provided a livelihood for metaphysicians for so long, and to have "cleared up two millennia of muddle-headedness about 'existence,' beginning with Plato's 'Theaetetus.' "[9]

From the metaphysician's point of view, the important implication of all this was the alleged disappearance of "exists" as

8. *Miracles,* An Exercise in Logical Mapwork (an Inaugural Lecture), Oxford, 1952, pp. 14–17, 20–1. Compare the same author's *Religious Language* (London, S.C.M. Press, 1957), p. 38.
9. Russell, *History of Western Philosophy* (London, Allen & Unwin, 1946), p. 860.

any kind of true assertion about any actual thing, and therefore the abolition of "existence" as an object of philosophical investigation. "Existence" can be predicated solely of a propositional function or, derivatively, of a class. "Existence-propositions do not say anything about the actual individual but only about the class or function." "When you take any propositional function and assert of it that it is possible, that it is sometimes true, that gives you the fundamental meaning of existence. . . . It means that propositional function is true in at least one instance." With regard to the "actual things there are in the world . . . it is a sheer mistake to say that there is anything analogous to existence that you can say about them." "Existence in the sense in which it is ascribed to single entities is thus removed altogether from the list of fundamentals." [10]

It is, however, notable that there is, in contemporary British philosophy, a considerable reaction against the Russellian theory of descriptions and its attendant logical atomism. This is, for example, one of the recurring themes in the representative selection from recent philosophical papers edited by Professor A. Flew and published as *Essays in Conceptual Analysis*.[11] The critics are not, of course, concerned to rehabilitate metaphysics. But the effect of the criticism has been to show that a particularly prevalent sort of anti-metaphysics was based on a logical mistake. The moral is that questions which arise in ordinary language cannot legitimately be pronounced meaningless or be dissolved by appeal to a special logical language. The attack on the theory of descriptions is part of the continuing struggle of British philosophy to free itself from the grip of the "metaphysics to end all metaphysics" of dogmatic empiricism, and to repudiate the imposition by it on philosophy of monopolistic criteria of meaning and truth, taken from mathematics, empirical science and formal logic.

10. Russell, "The Philosophy of Logical Atomism" (1918) in *Logic and Knowledge,* ed. Robert C. Marsh (London, Allen & Unwin, 1956), pp. 177–281; see especially pp. 229–34; compare "Logical Atomism" (1924), *ibid.*, pp. 323–43.
11. Macmillan, London, 1956.

There is no need to do more than cite some of the best-known papers in the above-named collection. P. F. Strawson ("On Referring") has shown that chief among the "fundamental mistakes" in Russell's theory is his confusion of "meaning" with "mentioning" or "referring." His "troublesome mythology" of the logically proper name is due to his mistaken idea that if there are expressions which have a uniquely referring use and if these are logical subjects, then there must *be* the objects which they are used to refer to. But "meaning" is not "mentioning" or "referring to." "Meaning" has to do with the directions governing the ways in which expressions have to be actually used to make true or false assertions; and these directions, like these uses, are too endlessly complex and unclassifiable to be reduced to any single formal model. Russell's model was the result of his preoccupation with mathematics and formal logic. "The constructor of calculuses, not concerned or required to make factual statements, approaches logic with a prejudice. . . . Neither Aristotelian nor Russellian rules give us the exact logic of any expression of ordinary language, for ordinary language has no exact logic."

G. J. Warnock, in his paper "Metaphysics in Logic," carries much further the same kind of criticism of the "logico-ontologists" and makes points which are of some importance for our topic. He is mainly concerned with the abuse of the device of the "existential quantifier." This convention assumes that there is a single, univocal meaning of "exists" or "does not exist" in ordinary language, corresponding to the meaning of "expressions allowed to be substituends for bound variables and expressions debarred from such employment" in quantificational logic. But this is to show "insufficient sense of the perils involved in imposing the neat simplicities of logic upon the troublesome complexities of language." There is an elasticity and variety about the use of "is" or "exists" in ordinary language to which no logical symbolism can do justice. To allow only one meaning to "exists" is to try to force "Pegasus," "23," "intelligence," "redness," "republicanism," into a single bag. "None of these designates a single object, but they fail to do so in ways utterly diverse." The question, are there or not abstract entities, is not just like the question, is there or not a city called Leeds. "The expressions supposed to correspond to the existential quantifier . . . are too diverse and intricate in their uses to yield the necessary results." The existential quantification device blinds logicians' eyes to the differences between phrases such as: There is . . . There is such a thing as . . . exists . . . Some . . . At least one . . . There is something which. . . . All are dealt with by the use of the existential quantifier, and it is thence assumed that they are interchangeable, that they all have the same meaning, even that logic has "proved" them to be the same. Warnock's conclusion is that the whole apparatus of quantificational logic has little or no application to the ordinary words and idioms in which the problems of ontology are initially expressed. "These problems arise from and can be settled in ordinary language and cannot be confined to or settled in a special language. If one cannot deal with the philosophical problems of ontology upon the field of discourse in general, one cannot deal with them at all. There are problems which we cannot look to the logician to settle for us, and the old problems of ontology remain among them." This is a conclusion which, he admits, amounts only to the "highly-charged platitude" that philosophy is not logic.

A sympathizer with the Thomist tradition in metaphysics will be pardoned for suggesting that what Warnock is really pleading for is a recognition of the analogical character of language. It seems to be in fact a feature of contemporary British philosophy that it has rediscovered, in the return to ordinary language, the traditional doctrine of the analogy of being. For what are Waismann's concepts of "language strata," "systematic ambiguity," "open texture of language"; or Austin's studies of how variously we use the terms, "I know," "I promise," etc.; or Urmson's investigation of the "grading term" "good"—what are these but reinvestigations in contemporary terms of the old problems of *analogia entis?* When Wittgenstein spoke of "family likenesses" between linguistic usages and said that "every statement has its own logic," he was, though not saying the same thing, at least grappling with the same problem, as Aquinas was when he wrote "Analogous prediction is intermediate between mere equivocation and complete univocity of meaning. Analogous terms are not used with the same meaning, as univocal terms are; nor yet with totally diverse meanings, as equivocal terms are; but when a term is used analogously, the meaning varies in the different uses, but there is a resemblance, different for each case, connecting together the various uses." [12]

Already it is clear that the purely logical criticism of Russell has removed many obstacles to metaphysics. But there is more to be said by way of showing that the problem of existence is a real problem, and by way of trying to uncover the philosophical meaning of Russell's and Ayer's attempts to exclude it from philosophy. It seems to me that G. E. Moore, in the 1936 Symposium, "Is Existence a Predicate?",[13] provided a pertinent logical enquiry into the meaning of "This exists" and unwittingly provided a logical prelude to a metaphysical enquiry into existence. He argued that in all cases in which one can say something like "This is a tame tiger" one can also say significantly "This exists." This is because in all such cases, "you can clearly say *with truth* of any such object 'This *might* not have existed,' 'It is *logically possible* that this should not have existed.'" The statement "It is logically possible that this should not have existed," seems to mean, "The sentence 'This does not exist' is significant," and if "This does not exist" is significant, "This does exist" must be significant too. It is not possible for "This might not have existed" to be true unless "This does in fact exist" is true and therefore also significant.

So far, Moore is stating in logical terms what metaphysicians have meant by the contingency of finite being. Heidegger's going-on about Nothing in *What is Metaphysics?* is not due to a blunder about the logic or grammar of the verb "to be," is not the result of thinking that Nothing is a name for "something peculiarly mysterious." [14] It is a phenomenological transcription of

12. *Summa Theologica*, 1.13.5.
13. *Aristotelian Society Supplementary Volume XV*, pp. 154–88.
14. As Ayer charged in *Language, Truth and Logic*, p. 44.

Moore's common-place logical observation that of any empirical object we can significantly say "This might not have existed"; or "This being might have been Nothing." There is sound logical sense as well as phenomenological depth in Heidegger's obscurities of utterance: "Nothing shows itself [in dread] as essentially belonging to what-is while this is slipping away in totality. . . . Only in the clear light of dread's Nothingness is what-is as such revealed in all its original overtness: that it 'is' and is not Nothing." It is because we know that any being *might not* be that "Nothing ceases to be the vague opposite of what-is: it now reveals itself as integral to the Being of what-is." For Nothing is Heidegger's name for the fact that we and things are contingent beings, that we are but *might* not-be. Only when we advert to the Nothing in us and in things do we really notice the *being* in us and around us. Existence then appears, not as something we can take for granted, but as something which should surprise us, awaken us to "the utter strangeness of what-is," call forth our wonder and our thankfulness, arouse our questioning and compel us to try to understand, "Why is there any Being at all— why not far rather Nothing?" And that is the whole meaning of metaphysics.[15]

Moore makes a second and very important point. He asks, what then becomes of the consecrated doctrine that existence is not an attribute? He suggests that "This exists" always forms part of what is asserted by "This is a book," "This is red," etc. Now "is a book," "is red," etc., are said to stand for attributes because *part but not the whole* of what is asserted by any value of "*x* is a book" or "*x* is red," etc., is "This exists." But "exists" in "This exists" does not, in that sense, "stand for an attribute," because the *whole and not merely a part* of what it asserts is "This exists."

To appreciate the significance of this, it is necessary to recall that the formula "existence is not an attribute" was called forth

15. See Heidegger, *Existence and Being*, Eng. trans. (London, Vision Press, 1949), pp. 368-9, 376-80. One may compare here M. B. Foster, who speaks of the necessity of a "repentance in the sphere of the intellect," as a preliminary to the recognition of God. [See *Mystery and Philosophy* (London, S.C.M. Press, 1957), p. 46.]

by and has always been connected with the refutation of the ontological argument, and of the associated doctrines of the priority
of essence over existence and of the possible over the actual. (A
great deal of contemporary anti-metaphysics is based on the erro-
neous belief that *all* metaphysics is committed to the ontological
argument and its implications.) Against this, it was important to
stress that existence is not "one of the attributes" or part of the
definition of a thing, and cannot be deduced from the definition
or essence of the thing. But this does not mean that existence
cannot be known, affirmed or enquired into. Existence is presupposed to any predication of attributes; it is the *toujours-déjà-
là* of all knowledge. It is not that it is the "Something-I-know-
not-what" underlying attributes. It is given with and present in
and co-affirmed with all attributes. It is so much everywhere and
so much everything that we do not notice it. It is so familiar that
we take it for granted. We cannot know anything, say anything,
do anything, except in terms of it. But it might not have been
there; and we might not have been there to encounter it. Therefore it is meaningful to say "Things exist"; and it is meaningful
to ask "Why is there anything?" and "What does being mean?"

When existence is "removed from the list of fundamentals"
and questions as to its meaning and causes are pronounced meaningless, this is because of the improper extension to philosophy
and to human thought in general of the criteria of meaning and
of truth, the assumptions and the methods which are proper to
the empirical sciences. Science puts men and existence in brackets.
It takes it for granted that there is a world of things and events,
and that man observes it. But it is of no interest to science *that*
the world is; only *how* it is. It is of no interest to science as such
that science is man-made; it matters only that science go on. It
is a condition of the existence of science that man and being be;
but science could not be if it called its own conditions in question.[16] Science must take the existence of objects as irreducibly

16. A. D. Ritchie has written recently: "Scientific investigation goes most
smoothly and easily when nobody enquires into fundamentals." (*Studies in
the History and Methods of the Sciences,* Edinburgh, 1958, p. 192.)

given; and proceed to observe, analyse, measure, correlate them. It must take the fact of knowledge for granted and try to make it as impersonal, objective and anonymous as possible. Its truth-tests, verification and falsification by observations, will never include the person of the observer, but only require that an experience occur or be possible.

The contemporary effort to restore metaphysics is essentially a struggle to prevent man himself from being depersonalized by the methods of impersonal investigation and anonymous verification he has devised for science. Metaphysics is part of the defence of humanism in an age dominated by the concepts and attitudes which are legitimate and necessary for science and technology but which become dangerous when they are thought to be adequate to explain all that man is and all that man seeks and needs to know. Hence Gabriel Marcel presents his metaphysics as the rejection of the omni-competence of the principle of verification, the refusal to leave man and being in brackets, the assertion of the primacy of *being* man over *having* tools and techniques. He writes: "When I am faced with a [scientific] problem, I work on the data in front of me; but everything proceeds, and quite rightly proceeds, as if I had no need to pay any attention to the 'I' who is at work; for the purpose in hand, 'I' am only a prerequisite. But when my question bears on being, the position is entirely different. Here the ontological status of the questioner comes into the first place. . . . Here we enter into the realm of the meta-problematic, that is to say of mystery. A 'mystery' is a problem which calls its own conditions in question" (and thus puts itself beyond the possibility of solution by the methods of the science in which it arose).[17] "To pose the ontological problem is to question oneself about the whole of being and about one's own self as a whole." [18]

Marcel's thought, on this point, is similar to Heidegger's. Heidegger criticizes the imposition on all thinking of the logical categories and the observational and mensurational procedures

17. *Être et avoir* (Paris, Aubier, 1935), pp. 144–6, 169 ff.
18. *Positions et approches concrètes du mystère ontologique* (Louvain, Nauwelaerts, 1949), p. 57.

proper to the sciences. For the sciences, "any particular thing is only what it 'adds up to' and any count ensures the further progress of the counting. . . . The 'coming out' of the calculation with the help of what-is (i.e. objects) counts as the explanation of the latter's Being. . . . Calculative thought places itself under compulsion to master everything in the logical terms of its procedure. It has no notion that in calculation everything calculable is already a whole before it starts working out its sums and products, a whole whose unity naturally belongs to the incalculable which, with its mystery, ever eludes the clutches of calculation." [19] Heidegger criticizes the science-derived correspondence theory of truth, as professing to make truth "independent of the explanation of the essential nature of all that 'is,' of its very *being* —which explanation always involves a corresponding explanation of the essential nature of man as the vehicle and perfector of the intellectus." [20]

Both G. Marcel and Heidegger might have had precisely Russell and Ayer in mind in their critique of scientism. The result of the Russell-Ayer brand of empiricistic logic is exactly to eliminate the "I" and "being" from philosophy, as they have been eliminated from science—for science is the source of their logic and methodology. (Russell doubted "whether philosophy as a study distinct from science and possessed of a method of its own is anything more than an unfortunate legacy from theology.")[21] Ayer, though considerably less brash in the last decade than Russell or his own younger self, has continually been haunted by the idea of non-personal or person-neutral knowledge and by the possibility of the elimination of the observer from experience and his reduction to the experienced. In his last book, he still relies on these devices to refute Descartes and to get himself out of the logical holes he falls into in explaining how we know the past and other minds.[22]

19. "What is Metaphysics," in *Existence and Being*, Eng. trans. (London, Vision Press, 1949), p. 388.
20. "On the Essence of Truth," in *Existence and Being*, pp. 324–5.
21. In "Logical Atomism," in *Logic and Knowledge*, p. 325.
22. See *Problem of Knowledge*, pp. 47, 154–70, 214 ff.

G. Marcel and Heidegger insist on bringing the "I" and "being" back into philosophy and declare that when "I" and "being" meet, metaphysics begins. For metaphysics is the "I's" quest for the why of being and for the why of the self as the questioner of being. There are no why's in science. But it is almost a definition of man in European philosophy from Socrates to Sartre that he is the being who demands to know the why of his own being and of being.

IV. THE METAPHYSICS OF HUMANISM

One does not prove that metaphysics is possible merely by showing that the available anti-metaphysics is mistaken. It would now be pretty generally accepted by philosophers that there are no good reasons for saying that metaphysical questions do not arise, or that they are meaningless or trivial. But there is still much doubt as to whether they can be meaningfully answered. There is a fairly general recognition nowadays of what D. F. Pears has called "the Protean metaphysical urge to transcend language." [23] But it is commonly felt that the urge is bound to fail. For, by definition, metaphysical answers would go beyond the limits of reason and of logic and of meaningful utterance.

The problem, therefore, remains of showing that metaphysics is positively possible. In the end, there is no conclusive way to show that anything is possible except to produce it. I must therefore try, however sketchily and imperfectly, to produce some specimens of metaphysics. I hope at least to show that metaphysics is not empirical science; or, to be more precise, show that the point of metaphysics is that empirical categories are not adequate to the reality which is given integral human experience.

1. *Being as Known by the Self*

Modern phenomenology, returning to scholastic studies of the intentionality of consciousness, has stressed that the starting point of knowledge is not consciousness but being. The point of de-

23. See *Logic and Language*, Second Series, ed. A. G. N. Flew (Oxford, Blackwell, 1955), p. 64.

parture of philosophical or second-order reflection is, therefore, not knowledge but things-known. The existentialists say that all reflection is reflection on the preflective presence of being to us and of us to being. They follow Husserl, who stressed that all thought is thought of some *thing*. And Husserl re-echoed Aquinas, who wrote: "That which is first known by the intellect and is present in all its knowledge, is being; and all our knowledge has to be expressed in terms of being." [24] That is why all pretence to deduce being from thought, to reduce being into thought, to define being, to analyse being, to put being in brackets or to explain it away, is futile. Being is always-already-there before I know it; always-still-there in everything I know and say. Just as I am always-already-there before I know anything, and always-still-there when I am explaining anything, or trying to understand myself. Being and the self are not like anything else I know; they are in my knowing of everything.

This is the source of all the talk about the meta-problematic, the mystical, the inexpressible, in modern philosophy. But does it follow that I cannot know or say anything about being and the self because these are the absolute presuppositions of all knowing and of all saying? This metaphysical agnosticism comes, I believe, from two errors. First there is the error of thinking that the "being" lies *beyond* things. In truth, it is *in* things, it *is* things, only we do not notice it; we see things, not their thingness, not the fact that they *are* and are not Nothing. With this we group the corresponding error of thinking that the self lies *beyond* knowledge. In truth it is *in* knowledge; but we do not notice it, because the self is knowing, not a thing known; is experiencing, not a datum of experience. Empirical psychology, as Bergson pointed out, always misses the *ego*, seeing only mental states. Secondly, there is the error of thinking that all knowledge must be clear, distinct, final, leaving its solved problems behind like milestones in its march to ever new discoveries. But knowing is not all or nothing; it has an "open texture." Because not all can be known about everything, it does not follow that reason-

24. *De Veritate* q. 1, a. 1.

ing is absurd. It is the unreasonable demand for all-explaining reasons that drove Camus to proclaim absurdity. "I demand that all should be explained to me or nothing. But reason is power-less before this cry from the heart. . . . To be able to say, just once, 'That is clear,' then all would be saved. But . . . nothing is clear, all is chaos, and man keeps only his clear-sightedness and the exact awareness of the walls that hem him in." [25]

But though not all can be known about anything, there is some-thing that can be known about everything that can exist: that it is something, and is not nothing. Here is something that is true of all that is or that could be or that must be.[26] When Alasdair Mac-Intyre says: "Our concept of existence is inexorably linked to our talk about spatio-temporal objects," [27] we feel bound to protest that the words "linked to" are ambiguous and their ambiguity can cause a serious misunderstanding. No metaphysician, no theist will deny that there must be empirical linkage, "empirical an-chorage," [28] for all talk about the metempirical. But such con-cepts as those of "existence," "reality," cannot be and are not limited to talk about empirical objects. My self exists, knowing exists, and they are, although involved in all spatio-temporal experience, yet certainly not contained within the limits of "our talk about spatio-temporal objects." It is impossible to deny the term existence to that without which spatio-temporal objects could not be known to exist. This is what is meant by scholastic philosophers in saying that knowing is convertible with being. Nothing can be thought of except in terms of being, in relation to being. Nothing can be that is not intelligible, or related to

25. *Le Mythe de Sisyphe* (Paris, Gallimard, 1942), pp. 44–5.
26. Compare John Wilson, *Language and Christian Belief* (London, Mac-millan, 1958), pp. 13–14: "God must be real in the same sense as physical objects are real, for the word real has in fact only one sense—either some-thing is real and exists or it is unreal and does not exist. 'Real' and 'exists' are definitely not ambiguous words, . . . Instead of the Vedantists' 'Not this, not this,' the Christian must be able to say 'At least this, and at least this.' . . ."
27. See "The Logical Status of Religious Belief," in *Metaphysical Beliefs* (London, S.C.M. Press, 1957), p. 202.
28. The phrase is Professor Ramsey's: see *Religious Language,* p. 14.

thought. There are as many different kinds of being as there are things. The application of the term *being* cannot be restricted to spatio-temporal objects. It must be allowed to all reality whose existence is involved in or is implied by or is a condition of the being of and our knowing of spatio-temporal objects. Hence there can be no *a priori* logical or linguistic disqualification of metaphysics. There cannot be, in the absolute sense, anything that is Unknowable or Inexpressible. Of the Unknowable, we know at least that it *is*, and the reasons for and implications of its unknowability. Of the Inexpressible we can at least say that it *is* and is different from the empirical things which we do know.

It is not that *un au-delà de la pensée est impensable;* but that *un au-delà de l'être est impossible.* Everything that I know is part of my world, my experience, and all that I can know, all that there can be for me, has the unitary character that it is being-known-by-me, being-for-me. The diversity of beings cannot be absolute. As we have seen in the case of Russell and Ayer, it is only by the logical trick of putting the *ego* in brackets, that absolute pluralism or logical atomism can be made to look plausible. All being is ego-unified. But there is no ego-centric predicament. The unity of being is not just a unity-for-me or a unity-in-my-thought. My thought is of things that are "there" independently of thought. Unity-for-thought is imposed by unity-in-things. There is at least the minimal unity in all being; that it somehow *is* and is not nothing. There is at least the minimal intelligibility in all that there can be: that it can be known that it is, and that at least some description of it has a reference. There are as many ways of being as there are things, as many uses of "exists" as there are meaningful sentences. But since all consciousness for me is consciousness of things-in-my-world, it follows that meaning for me is determined by meaning-in-terms-of-my-world. And my world is the world of empirical objects and of I-knowing-them. Hence, all that I can know or meaningfully say to exist is either an object or occurrence in, or a feature or description of, or an implication or condition or presupposition of, my knowledge of empirical objects.

2. The Self as Knowing Being

Hume was right, that "I can never catch myself at any time without a perception." Ayer was right, that "there is nothing that would count as having an experience of one's self." Merleau-Ponty was right, that "the true *cogito* is not a *tête-à-tête* of thought with the thought of this thought; they join hands only across the world." [29] But everything counts as an experience of my self-experiencing-something. The self is in the having of perceptions and the spanning of the world; but it is not describable in terms of the world nor analysable into a bundle of perceptions. That is "the mystical" of Wittgenstein, which we should rather call the metaphysical. My knowledge of empirical objects cannot be adequately described in terms of empirical objects.

Knowing cannot be defined, classified or understood, any more than being can be defined, classified or understood. You cannot *classify* "knowing" because the word "knowing" has the logically baffling quality that, unless what it *means* were the case, it could not exist as a word nor could any other word or thought or thing exist. "Knowing" is not a "kind" of a word, as knowing is not a kind of a capacity; just as, and for the same reason that, being is not a kind of a thing. This is what the scholastics meant by saying that being is not a genus but is transcendental, and that knowledge is convertible with it. You cannot, therefore, describe knowing adequately in language, for no term in language can be or have meaning unless knowing is already there. Yet we do *know* much about knowing and we are somehow describing it when we say that it is not like any empirical occurrence or object whatever. There is some knowledge of knowing involved in all knowledge of things; but the exploration of knowledge lies beyond our knowledge. As Wittgenstein said, "The metaphysical subject [is] the limit of the world." [30]

29. M. Merleau-Ponty, *Phénoménologie de la perception* (Paris, Gallimard, 1945), p. 344.
30. *Tractatus*, 5.641. One thinks here of Father Illtyd Trethowan's words: "If we take knowledge seriously, we cannot help being theists." *An Essay in Christian Philosophy* (London, Longmans, 1954), p. 87.

But is it then just the inexpressible, which shows itself, but of which no word can be said? The use of spatial and chronological metaphor is inescapable in this context, but it can be very misleading. (How much nonsense about Plato has come from taking literally what he says about *pre*-existence and the apartness of the Ideas.) The words "beyond," "outside," almost inevitably suggest that the philosophers who use them have believed in a "place" "outside the walls" of ordinary experience to which, in virtue of some peculiar super-cognition, they have a privileged access denied to lesser mortals. But philosophers have meant, or should have meant, that there is a mystery *in* all knowing and in all being; that there is a "beyond-experience" in all experience, an "outside-language" in all language; and that experience is not adequately described unless this metempirical in it is recognized.[31] When we find that we "run [our] heads up against the limits of language," we should not say that there is something beyond "ordinary" language that we could know in "extraordinary" language or non-linguistically. Nor, on the other hand, should we say that there is "nothing beyond" ordinary language in the sense that empirical concepts and terms describe without remainder all that there is. What we should say is that there is something *in* ordinary language which is not "ordinary" and not expressible in empirical terms.

But the metempirical is real. We know it. We *are* it. It is not just the inexpressible, the mystical. We can become progressively more aware of the implications of its inexpressibility. It is much to know that there is that in us which we cannot describe or understand. It is to know something about it when we say that it is not an object or a body, not-material, not-empirical, nor empirically limited. To be aware of limits is to think and to know and to be beyond those limits. Since metaphysical questions arise, metaphysical knowledge is possible. My questions reveal what I know and what I am. If my empirical knowledge forces

31. Malebranche said: "No. I will not bring you into a strange country, but I will perhaps teach you that you are a stranger in your own country." Cited by H. de Lubac, in *Les Chemins de Dieu* (Paris, Aubier, 1956), p. 88.

me to ask questions which *cannot* be answered in empirical terms, then I know that empirical knowledge is not adequate to the reality which I am. But to know that knowledge is inadequate is a valid and a most important kind of knowledge. It is a perpetual invitation to deeper reflection; but also an awareness that reflection will never come to an end of what there is to know.

It is not the metaphysicians who have professed to "explain" existence, "decipher the riddle" of life, "account for" morality, "solve the problem" of thought, of soul and body, etc. It is scientists, and "scientific" philosophers, who have professed and do profess to do so.[32] Lord Russell has written: "In favour of this theory [of Mind and Matter], the most important thing to be said is that it removes a mystery. Mystery is always annoying and is usually due to lack of clear analysis. The relations of mind and matter have puzzled people for a long time, but, if I am right, they need puzzle people no longer." [33] But what sense could it have to say, "I have solved the problem of mind and body. . . . Now that that is clear, we shall tomorrow turn to the next problem—we shall construct a machine which will make it clear what thinking and deciding are? . . ." These are not just problems which we solve, but realities which we are. The problem of "mind and body" is not a problem that could be *solved* by Russell's theory or anyone else's theory. It is something we shall be solving, by living it, realizing it, becoming it, until we die. If we could give a "scientific explanation" of morality, it would cease to be morality. If we could give a cybernetic account of thinking, what we would have explained would not be thinking. Gilbert Ryle, near the end of *The Concept of Mind,* remarks that philosophers may yet come to recognize that man perhaps is, after all, a man. But this is not, as he seems to suggest, the end, but the beginning

32. M. B. Foster, in *Mystery and Philosophy* (London, S.C.M. Press, 1957), p. 17, writes: "What is to be questioned is not the practice of analysis but the belief that nothing is really puzzling and that therefore there cannot be anything puzzling that we can legitimately want to say."
33. "Mind and Matter," in *Portraits from Memory* (London, Allen & Unwin, 1956), p. 153.

of philosophy. To resist all pretences to explain man in terms of the non-human; to strive for ever deeper realization of the human; but to know that there is always more to know about man than can be known, that is the task of metaphysics.

The accounts given by metaphysicians about the soul were not intended as "solutions to problems," as mathematics, formal logic or science understand solutions. Their language was a refusal to put empirical–science limits to man's reality, or formal–logical limits to man's self-awareness and self-discovery and self-fulfilment. The terms "mind," "soul," "spirit," are not clear and distinct and closed ideas which end puzzlement; but "open" ideas of inexhaustible fertility, which arouse wonder and are permanent invitations to the reflection and effort that will translate our assent to them from notional into real, that will convert them from theory into way of life.

3. *Truth as Adequacy*

But is metaphysics, then, only emotive or evaluative, not descriptive, factual or true? Does it only express an "interesting and challenging attitude to life?" Must we conclude, as Susan Stebbing once did, that metaphysical systems "are great as works of art are great. Hence their spiritual significance. They heighten the joy of living but they do not give knowledge; they are a source of inspiration, but they do not yield understanding?" [34] Platitudinously, but profoundly, it depends on what we mean by "true." And philosophers have been content for far too long with concepts and criteria of truth which scientists evolved for quite other reasons than their adequacy to human experience.

Science must, of its nature, be amenable to verification or falsification by observational tests. It is easy to conclude that the truth, perhaps even the meaning, of a scientific hypothesis is the sense-observations had or expected in respect of it. Whence it is easy to generalize that truth, perhaps also meaning, in all cases is the correspondence of a statement with observational or os-

34. "The Method of Analysis in Metaphysics," in *Proceedings of the Aristotelian Society,* n.s. XXXIII, 1932–3, p. 94.

tensive data, or with empirical objects. This is the source of
the correspondence theory of truth, as of the picture theory of
language. But neither of these theories is tenable. It has been
well said: "There are no that's in the world. . . . Sentences
and facts cannot correspond in any way that suits the needs of a
correspondence theory of language." [35] It is a fundamental mis-
conception of language that it grows out of gestures or is a substitute for pointing. Thinking and talking are not naming.

It is often thought that the Platonic-Aristotelian-Medieval
definition of truth is the same as this modern correspondence-
theory. Heidegger, who has devoted much labour to refuting the
modern theory, finds its prototype in Plato. This is a great misunderstanding. The fact is that Plato's notion of truth is a
better statement than Heidegger's own, of what Heidegger, to
my mind, wants to say, namely that truth is not a static, closed
correspondence of idea to thing, but a greater or less approximation of empirical datum to idea, essence, ideal; in Heidegger's
language, a "revelation of what-is," a "relationship of open re-
solve," "a directive to turn to what-is." [36] It was the doctrine of
Plato which, through Saint Augustine, came to Aquinas as the
doctrine of *adaequatio rei et intellectus;* where *adaequatio* is
closer in meaning to "adequacy" than to "correspondence," and
has little if anything in common with modern notions of "correspondence."

The fact is that language never fully corresponds to what we
know there is, in us and in things, to be described. A concept is
never just a record of an observation or a copy of an object; the
object always falls short of what it causes us to know.[37] In turn,

---

35. Miss E. Daitz, "The Picture Theory of Meaning," in *Essays in Conceptual
Analysis,* ed. A. Flew, pp. 66, 74.
36. "On the Essence of Truth," in *Existence and Being,* pp. 322–3, 328, 333–
4. Compare A. de Waehlens, *Phénoménologie et Verité* (Paris, Presses Uni-
versitaires de France, 1953), pp. 63 ff.
37. Compare David Pole, *The Later Philosophy of Wittgenstein* (Athlone
Press, 1958), p. 83: "There is always more meaning in an expression than
we have given it." He speaks of language as "a developing, self-correcting
system." Cp. Brice Parrain, *Recherches sur la nature et les fonctions du
langage* (Paris, Gallimard, 1942), pp. 154 ff.

our concepts and descriptions always fall short of their empirical objects; they can express everything about them except their *being*. Existence is not itself conceptualizable, but is the condition of all conceptualizing. That which is co-predicated in all predication is not itself a predicate. Furthermore, no empirical description can comprehend the reality of myself who am making it. The totality of empirical knowledge could not possibly answer my questions about myself and about my knowing and about being. By this, I know that I exceed the totality of empirical things.[38] Wittgenstein said "The feeling of the world as a limited whole is the mystical feeling."[39] We should rather say, it is that element within experience which makes metaphysics necessary.

A "correspondence" or "verification" theory of truth can be made plausible only by leaving the self and being out. The having of observations, the enumeration, even the ideally complete enumeration, of all the objects or facts or empirical data that there are in the world, would not be an adequate description of reality; it would leave out the describer and the being of the described. No statement about reality as a whole could be empirically verifiable, in the sense of its "being possible to describe in observational terms two different states of the Universe—one that takes place when the statement is true and another one when it is not."[40] A statement about reality as a whole *must* be compatible with all states of the Universe, or "neutral in respect of matters of fact." It is a commonplace that the principle of verification is such a statement and is not itself empirically verifiable. All metaphysical statements are of this kind. The question remains: how then can they be true?

I suggest that their truth is their adequacy to reality as a whole, or to the totality of experience. This is not to be interpreted as psychological adequacy, or capacity to reassure and inspire. It is a

38. Professor Ramsey speaks of "dissatisfaction with empirical descriptions" as a prerequisite to knowledge of God. See *Religious Language*, pp. 52, 62.
39. *Tractatus*, 6. 45.
40. von Mises, *Positivism*, p. 76.

question of allowing fully in one's descriptions and explanations for all that there is in human experience. I do not say "describing completely" or "explaining clearly." I have consistently argued that no language can succeed in doing either. But metaphysical language *can* be adequate to reality as a whole; first of all negatively—by exposing the falsity of claims that empirical descriptions are adequate, the falsity of all "nothing-buttery"; second, positively, by recognizing the existence of the metempirical within experience and by accepting the duty of making sense of it; third, by recognizing that what goes beyond experience and yet is involved in experience cannot be the infra-rational, the irrational or the absurd. It is this that Gabriel Marcel means by his concept of "mystery." "Mystery" is his name for the presence within experience of an "I" and "being" which are not adequately describable in empirical terms. Recognition of this "mystery" is metaphysics; he calls it "concrete philosophy" or the philosophy of complete experience, as Bergson had called metaphysics "integral experience."

4. *The Sense of the World*

I spoke of "the duty of making sense of" the metempirical within experience. But how do we know that the world makes sense? How can we know that the correct attitude is not that of Camus? —"Man finds himself before the irrational. He feels in himself his desire for happiness and for rationality. The absurd is this confrontation of man's demand and the unreasonable silence of the world.[41] . . . To live is to make the absurd live. To make it live is to look it full in the face. . . . One of the only coherent positions there is in philosophy is revolt. Revolt is a perpetual awareness by man of the irrational in his own existence. It is the demand for an impossible transparency." [42]

Something similar is often being said, though in less dramatic words and with less tragic accent, in contemporary British philosophy. The first thing I should like to say about it is that

41. *Le Mythe de Sisyphe,* pp. 44–5.
42. *Ibid.,* pp. 76–7.

it seems to suppose that "the irrational" (i.e. the self and being) somehow confronts reason, or stands opposite to and apart from reason, that reason has "the irrational" all round its edges. But I have argued that "the irrational," in the sense defined, is *in* all reasoning and cannot be the opponent or enemy of reasoning or be "beyond the edges" of reason. My existence as a reasoner cannot be absurd. It is I who recognize and challenge "absurdity." Camus was equating the rational with the completely understood; the irrational with all that I cannot completely describe in empirical terms. His "absurd" is only a misleading name for the metempirical elements in experience. But even Camus could not consistently regard these as absurd or even as unknowable. He defined man and humanism by them. It was in their name, and the synonymous name of humanism, that he revolted against the rationalism of empirical science. "Man in revolt" is another name for man-transcending-the-empirical world, or man-the-metaphysical.

Furthermore, metaphysics does not pretend to achieve the "impossible transparency" which Camus thought reason required. When I say that the metaphysician tries "to make sense" of the metempirical in the empirical; when I say that the theist posits the existence of God because otherwise the existence of anything would be inexplicable, my statements could be misunderstood. "To make sense of" is ambiguous, because it suggests that when the metaphysician has done, "all is now clear." "Inexplicable" is ambiguous in so far as its opposite may seem to be "completely explained." The theistic metaphysician does not pretend that the existence of God "makes everything clear" and explains away all problems. He does not make a "postulate of universal intelligibility" in the sense of demanding that reality shall be positively and exhaustively comprehended by us.[43] He postulates intelligibility only in the minimal sense that being shall not be self-contradictory, or absurd. All proofs for the existence of God are,

43. Hence Ronald W. Hepburn's objection is not merited: "Can *no* explanations be valuable unless *complete* and *ultimate* explanation is also possible?" [*Christianity and Paradox* (London, Watts, 1958), p. 181].

in one form or another, a *reductio ad absurdum et contradictorium* of the non-existence of God. They try to show that the non-admission of God is the inadequacy of description which amounts to a contradiction: treating part of experience as if it were the whole. Metaphysics begins with the recognition that there is mystery in being and in experience. But it is not merely the recognition of mystery. Metaphysics cannot end until it has rendered such reason of that mystery that it shall not become instead absurdity. The true alternative is not mystery *or* clarity, but mystery *or* absurdity.

The theist will not claim to understand Creation; but just that, without it, the existence of the world is impossible. He will not claim to comprehend God; but just to know that he is real and that his reality "exceeds by its immensity every concept that our minds can form." [44] The metaphysician is not dispensed from the need to turn to scientists for information about the "how-it-is" of the world. He is not dispensed from puzzlement about the "that-it-is" of the world. But the humility of his little knowledge is of vast importance for man. Aquinas said: "The least knowledge that can be had about the highest things is more desirable than the most exact knowledge about lesser things." [45] It is wonder, not curiosity which animates the metaphysician; and wonder is akin to admiration. "It is an indispensable condition of all true and lasting admiration that its object should be greater than our knowledge of it; and the growth of knowledge, far from touching the limits of the marvellous, should convince us more and more of their inaccessibility." [46]

44. St. Thomas Aquinas, *Summa contra Gentiles*, I 14.
45. *Ibid.*, I 5.
46. Abbot Vonier, *The Personality of Christ*, in *Collected Works*, Vol. I (London, Burns Oates, 1952), p. 107. Compare Camus in *Discours de Suède* (Paris, Gallimard, 1958): "Admiration is the supreme joy of the intelligence."

VI

God and the "Private-I"

WILLIAM H. POTEAT

I want to show certain, I think, quite obvious but perhaps important peculiarities of the role in our language of the first personal pronoun singular in order to suggest an analogy between the logical role in certain forms of discourse of the concept "I" and of the concept of "God." In the course of doing this, I think the use of certain theological concepts may be displayed.

I

Ever since the time of Hume all talk by ourselves about ourselves has been regarded as being in some way problematical, if not embarrassing. And the unavoidable use of the first personal pronoun singular by each man of himself has tempted us into assuming that each one of us enjoys a unique cognitive relation to himself concerning which, at any rate, the broadly empirical tradition in philosophy has made us feel slightly sheepish.

A recent, although certainly not the most unambiguous, assault upon what he himself has called the "privileged access" theory of self-knowledge is that of Gilbert Ryle in the *Concept of Mind*.

I want to begin my analysis with a look at part of his ingenious argument. Ryle says:

> John Doe's ways of finding out about John Doe are the same as John Doe's ways of finding out about Richard Roe. To drop the hope of Privileged Access is also to drop the fear of epistemological isolation: we lose the bitters with the sweets of Solipsism.[1]

Now, in fact, I believe Ryle is quite unsettled in his mind as to whether he wishes to stand on so bold a statement, as perhaps will be seen later on when we consider what he has to say about "the systematic elusiveness of 'I,' " and the functioning of the first personal pronoun singular. That is a technical question in Rylean exegesis which does not interest me. What I do want to show, using Ryle's remark above, is that such an analysis of self-knowledge is quite obviously false, and that the impossibility of accepting it shows us something important regarding the peculiar status and function in our language of the personal pronoun, first person, singular.

First, Ryle in having adroitly done away with the bitters of solipsism by denying the hope of privileged access has created a new problem. By making this move he has enabled us to overcome the haunting sense of being quite alone, and has shown us that we can after all know other minds. Alas he has done all this in such a way as to make everything about each of us something quite public, or at any rate in principle publicizable. Further, though we have on his terms an assured knowledge of other minds, there is now no longer the possibility of knowing of their *otherness*. If John Doe only comes to know or find out about John Doe as he comes to know or find out about Richard Roe, then John Doe would know of the differences between himself and Richard Roe only in the way he knows of the differences between Richard Roe and Mary Poe; and this would mean that he could never use the pronoun "I" of himself, "my" of his body or his past and his future in order to distinguish the

1. Gilbert Ryle, *The Concept of Mind,* London: Hutchinson University Library, 1949, p. 156.

things named by these from the things named by "his," "hers," "yours," etc.

Let me make my point in a preliminary way by putting it quite vaguely: without a "feeling" of myself still left over, and logically beyond the reach of any kind of behavioral reports I may make about myself after having put questions to myself as I might be imagined putting them to Richard Roe, including even reports about the linguistic behavior of using the pronouns "I" and "my," I cannot know of the *otherness* of other minds. It makes sense to talk about *other* minds only if "I" and "mine" mean something more for me than what can in principle be linguified in reports of actions, dispositions, thoughts, feelings and so on. To say, "No one knows what it is like to be me" is not at all to say something like, "I am shut up in my own mind," interpreted in such a way as to imply that I do not know what you are thinking or that you cannot know what I am thinking, providing I am willing to say.

In reply to this Ryle would want to say—"Yes, but the something left over, the I that cannot be assimilated to these reports of behavior or dispositions to behavior is systematically elusive." Indeed he says just this:

> To concern oneself about oneself in any way, theoretical or practical is to perform a higher order act . . . to try, for example, to describe what one has just done, or is now doing, is to comment upon a step which is not itself—one of commenting. But the operation which is the commenting is not and cannot be, the step on which the commentary is being made.[2]

Now, this analysis seems to me to be quite unexceptionable, as far as it goes. By means of it, in conjunction with his analysis of the question of privileged access, Ryle has succeeded in recalling to our attention some important facts. First, he has shown that "I" functions in a definite logical relation to empirical propositions about behavior or dispositions to behavior, so that even though John Doe may not know John Doe precisely

2. *Ibid.,* p. 195.

in the way that he knows Richard Roe, he certainly never knows something named "I" which is *entirely* independent of his own behavior, his thoughts, feelings or his own dispositions; even if this does not entail that, what is named "I" is just the *sum* of such behavior, reportable thoughts, feelings, and dispositions. Secondly, he shows that this knowing of his *own* acts and dispositions to act is knowing something which is genuinely part of what he means by "I." But most important, he suggests that "I" is a logically extended concept since what it names over and above what may be stated in and hence known by means of reports upon behavior or dispositions to behavior systematically eludes, at any given level of reporting, incorporation into the reports of that level. What I am taking issue with is the inference drawn by him from these discoveries. Do I not have a genuinely cognitive relation (in an unusual but permissible sense of cognitive) to what is named by "I" when I use it, which you in principle *cannot* have to what is named by "I" when I use it? "I" when I use it of myself, does not refer to a *ghostly* thing because what it names for me over and above what it names for you is not a thing at all since a *thing* is just what can be exhausted by terms in the predicate position of a sentence on any *given* logical level. From this it need not follow that we may not by analogy use the concepts "know," "thing," etc., in correlation with the first personal pronoun, if we can show that it is a logically extended concept which requires such unusual couplings. The issue really is just this: can *my* world be exhaustively described in straightforward "thing"-language, or is that "thing"-language brought under a peculiar kind of pressure when I try to describe my relation to myself and to my world *insofar as they are mine*? Is "person" a concept logically assimilable to "thing"-language without remainder?

Therefore, the statement: "John Doe's ways of finding out about John Doe are the same as John Doe's ways of finding out about Richard Roe," is false. To see that it is false and in what way false is to see something of the peculiar role in our language of the pronoun, first person singular. If we take seriously the logically peculiar role of "I," then we can explain how on the one hand it seems that what "I" names is assimilable to reports of behavior or dispositions to behavior, thus getting rid of all ghostly entities, and yet how it is possible on the other hand for *me* to be "aware" of its naming something which is not assimilable in this way. However publicizable what is named by "I" may be, there is always *for me* something which cannot be put into public discourse. It is this private relation which I have to myself, displayed in the logical fact that only I can use "I" of me, that underlies the urge to solipsism, which cannot be "said," but as Wittgenstein remarked, "shows itself."

The meaning of "I" is, for my hearers, certain behavior, etc., which is quite public. But "I" also means *for me* something more than this, something which is in principle not negotiable in ordinary public discourse about what I have done, and am now doing or am generally disposed to do, etc.; something which is, if you like, systematically elusive, but elusive of this kind of public discourse only, not completely elusive of my awareness. To put the matter metaphorically, when I use "I," I am talking both about what can be made public and what cannot; about what can be put into language and what cannot. "I" is a logically extended concept. It is about, I will now call them, *acts;* but it is, *for me,* also about something more, namely, *the actor.*

II

Suppose, however, that one wished to hold that this argument from experience is an inconclusive one, and that until this putative amphibious life of the term "I" has been exhibited by an analysis of its logical grammar nothing can be concluded. Is there support to be found for the view I am pressing against Ryle in the logical behavior of "I"? I think there is.

Suppose for the present limited purposes I were to define a language simply as a syntactically ordered system of terms having transferability. By "transferability" I mean that the various terms in the system are more or less adaptable to use by anyone in a wide variety of existential situations for calling the attention of others to particular features in these situations. For example, we can use verbs which designate certain kinds of actions or happenings to call attention to particular cases of such actions or events, nouns to denote particular things, adjectives to characterize these particulars, and so on. I will take it that proper names like Julius Caesar and Albertus Magnus are no part of language, since they lack the requisite transferability. Even so, if there were no surrogate names in language, it would be a wholly abstract analytic system like mathematics, with no existential reference. In English it is chiefly demonstratives and pronouns that serve to tie language to particulars. "This" and "that" are substitute names having maximum transferability. They may be used by anyone to make reference to any kind or any individual particular in any existential situation. "He" and "she" are also surrogate names having a high degree of transferability, but not so great as "this" and "that." Now, in terms of this admittedly simple-minded scheme, I want to look at some of the characteristic behavior of the first personal pronoun singular by comparing it with the pronoun "he" and with the proper name "William H. Poteat."

First, let us notice that, unlike the proper name "William H. Poteat," "he" and "I" may be used to refer to any number of different particulars, even if when they are actually so used, they are always equivalent to one and only one proper name. *Like* proper names "he" and "I" on the occasion of their being used name particular persons; in use they are equivalent to proper names. *Unlike* proper names however they share with other terms in language some degree of transferability. But while "he" and "I" are, unlike proper names, parts of our language, they do not possess the same degree of transferability. "He" may be used by an indefinite number of people of an indefinite number of people on different occasions; and when used by any given person may mean a different person on every single occasion. Whereas "I," though it may be used by an indefinite number of people, can, when used by any person, mean one and only one person

on every single occasion. We must say, then, that "I," unlike
"William H. Poteat," possesses transferability and therefore
qualifies as a part of language; but that unlike "he" it possesses
only minimum transferability, since whenever it is used by a given
person, "I" means one and only one person on every occasion
that it is used by that person. And this, of course, means that
"I" always functions reflexively; that is, it does not just name a
person, such as does "William H. Poteat." It names the *namer*.
It recoils on language and its user. "I" is a part of language like
"he" because of its transferability. It is a term like "he" or "the
man next door" with which we can make reference to a particular of which we want our hearers to notice certain characteristics which will appear in the predicate position of our
utterance. But at the same time "I" is *not* a part of language
like "he" because its transferability is minimal. That is, in any
given use, it always names its user, and hence always functions
reflexively.

Now, I do not pretend that there is anything very surprising
in this analysis. But I think we must not overlook the logical
grammatical fact that "I" has this amphibious status in language.
It behaves like any other subject term in a subject-predicate
sentence; and therefore it seems plausible for us to suppose of it,
what we would suppose of any other subject term, that whatever
the subject-term calls attention to can theoretically be exhausted
by adding a perhaps infinite number of terms to the predicate
position. "I" always functions reflexively. It not only calls the
attention of the hearers to a particular about which something
is being said, it refers reflexively for the speaker to his own activity of speaking, and this is not on logical all fours with *what*
is being said. We might show this by means of the following
case: I can theoretically give a complete report on Jones' activity;
I can never give a complete report on my own activity, because
after the last thing to be said, there would still remain one
further thing to be said, namely, a report to the effect that I
had just said the last thing.

This curious fact leads Ryle to speak, I think rightly, of the systematic elusiveness of "I"; rightly that is to say, if one understands that what is being eluded is incorporation into the language found in the predicate position. What he ignores, or is at least unclear about, is the reflexive activity of "I," which activity refers both to the speaker and to the subject of what he says, which is himself. "I" catches me in the activity of using language. It not only picks out a subject for predication, it reflexively picks out for me the activity of picking out, since the subject of the predication is, in predicating, engaged in the activity of picking out.

"I" not only names what it is about which something is to be said, it acts reflexively to allude *for me* to my activity of saying; it means *for me* my activity of meaning; it intends *for me* my activity of intending; it points *for me* to my activity of pointing. The systematic elusiveness of "I" shows that though others (my hearers) may correlate what I mean by "I" with straightforward reports of behavior or dispositions to behavior, it is impossible for me to do so, for when I use "I" in order to say something about myself at one logical level, there is the fact of my activity of saying this about myself at another logical level yet to be reported. Thus we see that whether we appeal to our actual experience or to the logical behavior of the first personal pronoun singular, the conclusion must be the same. I do have a privileged access to myself.

In light of this analysis, it may be possible to conclude with a suggestion as to certain analogies between the logical behavior of "I" and that of "God."

III

If it were true that the kind of relation which John Doe has to himself is precisely of the same sort that he has to Richard Roe; if, that is to say, the "I" when used by John Doe means nothing more for him than what can, at least in theory, be publicized in straightforward subject-object language; then everything there is is in some sense public or at least in principle publicizable.

There is no "private-I." The impulse to solipsism is a mere product of linguistic confusion; it not only cannot be said, it does not even show itself. Or, to put the case linguistically; there are not any logically extended concepts "on the borders of language" which put it under peculiar pressure. I have argued that there is at least one such logically extended concept and that when I use it of myself, it always alludes to a reality which is logically beyond all possibility of incorporation into the public world of subject-object discourse; and that therefore I do have a private relation to myself. Or, to put the matter ontologically, I, *as I see myself*, am always both in the world and not in the world.

If we understand that the world is just that which can be successfully incorporated into the conceptual structure of ordinary subject-object discourse, we will see that it is intelligible precisely because it has a conceptual structure—it is a world of essences. At the same time, if we accept the logical amphibiousness of "I," we will see that the extent to which "I" cannot be wholly assimilated into the structure of language, *i.e.*, the world of essences, is the extent to which we want to say that it precedes essence, that it is radically free, that it is irrational (systematically elusive, if you like), that it is a transcendent being, etc.

"I," as this logically extended concept, functions in theological discourse with such notions as, "freedom," "fellowship," "grace," and "reconciliation"; and this by reason of the fact, among others, that these concepts allude to "experiences" which are on the borders of our linguistically-limited experiences subject to the restrictions of this world, namely, the world where everything makes sense because it can be spoken of. Grace cannot be said, it shows itself.

In the Judeo-Christian tradition, we generally think of God as creator, that is, as actor *par excellence* and therefore, of the world of nature and history as his acts. Earlier on, I said that "I" when I use it, however well this may signify to my hearers what or who it is about which or whom something is being said, and consequently however plausible the assimilation of the

meaning of "I" to reports on behavior or dispositions to behavior may seem *to them,* can never mean *to me* just this, and
nothing more. "I" can mean to my hearers, and to me, the sum
of my acts or dispositions to acts. To me it always means both
the *acts* and *the actor, i.e.,* myself, because it always functions
reflexively.

In view of this parallel, I will say that the logical relation
holding between the ordinary subject-object discourse by means
of which we transact our ordinary public affairs and the concept "God" is analogous in certain ways to that which holds
between that same form of discourse and the logically extended
concept, "I." Just as we can meaningfully speak of the acts, behavior, intentions, etc., of the self, and even see that there is
some kind of correlation between acts and intentions, using our
ordinary subject-object form of discourse, and can do this without assuming that the meaning of "I" is entirely exhausted in
this discourse; so we can speak of God's acts, behavior and intentions, etc. in straightforward subject-object discourse about
the events in the world without assuming that God is just the
sum of these events. Yet to think of them as God's acts—*i.e.,*
to use "act" of them rather than "event," "occurrence," etc.—is
logically like calling *my* behavior "acts." In both cases an actor
who is not assimilable to his acts is the presupposition of the
form of discourse. And even as we can speak of certain events in
the world which on most occasions we would think of as the
acts of persons by using physical, historical, psychological or
economic concepts in the place of the concepts actor-acts; so, we
can also speak of events in the world in a non-theological idiom.
Just as saying: "Smith was killed when Jones' arm, holding a
heavy club at the end, smashed down upon him," is compatible
with saying, "Jones' act was one of wilful homicide"; so, saying,
"The Battle of Britain was the result of a concatenation of economic forces," is compatible with, "The Battle of Britain was
the Judgment of God." Settling the question as to whether there
is any reason for saying this sort of thing is, again, logically like
wondering whether talk about persons and their intentions is

licit. So too, the task of trying to infer the existence of God from certain characteristics of the world is analogous to trying to infer the existence of persons from the behavior of bodies. As to theological language and falsification: The problem of falsifying the proposition, "God loves us," that is, showing what would have to be different about the world for one to stop believing the proposition to be true, is analogous to the problem of falsifying the proposition, "She loves me." As Basil Mitchell has rightly shown,[3] the logical relation between statements about God's love of man and statements about what happens in history, etc., is such that certain things that happen do seem to be evidence against this claim. Yet, there can be no rule regarding when this would or should become decisive evidence against it. And furthermore, the difference between what is named by "God" and what is named by "she" is the difference between someone who is thought to be absolutely trustworthy and someone who is not.

None of this has shown any necessity for talking about God at all, and certainly not for talking about him in the ways traditional to the Jewish and Christian faiths. It has, however, shown that the Rylean attempt to fashion a flattened out logical behaviorism will not do; that "I" is a logically extended concept which demands a structure of mythical discourse to give body and meaning to each man's experience of his private-self; and, that finally, certain traditional elements of theological discourse have the same kind of use, hence the same kind of legitimation.

3. "Theology and Falsification," *New Essays in Philosophical Theology*, ed. by Antony Flew and A. MacIntyre, S.C.M. Press, 1955.

VII

Paradox in Religion

I. T. RAMSEY

I

In *Reasons and Faiths* Mr. Ninian Smart, after quoting a characteristic assertion from the *Īśa Upaniṣad:* "It is both far and near; It is within all this and It is outside all this," remarks that such "paradoxical pronouncements fulfil such a number of functions that by understanding the gist of them one can penetrate to the heart of the philosophy of religion." [1] In *Christianity and Paradox* Dr. Ronald Hepburn, considering more particularly theism, comments that "paradoxical and near-paradoxical language is the *staple* of accounts of God's nature and is not confined to rhetorical extravaganzas." [2] It seems then as if religious discourse not only revels in paradox but considers it illuminating. Here seem to be, if anywhere, what Professor John Wisdom would call revealing improprieties. [3]

But such reflections lead directly to the question with which I shall be concerned in this paper: can we do anything to distinguish illuminating and revealing improprieties from those

1. *Reasons and Faiths*, Ninian Smart. Kegan Paul, p. 20.
2. *Christianity and Paradox*, Ronald W. Hepburn. Watts, p. 16.
3. *Philosophy and Psycho-analysis*, John Wisdom. Blackwell, p. 112.

which merely bewilder and confound us? It is a question which Hepburn himself raises early in his book: "When is a contradiction not a *mere* contradiction, but a sublime Paradox, a mystery?" [4] Though Hepburn has a number of constructive suggestions to make I think he would say that for the most part the religious discourse he examines displays vicious muddle rather than revealing improprieties, so we are still left with the question on our hands. What Hepburn has done is to make the question all the more urgent and challenging. If certain paradoxes preserve and reveal something, what do they reveal, and how? Can we give any clues by which to recognise illuminating improprieties, revealing absurdities? [5] For our present purpose and without claiming that our classification is either definitive or exhaustive but merely an attempt to bring some sort of order into a vast and complex topic, let us begin by distinguishing the following brands of paradox: First, there is what we might call *avoidable paradox* which spotlights some confusion or other, as for example when a blunder in argument leads to a plain and obvious self-contradiction. Since the muddle can often be cleared up by retracing the steps of our argument, and since (at best) it may have a useful negative point to make, we might speak of this brand of avoidable paradox as *retrospectively negative*.

On the other hand, there is paradox which, while it is avoidable, is only avoided when we are led forward to a new assertion which somehow arises out of the two original assertions. Since there thus arises some positive significance from the paradox, as and when it is resolved, we may say that it is *subsequently significant*. This is the case with an antimony (as with Kant) and with dialectic in general, but not, I think with Hegelian dialectic in particular. For with Hegel, while any paradox of thesis and antithesis was resolvable in a synthesis, this immediately generated another paradox waiting to be resolved. So the Hegelian

4. *Loc. cit.*, p. 17.
5. *Cp.* Prof. Gilbert Ryle who concludes his article on *Categories* in *Logic and Language* (2nd series), ed. A. G. N. Flew, Blackwell, p. 81, with the question: "What are the tests of absurdity?"

dialectic would be a better example of unavoidable paradox claiming to have some sort of rational structure.

This brings us to our second group: *unavoidable paradox.* The significance of such paradox (it would be claimed) arises from and is bound up with its permanence and unavoidability. But within this group there arises the possibility of an important sub-division. Such unavoidable paradox may have a discernible, if curious, structure in virtue of which it becomes revealing; alternatively, the paradox may permit of no such structure being discerned. The paradox will then be permanent without permitting of any logical examination or assessment and we might call it (*b*) *logically inaccessible,* to distinguish it from the former brand which we might call (*a*) *logically explorable.*

What I propose to do in this paper is to examine cases of paradox in religion which fall into each of these two categories and their two sub-divisions.

II

Let us look first at what we have called avoidable paradox which is retrospectively negative, and begin with two examples from non-religious discourse.

(1) An example which Ryle gives: the child finding it a paradox that "the Equator can be crossed but not seen," [6] for whatever can be crossed, like roads, bridges, hills, can generally be seen. Here paradox arises because of a failure to distinguish cartographical language and physical object language. But the paradox might also arise as a declaration that, having distinguished these two languages, we are at a loss as to how to relate them.

(2) As a second example take the assertion: "Since all roots inevitably benefit from treatment with ammonium nitrate, so then must the roots of quadratics." But obviously the roots of quadratics cannot be treated with nitrate. Here is self-contradiction which arises from failing to recognise that here are two different uses of the token "root." Once we recognise this, it is clear that

6. *Loc. cit.,* p. 81.

the paradox is sheer absurdity, and its negative point of little value.

Now religious discourse includes examples of paradox which may be regarded as of this negative and resolvable kind, and we will try to give parallel examples to the two we have just given.

(1) As an example of religious paradox closely similar to the Equator case, let us recall an aphorism of William Temple's "I believe in the Holy Catholic Church, and sincerely regret that it does not at present exist." [7] Compare: "I believe I can cross the Equator, but regret that it does not exist to be seen." Here is paradox all right. But once again it has only a negative point to make, viz. that the word "Church" used in a credal profession, and the word "Church" used of a visible community, belong to two different logical areas. The problem of their relationship it leaves on our hands.

(2) As with our second general example, let us now take a case of religious paradox which displays sheer confusion and utter muddle. I am bold to say that this seems to me to occur at a certain stage in the development of Trinitarian doctrine as H. A. Wolfson describes it.[8] He argues that in Judaism there was a pre-existent Wisdom and a pre-existent Messiah, though (he says) the two were never identified. We might have expected that to be a merit, for how could we ever *identify* the ideas of Wisdom and Messiah? We could point at a Messiah once he appeared, but could we ever point in the same way at Wisdom? A Messiah exists in time and might pre-exist before birth, but how can we talk in the same way about existent and pre-existent Wisdom? However, nothing daunted, it was to Paul's credit (says Wolfson) to identify pre-existent Wisdom with the pre-existent Messiah and to use these terms interchangeably. Nor was that all. "While there is no explicit identification in Paul of the Holy Spirit and the pre-existent Messiah, he undoubtedly identified

7. *Life of William Temple,* F. A. Iremonger, p. 387, quoted by P. Hartill, *The Unity of God,* p. 139 and called (rightly) "a paradoxical bit of rhetoric intended to focus attention on the sin of disunion."
8. *The Philosophy of the Church Fathers,* H. A. Wolfson, O.U.P.

them." [9] Further, in the Fourth Gospel, the pre-existent Messiah was identified with the *Logos* of Philo's philosophy. So we then had:

pre-existent Wisdom = pre-existent Messiah = Holy Spirit
(St. Paul)
= pre-existent
Logos (Philo)

But from all this "identification" arises the question: "Is the Holy Spirit then pre-existent like *Logos,* or is it not?" which (since there was a one-stage and a two-stage account of this *Logos* pre-existence) develops into the question: "Was there a Trinity before, as well as after, the Incarnation?" But how can God, who is beyond change, undergo a radical constitutional upheaval? Here is paradox all right, and it arises (at any rate in part) from a failure to recognise that "pre-existence" like "root" in our general example, is being used interchangeably between vastly different logical areas. Utterly different uses of "pre-existence" have been illegitimately "identified." It only needed "pre-existent" to be then taken in all cases as straightforwardly descriptive (which presumably it might be in the case of a Messiah) and confusion was even worse confounded. Here is utterly unrevealing paradox generating bogus questions, which men were more anxious to answer than to examine. The overall result is the kind of increasingly profitless muddle which characterises not a little doctrinal speculation.

III

Let us now pass to the second brand of paradox we distinguished above: paradoxes which are avoidable but, in contrast with these last examples, positively significant.

Starting once again with a non-religious illustration, let us recall the familiar example of wave and particle theories in contemporary scientific method. To bring out the paradoxical

9. *Loc. cit.,* pp. 164–5.

character of this example, I think we have to formulate it as follows. Certain physical phenomena are best treated in terms of particle mechanics which presupposes that matter is discontinuous; at the same time, other physical phenomena are best treated in terms of wave mechanics which presupposes that matter is continuous. The world, therefore, is both continuous and discontinuous; a plain self-contradiction.

It might be said that this paradox belongs really to the first group, for "matter" and the "world" do not obviously belong to the same logical areas. But let us set that possibility aside and for the purpose of our present example notice only that the scientist working with this paradox does so with the intention that it must somehow and eventually be overcome in a more comprehensive and therefore more illuminating hypothesis. Whether or not this has been attained in the present instance by Bohm and others who talk about hidden parameters uniting the areas, I am not competent to say, but the possibility of their being right is enough to record for our purpose.

Granted that such paradox and procedure is not only justified but illuminating in science, what of possible theological parallels? Hepburn, who takes the example as a paradigm for understanding religious paradox, has no difficulty in showing that whether in assuming a parallel ontology, or some kind of similarity between a theological and scientific "hypothesis," the scientific near-parallel at crucial points breaks down. But could we ever expect it to be otherwise? If the theological case were identical with the scientific, theology, like science, would be concerned with no more than observables. But—to raise already a major point to which I return presently—can there be any distinctively *religious* language which talks of nothing more than observables?

Even so, let us agree with Hepburn so far as to admit that *some* religious paradox has a *prima facie* affinity with the scientific case and I may take specifically an example from Christology. The doctrine of the *Communicatio Idiomatum,* sponsored by Cyril of Alexandria and receiving Conciliar authority in the Tome of Leo, argued that while the human and divine natures of Jesus Christ were separate, the attributes of the one could be predicated of the other because of their union in the one person of Christ. Here is paradox indeed. Natures supposedly wholly separate are found to be united. On one interpretation it would certainly be a vicious muddle, *i.e.,* if it was supposed that a thing called a "person" united two other things called "natures" which were nevertheless utterly separate. Further, when the doctrine has been taken in this descriptive way, it has certainly led to what I would say is pointless controversy, *viz.,* as between Luther and the orthodox. But if the doctrine means to assert that while words about "human nature" and "God" are logically diverse, yet they have to be mixed to talk about Jesus Christ, so that as used of Jesus, words like "union" or "Person," or Cyril's phrase "hypostatic unity," are logical peculiars whose behaviour awaits elucidation—it may be right or wrong but it is not necessarily sheer muddle, and we may agree that some sort of encouragement for this task of elucidation can be derived from the scientific case. In this way the development of Christological doctrine can provide us with something close to the scientific parallel. But let us notice that it only does this by appealing in the end to crucial words and phrases which still await a logical placing. The original paradox may have been avoided, but only in a way which reveals more clearly than ever the characteristically preposterous core. In this way we are pushed on to the unavoidable paradox which is peculiarly religious.

It will be useful at this point to take an example from Nuer religion, for it leads us to the same sort of conclusion. In the religious discourse of the Nuer can be found assertions such as these: "The twin is a bird"; "The cucumber is an ox." Professor Evans-Pritchard elucidates these assertions as follows:

> When a cucumber is used as a sacrificial victim Nuer speak of it as an ox. In doing so they are asserting something rather more than that it takes the place of an ox. They do not, of course, say that cucumbers are oxen, and in speaking of a particular cucumber as an ox in a sacrificial situation they are only indicating that it may be thought of as an ox in that particular situation; and

they act accordingly by performing the sacrificial rites as closely as possible to what happens when the victim is an ox. The resemblance is conceptual, not perceptual. The "is" rests on qualitative analogy. And the expression is asymmetrical, a cucumber is an ox, but an ox is not a cucumber. A rather different example of this way of speaking is the Nuer assertion that twins are one person and that they are birds.[10]

Professor Evans-Pritchard continues a little later:

It seems odd, if not absurd, to a European when he is told that a twin is a bird as though it were an obvious fact, for Nuer are not saying that a twin is like a bird, but that he is a bird. There seems to be a complete contradiction in the statement . . . . But, in fact, no contradiction is involved in the statement, which, on the contrary, appears quite sensible, and even true, to one who presents the idea to himself in the Nuer language and within their system of religious thought. He does not then take their statements about twins any more literally than they make and understand themselves. They are not saying that a twin has a beak, feathers, and so forth . . . when Nuer say that a twin is a bird they are not speaking of either as it appears in the flesh . . . . they are speaking of the association birds have with Spirit through their ability to enter the realm to which Spirit is likened in metaphor and where Nuer think it chiefly is, or may be. The formula does not express a dyadic relationship between twins and birds but a triadic relationship between twins, birds, and God. In respect to God, twins and birds have a similar character.[11]

In such a case it is clear that what started as paradox concludes as a group of more transparent assertions, viz., that in respect of God or Spirit, twins, birds, cucumber and oxen have a similar symbolic function. The paradox only arises if, in Evans-Pritchard's words, we mistake the rules governing the assertions and think of the formulae as expressing a dyadic relationship rather than a triadic relationship. But this does not mean that the example falls into the negative class of avoidable paradox which we considered above. For while it is true that the paradox

10. *Nuer Religion*, E. E. Evans-Pritchard, p. 128.
11. *Loc. cit.*, pp. 131–2.

has disappeared when the correct structure of the formula has been recognised, it has only disappeared on the introduction of another concept, *viz.*, God or Spirit, whose logical behaviour remains unmapped. All we can gather is that such a concept, while it somehow refers to observables such as beaks, twin births, cucumber skin, oxen, refers to more than observables as well.

The same conclusion might be drawn from a less obviously religious example: "Hail to thee blithe spirit, bird thou never wert." [12] Bird, obviously the skylark is. Shelley is therefore saying that here we have something which is both a bird and not a bird. Paradox indeed. Yet he might say it was justified in so far as what has a beak, feathers and so forth, is a symbol of what is beak, feathers and more than any number of such items, *i.e.*, spirit. But, to reiterate our earlier point, the logical behaviour of "Spirit" is still on our hands.

Let us conclude this section with a further note on the Nuer tribe which will lead us conveniently to our next group of paradoxical assertions. Much earlier in the book Evans-Pritchard has remarked that Nuer prayers

> as is the case among other peoples, are often repetitions, but rather in the form of parallelisms than of tautologies, for they are variations of meaning within the same general meaning. Different images are used to express the same general idea, each stressing a different aspect of it.[13]

The important question which arises out of this remark is: Is the variegated and often conflicting discourse displayed by prayers only paradoxical and complex in so far as it contrives to bring together all kinds of ideas in curious concatenations,[14] thereby producing striking and unusual effects—the grotesque can often be the exciting and memorable—or does the discourse of prayer somehow contrive so to combine words and evoke images as to

12. *To a Skylark*, P. B. Shelley, ll. 1–2.
13. *Loc. cit.*, pp. 26–7.
14. Compare J. Newton's hymn (English Hymnal 405)
　　　Jesus! my Shepherd, Husband, Friend
　　　My Prophet, Priest and King
　　　My Lord, my Life, my Way, my End . . . .

tell some new kind of story altogether, a story about what can never be cashed in terms of such words and images taken at their face value, a story about something which is not merely observable, a story for which the rules (if there are any) still need to be elucidated? This brings us to what is most characteristically religious paradox: paradox claiming to be of the unavoidable kind.

IV

Let us begin with two typical examples of irreducible religious paradox arising as I shall try to make clear, from the attempt to describe what is both "seen and unseen" in language primarily suited to observables:

(1) "Religion is the vision of something which stands beyond, behind, and within, the passing flux of immediate things." [15]

(2) God is impassible yet loving, timeless yet purposive, both transcendent and immanent.

(1) Let us notice that if we take this sentence at its face value it is plainly self-contradictory. What is "beyond" cannot be "within." But the sentence has a religious point to make because it can be given (as I shall try to show) a different logical structure altogether, a structure which from the point of any descriptive language, is odd.

Let us begin with the "passing flux" of what's seen: the replacement of one noise by another, one view by another, night following day. From this beginning the writer hopes to evoke a "vision" said to be, preposterously enough, "of the unseen." To do this he offers us certain prepositions as operators or directives. *"Within"*: try to sub-divide and sub-divide, ever to penetrate more and more closely into what's seen. *"Beyond, behind"*: without leaving the "passing flux" extend our view, add, develop,

15. *Science and the Modern World*, A. N. Whitehead, C.U.P., 1933. Ch. XII, p. 238.

continuously. Now here, it will be recognized, is a technique very similar to that which Bradley set forward for evoking what he called "immediate experience" [16]—something which "is not intelligible . . . . in the sense of being explicable" but something which breaks in on us and satisfies us when no "relational addition from without (or) relational distinction from within" produces anything but "a sense of defect."

Whitehead's assertion likewise must be understood by reference to a situation which is "the passing flux" and more, a situation which breaks in on us (we must hope) as we practise the technique of sub-division and continuous expansion.

Further, the example supplies us, I suggest, with a general clue to the structure of *some* unavoidable religious paradox at any rate. Religious discourse in its most characteristic areas arises, we see, from the claim that there is something to be talked about which is not only spatio-temporal, but more than spatio-temporal as well.[17] Now supposing that we agree on this basic claim, what should we expect to be appropriate currency for such discourse? How should we expect to talk, in terms of observables, about what is observables and more, a "more" never compassed by observables however far these are enumerated?

One answer—and I do not claim it is the only answer—will be that we may properly speak of a characteristically religious situation in terms of an infinite series of observables, and this suggestion may help to illuminate another sort of paradoxical utterance which follows immediately on the assertion from Whitehead quoted above. He continues: (Religion is) "something which is real, and yet waiting to be realised . . . . something whose possession is the final good, and yet is beyond all reach." [18] We may conveniently take with this, such Christian

16. *Essays on Truth and Reality*, F. H. Bradley, O.U.P. Ch. VI, esp. pp. 188–189.
17. Christian paradox is a special case which arises when an attempt is made to use the historical to talk about what is historical and more. While Christian assertions are in part "about history," they do not stand or fall on historical criteria alone; nor is their historical reference always very determinate.
18. *Loc. cit.*, p. 238.

assertions as "Salvation is both attained and yet not attained"; "The kingdom of God has come and yet is to come." "Revelation is both final and progressive." In all these cases there is on the one hand a characteristically religious situation which is the topic of the utterance, something called merely "Religion" or more specifically "Salvation," "The Kingdom of God," or "Revelation." From this standpoint religion is "real" and "the final good," Salvation is a "state," the Kingdom of God is "here and now," Revelation is "final." But if we talk about such a situation we must talk of it in terms of a never-ending series of observables. So *our talk* will be of religion as "waiting to be realised," "beyond all reach," of Salvation as a "process," of the Kingdom of God as "yet to come," or Revelation as "progressive." But the paradox is not that there are, so to say, two different—and incompatible kinds of religion, salvation, kingdom, revelation. The paradox merely calls our attention to the fact that *our* talk about what we are given in the characteristically religious situation discourse in terms of observables will never be finite and complete. The situation will be talked about in terms of language and imagery whose span is in principle infinite.

It is with such a background that I have used, and I think justifiably used, on more than one occasion[19] mathematical parallels for religious paradox. For in mathematics, too, we meet unavoidable paradox. A series can "have" an "infinite sum" (or a "sum to infinity") which at some point or other in a mathematical argument we "see," without the series ever having a sum which is given by straight addition. It is sometimes said that a circle is a regular polygon with an infinite number of sides, even though no polygon, however many its sides, is a circle. This second paradox is specially illuminating because it gives us a technique for developing a sides story until we "see" what a circle is. The mathematical case thus resembles the theological in so far as we have unavoidable paradox which (if the formalists will allow me to say so) is significant and illuminating in so far

19. See *e.g.*, *Religious Language*, pp. 59, 69, and *Mind* LXV(NS) 258, April, 1956, Note on *The Paradox of Omnipotence* (pp. 263–6).

as it grounds characteristic phrases in a discernment and a disclosure, and gives them a logical structure of an unexpected kind.

A further point: on this background we may usefully take some theological phrases—I do not say all—as phrases generative of an infinite series, and it is this consideration which lies behind my suggestion of models and qualifiers[20] as a guide to the structure of some—I do not say all—religious phrases. It is in terms of "models and qualifiers" that we shall treat the second example of typical religious paradox.

(2) *God is impassible yet loving, timeless yet purposive, transcendent and immanent.* If these phrases are taken at their face value, if they are given the logic which their grammar suggests, self-contradictions abound. How can what is impassible be loving, how can what is timeless display a purpose, do not immanence and transcendence mutually exclude one another? But suppose that the phrases are not to be taken at their face grammar. Then, while self-contradiction as such disappears, impropriety and unavoidable paradox inevitably remain. What can we do about it? Let me give even in outline, a possible treatment of this paradoxical assertion.

God is impassible yet loving. Take first: *God is impassible.* Read "impassible" as "im-passible," and as such directing us to try to effect a disclosure by operating ("im"-like) on situations displaying "passibility" *i.e.,* in such a way as tries to overcome and deny that feature. In this way the theological word "impassible" first presents us with a model situation, *viz.,* a situation characterised by "passibility," something which everyone, religious or not, can understand. We then operate on this model with the qualifier "im" in the hope that sooner or later a disclosure situation will be evoked. The idea is that starting with something which displays passibility we must endeavour to reach something which is stable, and recalling Bradley's example we may obviously try to do this by relational division from within, or relational addition from without. This technique must continue until (or so we hope) a disclosure situation is evoked.

20. *Loc. cit.* Ch. II and pp. 175–6.

When this happens the phrase "impassible" has a second point—though a very negative one—to make, a point about language. It suggests that the word "God," used to talk of what is disclosed, must have a logical placing away from all language suited to passible things.

What now of *God is loving*? Here we must notice at the outset, that the sentence as it stands is already misleading, "incomplete" in a sense not unlike that which Russell [21] introduced. So our first task is to substitute for the original sentence one of the following more complete versions: *God is infinitely loving; God is perfectly loving; God is all-loving*. What we have to do now to understand such an assertion is to construct a series of situations characterised by love (being in this way models) in such a way that there will (or so we hope) dawn on us a situation which includes and is more than them all. "Perfect," "infinitely," "all" are qualifiers directing us to continue such a series along the right lines: to think away any imperfect, finite, limited features of any and all terms in the series. In this way the qualifiers enable the construction to be developed to any length until the disclosure occurs.

Then, and secondly, the qualifier has again a point to make about the logical placing of "God." If, for instance, we have used the qualifier "infinitely," the assertion that "God is infinitely loving" makes the point that the word "God" stands to language about loving somewhat as the "sum" of an infinite series stands to any finite summation of its terms. We may remind ourselves indeed that people have spoken of God as "Infinite Love" which makes the parallel with the infinite series exceedingly close. Alternatively, if we have used a qualifier like "perfect" or "all," I suggest that their claim would be that the word "God" is a unique and ultimate key-word dominating the whole of a theistic language scheme, an "irreducible posit" [22] to which the theist appeals as his end-point of explanation.

21. *Principia Mathematica*, Introduction. Ch. III, p. 66.
22. In a sense not unlike that used by W. v. O. Quine in *From a Logical Point of View*, Harvard, p. 44.

The same treatment might be given to "time-less" on the one hand, and to "purposive" on the other. Both are examples of qualified models, though before the last can be developed it must once again be completed by a qualifier—this time by "eternally."

Both elements of each pair of assertions in the original para-doxical utterance are thus harmonised by being tracked back to the same kind of situation. Nor is there any self-contradiction for we do not take the assertions at their face grammar. The logical structure, for instance, of "God has an eternal purpose" is on our view as much like that of "$2 = \sum_{r=1}^{r=\infty} \left(\frac{1}{2^r - 1} \right)$" as it is like that of "Aneurin Bevan has a long-term purpose." But as often in philosophy, to clear one problem is to make another more prominent, and certainly, a major logical problem remains: how to connect the word "God" with verifiably descriptive words—something about which the theory of models and qualifiers makes only outline suggestions; how to maintain both the logical unique-ness, distinctiveness, and so on of "God" and yet provide some account of its union with descriptive words. And this, I may say (to complete this section) is the theme of the paradoxical assertion that *God is immanent and transcendent*. Here is the crucial theological paradox. But it is for the most part a proposition about the use of words, *viz.*: how can the word "God" be united with words like "table," "human beings," "goodness," "evil," "beauty," and so on ("immanent") and yet be a word of unique logical status different in its logical behaviour from all other nouns? This latter is at one and the same time the claim of "transcendence," and the point of the ontological argument.

So for the theist, at any rate, it looks as if any defence of the preposterous must finish up by facing this logical problem set by the word "God," or "Spirit," a problem which in its Christian version concerns also words and phrases like "Person" and "hypo-static unity." The basic problem in assessing and defending un-avoidable religious paradox is how words can be both united with yet distinguished from verifiably descriptive words—however

many sorts of "description" there be; what logical behaviour can
we give to words which are to be united with verifiably descriptive words, without themselves being verifiably descriptive? Here
is the basic problem and it arises from the claim of religion to
talk of what is seen and more than what is seen, using as the
basis of its currency language suited to observables.

V

It is at this point that there comes the great divide amongst those
who are otherwise united in holding that paradox in religion is
unavoidable. For some would say that no sort of reasonable
account can be given of this unavoidable paradox; that theological phrases are logically inaccessible; that the problem we
have just raised can never arise. Contrariwise, others would say
that this unavoidable paradox is logically explorable, and they
would try to make some suggestions as to the solution of the
problem.

The difference between these viewpoints may be illustrated
by reference to what has been called Tertullian's paradox: "The
Son of God died; it is by all means to be believed because it is
absurd (*ineptum*). And he was buried and rose again; the fact
is certain, because it is impossible (*impossibile*)." [23] Some, recalling passages in Tertullian where he is critical of philosophers
would interpret this to be a rejoicing in paradox which was
logically inaccessible. Here (they would say) in the Incarnation
was something quite opaque to all examinations of prying
philosophers; something calling only for (I suppose, blind) acceptance. Here is an anticipation of views which we find in
Kierkegaard and most obviously in Karl Barth. But considering
that the treatise is written against Marcion, and that its overall
purpose is to reject what Tertullian himself called the "docetic
parody" which would have denied the "reality" of Christ's earthly
life, it can be argued that what is by contrast *ineptum* and *impossibile* is the original unparodied story which must talk of In-

23. *De Carne Christi*, Tertullian, Ch. 5.

carnation using words about observables like human flesh. And in so far as Tertullian used phrases which anticipated orthodox Christological doctrine, we may say that the paradox which he considered quite unavoidable he also considered logically explorable. Here is the second position with regard to unavoidable paradox. It is the position I would myself wish to defend and among other companions I think I would have at least Professor C. A. Campbell who argues both for a "symbolic" theology and for non-theological clues to it.[24]

But let us look first at some of those who would say that the unavoidable paradox of religion is logically inaccessible. First, Kierkegaard. While all of us may welcome Kierkegaard's insistence that the basis of religion is in some curious empirical situation in which I am "existentially" set, and while we might well agree that super-scientific descriptive metaphysics is not appropriate currency for what the religious man desires to talk about, yet in the end faith for Kierkegaard involves a "leap" which, he would say, is unbridgeable no matter how peculiar the structure of any proposed bridge. Or perhaps it is fairer to say that in his time nothing was available but metaphysical bridges of super-scientific design, and such bridges he uncompromisingly rejected. Now we may agree that faith involves some sort of "going beyond"; we have ourselves spoken of "more than what's seen" breaking in on us in a disclosure—a discernment to which the religious man responds with an appropriate commitment. But this is not so much a "leap" into some new territory as that we find ourselves being carried over into it, and then retrospectively have the job of mapping the track by which we travelled, peculiar though it be. And since Kierkegaard's

24. *On Selfhood and Godhood*, C. A. Campbell, esp. Lecture XVII *et seq*. Here, too, I think, would come H. H. Farmer who, with Paul Roubiczek would argue in effect that while paradox is unavoidable in theology—for like all thinking it works by contraries—its oppositions are to be so plotted as to issue in a progressive transformation of our "feelings." Here would be paradox which, if successfully explored, would lead us to "feel" what any assemblage of contrary concepts is bound paradoxically to express. Here, too, perhaps, should be placed Tillich: "Paradox has its logical place" (*Systematic Theology*, Vol. I, p. 64).

time the possibility of very peculiar paths such as he never contemplated has shown itself.

In our own day the most notable representative of this view is undoubtedly Karl Barth, who starts from the position that God is not man. God is "wholly other." Man must not formulate theologies which "rob God of his deity." [25] But then there is Jesus—God *and* man—therefore any talk about Jesus will be paradoxical indeed, for it will bridge the unbridgeable. Here, let us notice, is a double degree of paradox. We have first the necessarily paradoxical character of any theology of the "wholly other." An Incarnational theology however has to go even further—and here Barth closely follows Kierkegaard. An Incarnational theology must somehow bring together in one discourse talk about this "wholly other" and about man. Barth's answer is to make such Incarnational discourse unique and inaccessible, and to do this at the cost of declaring that we never understand the "real" meanings of words when these are taken outside a Christian setting. There may be something in such a claim. But how on Barth's severe dichotomy words outside Christian discourse have any meaning whatever is not clear. Granted that it is a blunder to rob God of his deity, is it not also a blunder to rob God of his world, a world which everybody, Christian or not, manages to talk about? If, like Barth, we have paradox which is logically inaccessible, how do we write intelligible books or begin to talk significantly about religion to unbelievers? Perhaps (he would say) we don't. The truth is that Barth can never do with logical links between Christian theology and ordinary discourse; but neither can he do without them; and the only conclusion is that in fact there must be peculiar links whose logical behaviour awaits elucidation.

Meanwhile, from the philosopher's point of view Barth's mistake is at least two-fold:

(1) Recognising the uniqueness of the word "God" whose logical behaviour is indeed (as we are willing to grant) "wholly

25. *Church Dogmatics*, Karl Barth. Vol. II. Pt. I (authorised translation). T. and T. Clark, p. 281.

other," Barth translates this proposition about words into one of supposed facts which the words picture. How much of the paradox and the absurdity in which Barth revels arises from the consequent ontology which sponsors two worlds?

(2) Barth further supposes that with a uniquely distinctive and compelling revelation—"self-authenticating" as he would call it (and let us allow that phrases like this may be apt labels for the exceptionally peculiar religious situation to which the Christian *qua* Christian makes appeal)—there must necessarily go a unique and self-guaranteeing theology. Here we have an opposite blunder from (1); in this case we have the characteristics of a situation illegitimately transferred to language. In these ways then we would say that Barth has a mistaken view of the logical character of religious language and of its empirical anchorage, and we need not be put off from any logical exploration of paradox by the old-fashioned epistemology which lies behind Barthian theology.

But there have been others less theologically minded who have taken a somewhat similar view of the logical inaccessibility of religious paradox. Mr. Thomas McPherson has spoken of religion as the inexpressible,[26] arguing that the improprieties and paradoxes of religion can never be demonstratively linked with what religion talks about, and this is a point of view very similar to that of Mr. Alasdair MacIntyre. For MacIntyre the religious man becomes religious by a total unquestioning acceptance of some authoritative demand. On this view "belief cannot argue with unbelief: it can only preach to it." [27] But *how* can it preach? *How* can its words manage to "recount the content of its faith"? [28] Have we to say that these are bogus and unanswerable

---

26. *New Essays in Philosophical Theology,* ed. A. G. N. Flew and A. MacIntyre, S.C.M. VII.

27. *Metaphysical Beliefs,* ed. Alasdair MacIntyre, S.C.M., p. 211 [Both McPherson and MacIntyre have changed their positions on this since Ramsey's essay was originally written. See McPherson's contribution to the present volume and MacIntyre's contribution to *Faith and the Philosophers,* ed. John Hick, St. Martin's, 1964. Ed.]

28. *Loc. cit.,* p. 211.

questions? The question is even more serious for MacIntyre because he rightly makes a point of emphasising the extent to which
theological language uses ordinary words, "the large degree of
resemblance between religious language and everyday speech." [29]
Must we never attempt to map these resemblances, however peculiar their logical connexions?

What light has this negative position to shed on the paradoxical character of religious assertions? All its advocates rightly
claim that religion deals in unavoidable improprieties; that if
religion uses ordinary words it uses them in a very special sort
of way; that religious discourse is not somehow high-powered
scientific theory offering some kind of scientific explanation;
that religion concerns us as persons in a vital total loyalty. But
are they right in supposing that no account can be given of the
logical structure of the phrases appropriate to this loyalty? There
can, I suppose, be only one answer, and that is to try ourselves
to do some logical exploration, and look for the results.

Here we may return to the starting point of this present discussion by reflecting that what this group does—apart from the
many differences among its members—is to take such a word as
"God," and to make it so distinctive and ultimate as to exclude
all connexion with non-theological language. We are back with
what we called the crucial problem in assessing unavoidable paradox in religion. So let us face the challenge put to us by such
as Kierkegaard and Barth by returning to this crucial problem
to see if there is any hope that the unavoidable paradox displayed
by religious language can nevertheless be given some kind of
recognisable logical structure. Can we do anything—albeit in
outline—to suggest that logical exploration of unavoidable paradox may be worth while?

Let us start by taking one of the points which Kierkegaard
and others emphasise, viz., that religious loyalty involves the
whole of ourselves. In this way they direct our attention to the
significance of the word "I" for understanding religious dis-

29. Loc. cit., p. 178.

course.[30] It is with some reflections on the importance of "I" as a clue to religious paradox that I will end this paper.

Though normally we can ignore the point with impunity, there is in fact a lack of logical fit between my assertion "I am doing x" (a state of affairs not restricted to "objects," for how can "I" to myself be wholly a matter of objects?) and "He is doing x" said of me by another (wholly a matter of "objects" or what we have called "observables").[31] The difference—and it then gives rise to paradoxical assertions—is revealed in certain unusual cases. "Did you lecture yesterday?" we ask Dr. X, and when in Descartes' phrase he had let his mind go on holiday while he expounded for the eighty-fifth time his favourite theory about the date of *Galatians*, he replies with engaging frankness: "I did and I didn't." Paradox indeed. We say of the athlete coursing round the track: "He is running magnificently to-day"; but the athlete says "Not a bit of it—it's the new B.D.H. drug that is taking my legs round." The athlete runs yet he does not run. Alternatively, on some other occasion the coach and the medical director may say: "We cannot understand how he keeps on running," "He's running and yet he can't be." Whereupon the athlete comments: "Oh yes, I am running—it's something like will-power!" And the coach comments more significantly than he suspects, "God alone knows what's happening," for the paradox is near-theological. Or there are cases of depersonalization when "I" known to the world as Charlie Bloggs dissociate myself wholly from Charlie Bloggs who is laughing heartily over someone's misfortune. Charlie Bloggs is both laughing and is not laughing. In these ways "I"—somewhat like "God"—gives rise to unavoidable paradox in virtue of having to be both associated with verifiable descriptions, yet distinguished from any or all of them.

30. *Cp. Subjectivity and Paradox,* J. Heywood Thomas. Blackwell. Esp. Chapter VI. C. A. Campbell (*loc. cit.*) makes the same kind of point from a quite different direction.
31. *Cp. Proceedings of the Aristotelian Society,* Suppl. Vol. XXX. "Self-Knowledge." J. R. Jones and T. R. Miles, pp. 120–156, and *Proceedings of the Aristotelian Society,* 1958–9. VI. "The Two Contexts of Mental Concepts." J. R. Jones.

Secondly, we might notice that "I" is only given its full—more than "objects"—use in a disclosure. If we ask: "What does 'I' talk of?" we shall only know the answer when we come to ourselves, when we are aware of ourselves in a disclosure situation,[32] when according to Hume we "feel a connexion" [33] between all our "distinct perceptions" which is something more than any and all such distinct perceptions or observables—hence Hume's perplexity. The logical behaviour of "I" then, being grounded in a disclosure and ultimately distinct from all descriptive language while nevertheless associated with it, is a good clue to that of "God," and we can expect the paradoxes of "I" to help us somewhat in our logical exploration of unavoidable religious paradox, to help us distinguish the bogus from the defensible.

Incidentally, it may be helpful to summarise these suggestions by reference to the theory of types:

(1) Many ordinary absurdities—avoidable paradoxes, retrospectively negative—are admittedly species of type-trespass.

(2) The paradoxes most characteristic of religion would also be cases of type-trespass if the key-words of religious discourse such as "God" were native to any one type-distinguished area, to any one language frame.[34] For it is characteristic of such key-words to be associated with any and all verifiable descriptions, i.e. to be frame-transferable by nature. This incidentally is the linguistic version of the doctrine of creation.

(3) So if religious improprieties are to be revealing and not absurd, they must centre on categories which, while they have freedom of association with all type-distinguished categories, are not themselves native to any one language frame. The crucial question is: are there any categories which in this way fall outside

32. *Cp.* "The Systematic Elusiveness of 'I,'" I. T. Ramsey, *Philosophical Quarterly.* Vol. 5, No. 20. July 1955, pp. 193–204.
33. *A Treatise of Human Nature,* David Hume, Vol. II, Appendix (p. 319, Everyman edn.).
34. Adopting this phrase from Ninian Smart's *Reasons and Faiths* (p. 10) and using it as he does, against the background of Dr. Waismann's article on Language Strata (*Logic and Language,* 2nd Series, ed. A. G. N. Flew, Blackwell).

a theory of types, and my suggestion has been that there is at least one word: "I."

(4) "I" and its paradoxes may then provide a paradigm for reasonable paradox in religion, as solipsism is the primitive metaphysics.[35]

If this seems too vague and generalised a note on which to end, let me point to two practical conclusions which follow from our reflections:

(i) Any unavoidable religious paradox will be defensible only in so far as it can be so structured as to be evocative of a disclosure situation comprising "what is seen and more." Failure to do this results in an irreligious theology.

(ii) Any unavoidable religious paradox will be the more defensible in so far as it can be explored in characteristically personal terms. Paradoxical theism centering on friendship will thus be more reliable than paradoxical theism centering on the Law Courts, on Judges, Generals, or Despots, and much more reliable than that which clusters around wholly impersonal models such as are used in mechanical and hydrodynamical theories of grace.

VI

Summary

There are presumably countless types of paradox, not least in religious discourse, and what I have tried to do has been to separate out and comment on a few specimens. Some of the paradox in religion may be sheer muddle, and we mentioned some patristic discussions of the Trinity as an example. Other paradox may plead, in a negative sort of way, the oddness of certain religious phrases—Temple's aphorism was a case in point, though here we are left with words whose logical behaviour is still to be elucidated. The same is true about that kind of paradox in religion which we called positively significant, and of which we took the *Communicatio Idiomatum* as our example. What it

35. *Cp.* Wittgenstein, *Tractatus Logico-Philosophicus.* 5.62.

leaves on our hands is the logical placing of key Christological phrases.

When we came to what we called unavoidable paradox in religion we saw that its basic justification was that religious discourse must contrive to talk about "what's seen and more" in terms of the language suited to observables, and I tried to show how some typically theistic assertions, paradoxical in character when regarded as directly descriptive, could be so structured as to be suitable currency for the religious situations they were meant to evoke and express. But this presented us with what I call the crucial problem of unavoidable religious paradox: How words which are not verifiably descriptive in any way can be linked with words that are.

Some would say that this question is bogus and that the unavoidably paradoxical character of theological language is logically inaccessible simply as a matter of fact, being revealing to the converted and unrevealing to those who are not. Sheep and goats must be most decisively separated. But part of the logically inaccessible paradox of theological language, at least for Barth, arose (we saw) because of an illegitimate supposition that theological words mirror and picture what they talk about.

On the other hand I suggested that some kind of logical exploration of unavoidable religious paradox was possible, and that we might be encouraged in such exploration by having as our paradigm the word "I," the paradoxes associated with it, and the empirical anchorage it must be given. What I have tried to allow for is genuine mystery in the sense that "what there is" is not restricted to observables, and to suggest that it is as apt currency for such mystery that there arises "mysterious paradox," which is then neither a vicious muddle nor an inaccessible incantation, but paradox whose structure can be investigated and explored under the guidance of the logical behaviour of "I." "I" is the best (perhaps the only) clue to all genuine mystery, all sublime paradox, and all revealing impropriety.

VIII

Birth, Suicide and the Doctrine of Creation: An Exploration of Analogies

WILLIAM H. POTEAT

Prima facie, nothing would seem to be more unlikely to clarify the peculiar nature of certain concepts in theological discourse than an analysis of the expression "I was born" and an examination of the nature of a decision to take one's own life. Nevertheless, I believe that such an inquiry will be of value in explicating certain features of the language of "beginnings" which is a familiar part of theological discussion, and one which has perhaps presented peculiar difficulty in the one hundred years since the publication of Darwin's *Origin of Species*.

One of the many things that Christians profess to believe about God is that he is "maker of heaven and earth"—where this is taken to mean that before the divine act, through the utterance of God's Word whereby the world with which we have to do is thought to have become what it is, there was nothing. Hence the so-called doctrine of *creatio ex nihilo*. This view, it is supposed, is a characteristic of both Christian and Jewish belief which sets them apart from the beliefs of all religions—such as Hinduism, Buddhism, etc.—which are either explicitly or implicitly a-theistic, and also against metaphysical systems where either there is no God, in the theistic sense, or where, if there is, he is thought to be no more than an artificer, working upon some antecedently given matter.

Along with this belief, it is also asserted that man is made in the image of God. Let me, as preliminary, take this to mean, so far as the present inquiry is concerned, that man, himself a creature, stands to the created world (understood as the subject of our public, common sense, or even our scientific curiosity) in a way analogous to that in which those who believe in *creatio ex nihilo* suppose God to stand to this world.

Now, it is notoriously difficult to assimilate logically what is thought to be meant by *creatio ex nihilo* to the many other things that we say about the world (whether we interpret the concept "world" here in the Kantian sense as a regulative principle for *cosmologia rationalis,* or merely as any given finite sum of synthetic propositions about phenomena that may be thought of as being "in" the world, taken in the Kantian sense). Theologians have declared the notion to be a mystery,[1] and philosophers, beginning in the modern period with Kant's antinomics, have generally regarded it as having no definite meaning.

I propose to show that though *creatio ex nihilo* is indeed a queer conception, which leads theologians to speak of mysteries and philosophers to speak of nonsense, in fact the notion is not so remote as has been supposed from certain demands within what is nowadays called our ordinary ways of speaking; and that within these ordinary ways of speaking where we are talking in a logically extended way about matters which are both meaningful and important to us as persons, there are displayed analogies with the sort of thing the theologian has in mind when he uses "creation" and "image of God." To anticipate later argument, I think it can be shown by an analysis of some of the things we normally say and think of ourselves as persons that

---

1. ". . . In the history of religion the idea of real creation first appears when God, instead of being considered a merely natural force, becomes a transcendent Being. We do not know this God through experience or reason but through faith, and we know of the mystery of creation by the same means." E. Frank, *Philosophical Understanding and Religious Truth,* New York, 1945, p. 58.

what we mean when we say them is logically heterogeneous with certain other things we say about ourselves, and therefore they may be said to be both "queer" (if we take as our paradigm for what is "unqueer" these other things we say) and yet meaningful; and that in them some analogy with what one might mean by *creatio ex nihilo* is to be found.

While, of course, this does not necessarily accredit the use of analogies drawn from these tracts of our ordinary ways of speaking for describing God; and while it certainly does not authorize the use of theological language in general; it does give us some genuine insight into what it is that the Christian might mean when he uses them.

This, I propose to do by exploring suicide as in some sense an act of absolute and radical destruction; and by analysing certain features of the expression "I was born."

I

The impulse to see man as in the image of God, and especially to see that image manifest paradigmatically in a dark and violent gesture of defiance, destructiveness and nihilism is of such antiquity that we cannot but wonder what kind of posture man is thought to achieve in relation to the world and to himself in these acts in which it seems so natural to see the image of God. Adam and Eve are promised that, if they will eat of the tree of the Knowledge of Good and Evil, they will become as God. While this is a calamitous act, it is nevertheless one in which man is felt to exhibit a real if perverted likeness to God. Man's act of rebellion is in certain respects logically like God's act of creation! The logical parallel between God's act of creation and man's act of destruction is clearly assumed. If this be so, it is necessary to explore some of the features of the way we think of ourselves that are built in to our talk about ourselves as persons.

St. Augustine, in his *Confessions,* reflecting in later life upon a boyhood act of wantonly stealing pears which he did not want and could not possibly eat, and concluding that the only possible answer to the question "Why did I do it?" was: "It was forbidden," goes on to make even more explicit the curious logical connexion between God's creative activity and man's wilful rebelliousness. He says, "And wherein did I, even corruptedly and pervertedly, imitate my Lord? Did I wish, if only by artifice, to act contrary to Thy law . . . so that . . . I might imitate an imperfect liberty by doing with impunity things which I was not allowed to do, in obscured likeness of Thy omnipotency?" [2] And then, elsewhere, doubtless having the same case in mind says: "For souls in their very sins strive after nothing else but some kind of likeness to God, in a proud, preposterous, and, so to speak, servile liberty." [3]

A similar tie between God the radical creator and man the radical destroyer is shown in Albert Camus's brilliant essay, *The Rebel*. He says of modern revolt: "Metaphysical rebellion is the means by which a man protests against his condition and against the whole of creation. It is metaphysical because it disputes the ends of man and of creation. . . . When the throne of God is overthrown, the rebel realizes that it is now his own responsibility to create the justice, order and unity that he sought in vain within his own condition and, in this way, to justify the fall of God" [4]— that is, to become God himself.

Again, the American poet, E. E. Cummings, seems to suggest that man as a radical destroyer of the world is the most apt antithesis to and hence the best source of analogies for God as creator *ex nihilo* when he writes:

> when god decided to invent
> everything he took one
> breath bigger than a circustent
> and everything began
>
> when man determined to destroy
> himself he picked the was

2. *Confessions*, Bk. II, ch. vi.
3. *On the Trinity*, Bk. XI, ch. v.
4. *The Rebel*, trans. by Anthony Bower, London, 1953, pp. 29–31.

of shall and finding only way
smashed it into because[5]

Finally, in Dostoyevski's novel, *The Devils,* we are confronted by Kirilov who, believing that God does not exist, nevertheless so conceives of the God who does not exist and who therefore must be replaced, that only an act of suicide by him is a genuine earnest that he himself may be thought to have become this God. He says: "Full freedom will come only when it makes no difference whether to live or not to live . . . a new man will come, happy and proud. To whom it won't matter whether he lives or not. . . . Everyone who desires supreme freedom must dare to kill himself." [6] In other words, the indifferent contemplation of suicide seems for Kirilov to exhibit a posture in relation to oneself and the world that is in some way or other like that which God has been thought to have to the world which is his creature.

Preliminary to analysing further the significance of these striking parallels, it is necessary to consider what can be meant by the concept "world," for it seems to me to be a very ambiguous one, and its ambiguity is the source of much confusion concerning what is meant by God as the creator of the world. Being perforce brief, this will be vague.

Doubtless there are many more uses of the concept "world," but let us consider here only three.

"World" can be used, as Kant seems to have thought, as an idea of the Transcendental Reason, and as such functions as a regulative principle for a *cosmologia rationalis.* The concept in this use has no content—in Kant's sense—but nevertheless provides us with guidelines in the pursuit of a goal which, though never to be achieved, nonetheless governs the progress of scientific understanding. This use of the concept is largely irrelevant to my present inquiry.

The world may also be thought of as that which can be exhaustively catalogued by a, practically speaking, infinite number of straightforward subject-predicate sentences in a language sys-

5. *Poems:* 1923–1954, New York, 1955, p. 404.
6. *Penguin Classics,* trans. by David Magarshack, London, 1953, pp. 125–126.

tem which we will, in order to educe the distinction essential to my purposes, imagine as having no use of first personal pronouns, singular. In fact, of course, if we eliminate first personal pronouns, singular, it is difficult to imagine what pronouns like "we" and "you" could do in the language (where they are steadfastly held to be unanalysable into demonstratives like "this," "that," "these," and "those"); and therefore we may eliminate them as well. Now we have a language with only the demonstratives, and the third personal pronouns. But surely, a language which does not use the first personal pronoun would have to reduce even the third personal to "it," i.e. "he," "she" and "they" could only mean what could be catalogued in reports of behaviour (actually we should have to say "events") or dispositions to behaviour. We now have a language in terms of which nothing can be said about persons.

In the language thus truncated, the world will be the sum of synthetic propositions that could conceivably be shown to be true or false. It would, in other words, be the world that could be known to us, and which is thought of in our scientifically dominated culture, as the world of common sense, and of all of the sciences themselves. Therefore it will be the world as it is "known by science." It will be objective, that is, it will be what can be catalogued exhaustively in a language having no personal pronouns. It will be in practice, a third person world, remembering that the only pronoun in the third person which remains is "it." It will be, in other words, the public world as it must be imagined to be apart from anyone actually experiencing it. It is the world as we would all agree it *must be;* all epistemological relativism aside, in the language of our model, it cannot be described as being experienced by anyone in particular.[7] It is a world in which there are no persons, because "I" and "my" cannot be used in the language that describes it. Therefore, it cannot be the world *of* or *for* anyone. No doubt a description of the world in this way

7. Given the purposes of my model, it is an irrelevant criticism to observe that modern physics has had to argue that an ideal observer or at least an observation point always has to be posited.

would be a *tour de force*, and would involve a language which is very awkward, when compared with our ordinary ways of speaking about the common sense world. Nevertheless, I think it an imaginable one, and is in fact the ideal goal of all objective scientific knowledge, albeit the concepts that may be meaningfully used vary among sciences.

In contrast with this, and as our third use of the concept "world," let us imagine what we could speak of in a language in which there *are* first personal pronouns. What differences would immediately appear?

First the world would be *of* and *for* someone. What I would mean by the world would be *my* world—though, committed as I believe we usually are to using "world" in the second of our three senses, this may be obscured. What is meant by "world" in this sense would include all of those features which could be catalogued in "third person" language as in sense two. But by adding the first personal pronoun all of this would be radically transformed by the additional characteristic of the world being mine; not just the world as I experience it from a particular point of view in a third person way like the third person way in which you, from a different particular point of view, also experience it (in other words, the first personal pronoun does not merely introduce the possibility of epistemological relativism); but mine in the sense that I have a relation to the body, its behaviour and the environment of its actions (which is the world *for me*), which is part of what I mean by "I," that can never be identical with the relation which *you* have, and that cannot be expressed in the language lacking the first personal pronoun singular. That this statement would seem to be analytic does not weaken the force of the distinction.

Perhaps this can be illustrated in the following way. In the terms set forth above, the expression "I will die" when used by me cannot be exhaustively analysed into a purely third person reading of "This body will undergo a radical change, including ceasing to behave in certain ways, etc." References by me to the body and its behaviour which is part at least of what I mean

by "I" can never be made to be logically equivalent to references
by me to bodies and their behaviour which are not. "I will die"
can never mean for me just the same thing as "There is a body
in the world (in the second sense) which one day will cease to
behave as it now does." What is being asserted is not just about
an object in the world (in the second sense) in the way that "This
body (as a component of the world in the second sense) will die"
is about an object in the world. My body and its behaviour is
not in the world *for me* in the same way that your body (to
avoid the possessive pronoun, we'll call it "Smith") and its behaviour is in the world for me. For me to describe my death as
the end of certain kinds of behaviour in the world is not *for me*
the description of an occurrence *in the world* at all like an account by me of Smith's death as an occurrence *in the world*.
For myself, I am not *in* the world as Smith is in the world.

Now, taking as our paradigm Kirilov's suggestion that the act
of suicide will be the earnest of his having achieved Godhead
because it will exhibit a characteristic in himself which he conceives to be essential to Godlikeness, how may the posture of a
man to himself and to his world as he contemplates suicide be
likened in certain respects to the posture of God when he is
thought to be the "maker of heaven and earth"?—and it must
be remembered that the parallel we are here drawing is between
God as radical creator and man, as in some sense, a radical
destroyer.

If we take seriously our distinction between the use of the
concept "world" in the second sense above, where what is meant
in the nature of the case cannot be something that is *of* or *for*
someone in particular; and its use in sense three, where it is
always *my* world; then I think it is quite meaningful, using
"world" in sense three, to say that my suicide is an act of destroying *my* world. If, that is, we keep in mind how "world" is functioning here, we may say that when I take my own life, I destroy
the world! As destroyer of the world, in this sense, I stand to the
world in my act of radical destruction, as God seems to be
thought to stand in his act of radical creation. The posture I

assume toward myself and the world (in sense three) as radical disposer is logically different from that I assume as disposer of this, that, or some other characteristic or feature of myself or the world. I am not destroying something or other *in* the world. I am destroying the world as a whole. I may be thought, in other words, speaking metaphorically, to take up a relation to myself and the world *as a whole,* to stand "outside" myself (in our ordinary uses of "myself"); and this bears some analogy to what the Christian seems to be believing about God's relation to the world when he declares him to be "maker of heaven and earth."

Or, to put the case in a slightly different way, in the act of suicide I am, with reference to what I name with the personal pronoun "I," bringing something radically to an end. Just as Hamlet's question "To be or not to be . . ." is logically not like "To be or not to be a doctor, lawyer or merchant chief . . . ," so contemplating the ending of my life is logically not like ending a job or a marriage. It is an end of *all* possibilities for something, namely, for what I name with the personal pronoun "I," and not just the ending of certain possibilities such as this or that. We can say "After his divorce he was remarried," or ". . . he was sadder but wiser." To go with the expression "After he died . . ." there are no expressions logically like "he remarried" or "was sadder but wiser."

I want to say then that though the act of suicide may not be thought of as destroying the world insofar as it is taken as an object for thought in the third person, nevertheless, the world as *my* world, *in* which part of what I mean when I use the pronoun "I" of myself is to be found, which is the environment of the acts of the body that is part of what I mean by "I," and is accordingly the world in our third sense, *is* destroyed. And the posture which I have in relation to the world, thus construed, is analogous to that which God is thought to have to the world (in either of our first two senses) as its radical creator.[8] There are

8. There is a dangerous pitfall in the analogy here, for we may be tempted to infer from it, at this stage, that God and his world are identical. But this would be an invalid inference for, as I shall show, I and *my* world are not identical either.

three equally important features of this analogy to be emphasized. First, as destroyer of the world (in sense three), I have a
view of myself as what may be called a radical agent. In the act
of suicide, I perform an act which makes nothing out of something. My act is the reverse of God's who makes something out
of nothing. A world which can be imagined, in terms of the
present analysis, to have an end can equally be thought to have
a beginning. When I imagine the end of the world by imaging
a state of affairs in which there is no longer the world *for me,*
I am thinking of a situation logically no more nor less queer
than when I think of the world as having been created.

Secondly, in thinking of suicide as an act of destroying the
world, I am thinking of the world as coming to an end, that is,
as being finite. There is in this the greatest possible contrast
with the way that we, quite properly, think of the world when
using the concept "world" in sense two. The world in the third
person, the subject of our purely scientific curiosity, is in practice, and rightly so, open-ended, infinite, and therefore not a
possible object of experience, as Kant seemed to imply in his
refusal to make the concept either an empirical one or one of
the understanding. Accordingly we can derive no analogy for
God's relation to the world which is his creature, from our relation to the world in sense two, for nothing ever radically begins
or ends in *this* world.

Thirdly, it is having this kind of relation to the world (in
sense three) which I have as a radical agent, that consitutes, for
the Christian, my being in the image of God.

II

It still remains for me to show that there are certain logical pressures within what we ordinarily say and think about ourselves
as persons which are not less "queer" than, because logically
analogous to, saying of God that he is "maker of heaven and
earth." To do this I will undertake to analyse the expression
"I was born."

Frequently we find ourselves answering questions such as "When were you born?" And we do not take these questions to be odd in any way. We answer by giving a date, such as "In April of 1919" or "Shortly after the First World War" or if the context is appropriate, we may say "In the year of the great earthquake," etc., or we may be asked "Where were you born?" and answer "In Kaifeng, China" or "In the Presbyterian Hospital." If we are to take these questions as in some way mystifying we would probably be taken to be resorting to, perhaps suspicious, evasion, or to be mere trouble-makers. For the questions obviously presuppose possible answers in terms of straightforwardly datable and locatable events, which occur in the objective world which is spread out in time and space; and which, in practice, extends infinitely backward and forward from the event expressed by "I was born." As such, the event may be thought to have all the complexity that any of the events in this world has: one may, for example, consider it from the standpoint of historical chronicle, from the standpoint of biology and genetics, or from the standpoint of obstetrics. And saying that "I was born" is true will certainly entail that certain historical, biological and genetic, or obstetrical propositions will be true. One may even wish to go so far as to hold that the proposition "I was born" can be exhaustively analysed into all the propositions of the same logical sort as those above, the truth of which would be entailed by the truth of "I was born."

We take "I was born" in this way most of the time, and quite rightly so, as is evinced in our willingness to answer the question "When were you born?" by straightforwardly offering a date, and not precipitating any philosophical quarrels about it.

But if we take this legitimate because, in most cases, quite adequate interpretation to be the paradigmatic or only one, we are left with some serious puzzles. For this puts me in the curious position of *celebrating* a chronicle of events, or biological and genetic or obstetrical facts, and the like when I celebrate my birthday! To honour and observe duly with solemn rites only certain obstetrical facts seems a very odd form of behaviour. And in fact I do not think any of us is doing this when we celebrate our birthdays, however impossible it may be to conceive of there being something to celebrate unless there *were* or *had been* some obstetrical facts. If we analyse "I was born" into the sum of true propositions about obstetrical and other facts, and the like, which are entailed by the truth of the proposition "I was born," then there seems to be nothing left of the sort that as persons we celebrate—nothing, indeed, in which we could take other than a purely obstetrical interest.

Now, why is this so? I believe we can say that it is because concealed in the language in which we are asked "When were you born?" and in the answer "In April of 1919" is a subtle commitment to the objectivist language which possesses no personal pronouns or else does not take them seriously; and therefore a birthday can never be described as *my* birthday. Or to put it differently, if we take the question "When were you born?" to be like "When did you come into the world?", we answer the question in such a way as to predispose us to take the meaning of "into the *world*" in the second of the two senses above. It is obvious that in this view, my "coming into the world" is not a radical event. When do we start counting "being in the world"? At conception? At the moment I leave my mother's womb? Or do we start with the gleam in my father's eye? Birthdays are celebrated only by persons, for a birthday is not what we understand it to be unless it is *of* and *for* someone, unless there is only one person who uses the pronoun "mine" of it. Only what can be *of* and *for* someone can be celebrated; and nothing in a world described merely in a language lacking personal pronouns can be so described. The fact that we celebrate birthdays therefore suggests that "I was born" cannot be exhaustively analysed into reports upon obstetrical events, etc., in our language having no personal pronouns.

If, however, "I was born" thus analysed tells some of the story of my coming into the world because the proposition "I was born" entails that there will be certain obstetrical and other facts, what is left out? The answer is of course that the world

into which I am described as having come is the world in sense
two above. And there is not *for me* any world in sense three until
I use "I" and "mine." With this act, the world in sense three
comes into being, the world which is *my* world. And it is an
absolutely novel act, for only I can use "I" and "mine" *for* and
of me and *my* world. The absolute discontinuity between there
being no world in sense three for me and there suddenly being
such a world because someone uses "I" and "mine" of it is the
same as the logical discontinuity between language two having
no personal pronouns and language three which does have them.
And this is paralleled in the ontological discontinuity between
there being nothing and there being something which is involved in the doctrine of *creatio ex nihilo.* In the act of suicide
I make nothing out of something, the reverse of God's act of creation. In using the first personal pronouns singular, I make
something out of nothing. It is from this that our analogy for
God as "maker of heaven and earth" must come. To speak of
God as creator is not the same as saying "I was born," but it
is in certain respects logically like this.

III

Let us then ask in conclusion how some of the apparent conflicts
between science and religion—with particular reference to the
notion of creation—can be shown to be the result of a confusion
concerning the logical status of their respective claims.

Earlier on, I suggested that the implicit ideal of all objective
scientific inquiry is a catalogue of everything there is in a language from which we might imagine all the personal pronouns
to have been dropped out, for such a catalogue yields a world
which is as it is independent of its being known from any particular point of view or by anyone in particular. I also suggested
that within limits imposed by the programme itself this is a
perfectly legitimate enterprise. Let me now anticipate what is
to follow and suggest that the putative conflict between science
and religion—between Fred Hoyle and Genesis—respecting cre-

ation is the result of failing to notice the subtle commitment in this programme to the concept of "world" as I have defined it as sense two above; and further because of a failure to notice that many of the things we say and think quite ordinarily about ourselves as persons rather operates with the concept in sense three. Finally, if our analogy for creation is to be drawn from the kind of discourse in which I say of myself "I was born," where this expression is analysed as unassimilable to a language having no personal pronouns and therefore must be understood as at once saying more than can be said in such a language while entailing all of the sorts of things that can, a compounding of the confusion is always possible. For this means that what is named by "I" and "world" in our language possessing personal pronouns is not entirely unrelated to the body and its environment that is described in the language which lacks them, because the concepts "I" and "world" (in sense three) could not be used were not the concepts "body" and "world" (in sense two) already in use—while the converse is not the case. Our language having personal pronouns says more than one lacking them, but not more in the sense of adding further information of the same logical sort as already known through the pronounless language. Adding personal pronouns changes *the whole* picture, but it is an already familiar picture that is *transformed,* seen in a different light. This means that, in speaking by means of our analogy, of the world as having been created, we run the risk of misconstruing the relation of religious claims about creation of the world to scientific claims about the world in either of two ways; (1) supposing there to be absolutely no connexion between them;[9] (2) supposing the connexion to be of the sort obtaining between two propositions within one of the language systems in our model. To say that the world is created, using our analogy, is not to report an additional fact about it like saying that there are material objects in it. Saying of the world that it is created stands to the fact of its being extended in a way analogous to

9. Karl Barth and Rudolf Bultmann, in different ways, seem to me to come very close to suggesting this view.

saying of a body that it is a person stands to its having three dimensions.

Now, perhaps the difficulties can be elucidated in the following way. Let my body—in so far as it is extended, an organism, and capable of what might be called directed activity—be the kind of being about which the physicist, biologist and psychologist speak. Within their conceptual schemes the notion of creation as the emergence of absolute novelty does not appropriately operate. Why? Because of everything that may be conceived as being reported in the concepts of the aforementioned disciplines we can imagine asking "What was the cause of *that*?" (where "cause" functions in a straightforward explanatory way), and we would expect to be given an answer by reference to some antecedents on a common logical footing with the events or behaviour reported by these disciplines, using a covering law which embodies the concepts of these disciplines. Each of them, in other words, takes any given event or piece of behaviour reported by means of their concepts to be continuous with other events or behaviour of logically the same order prior to the one reported and so on *ad infinitum*. While obviously the physicist, biologist and psychologist operate with differing concepts appropriate to their own modes of explanation; and even though one may wish to hold that for this reason there is logical discontinuity of a sort among these modes of explanation, since, e.g. no complex of *physical* facts *qua* physical logically entails any biological fact; there *is* an analogy among these modes in the respect that within the limits of their explanatory interests any fact, event or piece of behaviour is preceded by a theoretically infinite series of facts, events or pieces of behaviour of the same logical order. And their explanatory interests, far from requiring a notion of a radical discontinuation of these series, would in fact be frustrated by it.

The implicit ideal of these accounts of the world is a catalogue in a language in which there are no personal pronouns.

When, however, we add the personal pronouns everything is changed. However much the use of this new and enriched language may imply the appropriateness, within the specified limits, of the truncated one, we are now speaking of the world as *my* world and *yours*. A body and its environment may be thought of as becoming *my* body in *my* world—which is to use "world" in the third of our senses—when someone, namely you or I, can use of them the expression "*my* body in *my* world." Since nothing in the truncated language logically implies the new components of the richer one, we may say that *my* body in *my* world is, as *mine,* radically discontinuous with *this* body, *a* body, *the* body, etc., in the world (taken in the *second* sense). And it is this fact that makes it possible to speak of *me* and *my* world as having come into being *out of* nothing, i.e. as having been created.

To have shown the source of the analogies by means of which the Christian speaks of God as "maker of heaven and earth" is not the same as showing that these analogies ought to be used.

I have attempted here only to argue that the doctrine of creation *ex nihilo* is a logically queer notion; but that it is not as remote as is supposed from many things we say and think about ourselves in quite ordinary ways, and that an analysis of the kind of posture a man may be thought to assume to himself and his world in contemplating suicide and of the expression "I was born" display this fact. Persuading a man that he ought to think of the world as having been created is not unlike persuading a man who speaks a language having no personal pronouns that there are persons.

IX

The Justification of Religious Belief

BASIL MITCHELL

I want in this article to examine a particular view of the nature of religious belief. Put very crudely the view is that religious belief is a matter of "plumping" for one authority rather than another (or none), and that this activity admits of no logical justification. It is a view which has received effective expression in Alasdair MacIntyre's contribution to the symposium *Metaphysical Beliefs,** and, in order to avoid the imputation of constructing a man of straw, I propose to discuss his formulation of it.

MacIntyre's general thesis is that "to ask for reasons for or a justification of religious belief is not to have understood what religious belief is." Upon this conclusion, he says, two considerations converge. The first is logical: "every chain of reasons must have an ending. Religious belief can in no sense be translated into and cannot be derived from non-religious beliefs. To ask for a justification of a particular religious belief can only be to ask that it be placed in the total context of belief. To ask for a justification of religious belief as a whole is to ask for a something more ultimate than a fundamental conviction. If religious

[* SCM Press, 1957. Ed.]

belief was not fundamental, it would not be religion." The second is theological: "suppose religion could be provided with a method of proof . . . all possibility of choice would have been done away. Any objective justification of belief would have the same effect . . . faith would have been eliminated" (p. 209). It follows that "we ought not, therefore, to be surprised that to accept religious belief is a matter not of argument, but of conversion. Conversion because there is no logical transition which will take one from unbelief to belief. The transition is not in objective considerations at all, but in the person who comes to believe. There are no logical principles which will make the transition for one. There are no reasons to which one can appeal to evade the burden of decision."

My fundamental criticism of this will be that it is based on a set of false alternatives, between conversion and argument, deciding freely and having reasons, applying rules of logic and being non-rational.

I

But before proceeding to criticize the main thesis I think it may be helpful to consider in some detail one application of it, which is of central importance. As MacIntyre recognizes, some articles of belief are about history and it might seem that in these cases, at least, it was appropriate to talk of evidence for or against religious beliefs, for surely such beliefs are open to test by ordinary historical methods; and Christian theologians have been at great pains to vindicate the historical authenticity of scripture. How will a philosopher react who wishes to claim that Christianity is a historical religion, but to deny that there can (logically) be evidence for or against it?

MacIntyre takes a bold, not to say heroic, line: "what I want to suggest," he says, "is that everything of importance to religious faith is outside the reach of historical investigation. That, for instance, in asking whether the Resurrection happened we are not in fact asking a question which future historical investigation might settle is apparent if we consider how any evidence that might be discovered would be assessed. Suppose a document alleging the Resurrection to be genuine certified by Caiaphas were discovered: those who at present see the Gospels as fabrication would have the same grounds for seeing in the new discovery yet another piece of Christian propaganda. Suppose, conversely, that a document alleging the Resurrection not to have occurred, certified by the apostles, were discovered. What more probable, Christian scholars would say, than that this kind of anti-Christian forgery should be found?" (p. 206). "Even if it could be established," he goes on ". . . that Jesus died and left the tomb three days later, this would only establish a necessary condition for belief in the Resurrection. . . . This is only part of the belief that God raised Jesus Christ from the dead. To the reference to an act of God historical inquiry is irrelevant" (p. 207).

The first move, then, is to distinguish between the act of God and the historical event. The latter only is open to historical investigation, which to the former is irrelevant. But religious belief asserts some *straightforward* historical statements and to these, at least, it might be thought historical research is relevant. However, in the interests of his thesis, MacIntyre must deny this, and he does so by way of a distinction between historical event in the sense of "past event" and in the sense of "event to be investigated by historians." "To believe that a past event happened is usually only reasonable if historical inquiry warrants the belief. But the essence of the New Testament claim, as we have seen, is that certain past events can be part of a religious belief, that is that they can be believed in on authority" (p. 207).

This account is said to be confirmed by the way believers treat historical documents. "When it is asked, for example, why the Church receives the canonical Gospels but not the apocryphal, the answer commonly made by theologians is that, to anyone who reads both, the former will carry an immediate conviction which the latter do not. . . . But this is to distinguish the two on quite other than historical grounds. It is to look for the effect of each narration upon the reader. It does not offer a justification, so much as it looks for a conversion" (p. 208).

To begin with, even on his own assumption, MacIntyre has overstated the case against the relevance of historical investigation. For if, as he concedes, the occurrence of certain historical events is a necessary condition of there having been a certain act of God (as the empty tomb of the Resurrection) then historical investigation is certainly *relevant* to the question of whether such an act took place, in so far as it is relevant to the occurrence of the historical event. No doubt historical investigation cannot "settle" a theological question by proving a theological doctrine, but it may well "settle" it by disproving it. But this does not take us very far, because MacIntyre, even if he were to admit this, is not prepared to admit that anything *discoverable by historical investigation* is relevant to the truth of a religious belief. What may be relevant is the occurrence of a *past event;* but, he insists, belief in past events need not be and, in the religious case, cannot be based upon historical inquiry. This is the conclusion of two arguments, one logical, the other theological.

(1) The logical argument aims to show how very different is the way theologians treat recalcitrant evidence from the way historians treat it. It succeeds, however, rather in pointing the resemblances. This is just how historians behave. A Roman historian who set out to whitewash Tiberius would dismiss much of Tacitus as the product of propaganda against the Emperor. Greek historians have little hesitation in dismissing inconvenient Delphic oracles as forgeries by interested parties. It is very often impossible in historical inquiry to work out a consistent account of what happened by taking all the available evidence at its face value. Prejudice, error and downright deceit in your original sources can never (or scarcely ever) be entirely ruled out. Where you decide to impute them will depend on what you take to be the most convincing over-all account. So far as I can see the procedure which MacIntyre regards as peculiar to theological debate is simply a commonplace of historical method. Of course

the case would be otherwise if it were clear that theologians (and their opponents) stick to their conclusions, no matter what the evidence, for this historians do not do. This may be what Mac-Intyre in fact believes to be the case; but his hypothetical examples do not show it.

Nor is it shown by his other example of the treatment by theologians of such historical documents as the apocryphal Gospels. Why these came to be rejected in favour of the canonical Gospels is itself a historical question of some difficulty. I should myself be surprised to learn that no other historical considerations played a part in the choice, but, be that as it may, it is not obvious to me why it should be unhistorical to prefer a document which carries immediate conviction to one which does not. The sort of appeal a theologian makes is instanced in this remark of Bishop Gore's: "if our imaginations are purged of this prejudice [against the miraculous] and we approach the Gospels with open minds, we find ourselves presented in the synoptists with a picture of Jesus of extraordinary impressiveness, *such as we cannot conceive to have been an imaginative invention*" (*Knowledge of God*, p. 253). Gore is at this point concerned to vindicate the historicity of the Gospel narratives. He does, indeed, "look for a conversion," but this is not for him independent of offering an historical justification. The question of the extent to which, and the sense in which, the Gospels present "the historical Jesus" is an immensely difficult one, and I do not want to presume a simple answer to it. I simply wish, at this stage, to argue that MacIntyre does not prove his point that the preference for the canonical Gospels is *in no way* determined by historical considerations.

Consider a non-religious parallel, the problem of the historical Socrates. The Platonic Socrates differs from, shall we say, the Xenophontic Socrates in showing greater interest in mathematics and metaphysics; he argues more acutely and profoundly and he is decidedly less commonplace. Xenophon claims to be presenting an historical portrait, Plato does not. Which Socrates shall we accept as historical? Well, there are all sorts of considerations, but if someone said "the Platonic Socrates carries immediate con-

viction; the Xenophontic Socrates does not" we should admit
he had a point—not a decisive point, but a point nevertheless.
Of course the parallel is not exact. Plato was a literary genius of
the first rank, which the evangelists were not. Perhaps Plato could
have invented a really convincing Socrates. To this extent the
argument in the case of the Gospels is somewhat stronger. But I
am not concerned to assess the strength of the argument. I simply
maintain that it is, so far as it goes, a perfectly respectable *historical* argument.

What does emerge from these considerations is that the conclusions which historians draw from evidence are liable to be
influenced by their antecedent presuppositions; though it does
not follow, and is not, I should have thought, the case, that these
presuppositions are themselves incapable of rational justification.
An historian's assessment of the evidential value of the Delphic
Oracle might well depend on whether he accepted the possibility
of genuine precognition, but this is not a question that is beyond
argument.

I am unimpressed, therefore, by these reasons for holding that
theologians are in no way concerned with historical evidence.
Indeed, I shall argue later that, although theological thinking
cannot, for obvious reasons, be identified with historical, there
are important analogies between the two, and MacIntyre's analysis
suffers through neglecting them.

MacIntyre's positive doctrine about the relation between religious belief and history is perplexing. The suggestion seems to
be that, quite apart from what historians may have to say, religious
authority requires assent to certain statements about the past.
This might be all right if one could think of the past, which
history studies, as containing a number of absolute blanks, into
which could be inserted the revealed historical facts; but no
historian can countenance such blanks. Any belief about the past
which piety enjoins will have to rub shoulders with a crowd of
ordinary historical facts, established by straightforward historical
inquiry and liable to revision in the light of further evidence. It
will not do to rule by fiat that no logical relations shall hold

between the two sets of beliefs about the past. If historical investigation were to prove, as conclusively as it can, that Jesus Christ was not crucified under Pontius Pilate, no amount of logical ingenuity can render this compatible with the statement in the Creeds that Jesus Christ was crucified under Pontius Pilate; unless the expression "crucified under Pontius Pilate" is differently understood, as it would be, for example, in a work of fiction, or unless, perhaps, one were prepared to identify the meaning of a statement with the method of its verification.

This is a case in which the event to be believed in on authority is of a kind generally agreed to be entirely open to historical investigation; but what I have said applies equally to other more theological articles of the Creed, in so far as they contain historical elements, e.g. the Resurrection. MacIntyre, rightly I think, resists the temptation to interpret belief in the Resurrection in such a fashion that no historical event is asserted: "to understand that belief in the Resurrection does not rest on historical grounds is quite different from saying that such a belief is not a belief about history. To believe in the Resurrection is to believe more than that Jesus walked out of the tomb, but it is at least to believe this." But this only heightens the paradox.

It is a paradox which, one feels, no one would embrace unless he were maintaining a thesis; and the question inevitably presents itself why MacIntyre should feel constrained to put forward this unlikely thesis. It seems clear that he is driven to it by certain very general assumptions about religious belief and about "reason"; and it will be my task in the rest of the article to examine these.

II

What are these assumptions? There is, first, an argument about the nature of religious belief, to which he attaches overriding importance, and which provides, in his view, an entirely sufficient reason for removing historical beliefs of a religious kind from the realm of historical evidence. It is this: "since a belief in a historical event is always a factual belief, it is always provisional in the sense that new evidence as to the facts could always turn up. But religious faith, as we have already argued, is never provisional . . . the gladness of Easter morning is never a conditional joy" (p. 207). The backward reference is to an earlier passage in which he criticizes Crombie's suggestion in his "Theology and Falsification" that, where evil is concerned, "we do not see all the picture, and the parts which we do not see are precisely the parts that determine the design of the whole." To this MacIntyre objects that "if this be correct, in this present life religious beliefs could never be anything more than as yet unconfirmed hypotheses, warranting nothing more than a provisional and tentative adherence. But such an adherence is completely uncharacteristic of religious belief. . . . For part of the content of Christian belief is that a decisive adherence has to be given to God. So that to hold Christian belief as a hypothesis would be to render it no longer Christian belief."

This argument is, in purpose, a dilemma. If religious belief is to be in any sense rational, then *either* the reasons offered are less than conclusive, in which case belief is tentative and provisional; *or* they are conclusive, in which case there is no room for decision. Since it is of the essence of faith that it should be freely chosen, and also that it should be fully committed, religious belief cannot in any sense be rational. It follows that it is "logically inappropriate" to give reasons for a religious belief. The dilemma, however, is a false one, and both its horns lack force. I am entirely free, in life though not in logic, to reject conclusions for which the evidence is overwhelming; and I can, and sometimes should, commit myself fully to beliefs, for which the evidence is less than conclusive. "In questions of difficulty," says Bishop Butler, "where more satisfactory evidence cannot be had, or is not seen: if the result of examination be, that there appears on the whole any presumption on one side, and none on the other, or a greater presumption on one side, though in the lowest degree greater; this determines the question, even in matters of speculation; and in matters of practice will lay us under an abso-

lute and formal obligation, in point of prudence and of interest,
to act upon that presumption or low probability, though it be
so low as to leave the mind in very great doubt which is the
truth . . ." (*Analogy*, Introduction §4).

There are certain questions which in practice a man has to
decide, or to live as if he had decided. They are no longer open
questions for him, though they may once have been and may
conceivably become so again. His attitude to them may thus vary,
but this variation in his attitude does not affect their logical
status. They may be, from a logical point of view, hypotheses,
based on evidence and liable to be confirmed or refuted by further evidence; but so long as he is trying to live by them he does
not, and cannot, treat them as hypotheses. They may become
for him ultimate and fundamental convictions, which determine
his priorities and decisively shape his attitudes and interests, and
help to make him the sort of man that he is; but this does not
dictate an answer to the question whether or to what extent
they can be justified. It certainly does not imply that no question of justification can arise. A man does not contradict himself
if he is prepared to give reasons why, ultimately, he is a Christian
or a Marxist.

This predicament is characteristically human. It is *felt* as a
predicament only by reflective people who recognize an obligation to be critical of accepted opinions. It is, however, a more
pressing predicament for the religious believer than for the un-
believer, because one of the things he commits himself to, when
he *becomes* a believer, is, as MacIntyre insists, an unconditional
adherence to God.

It is important to be clear just what the difficulty is. It is presumably that he is under an obligation both to be loyal to certain beliefs and to be loyal to truth, and these are both aspects
of his Christian duty. If it is conceded that any of his Christian
beliefs are such that evidence might turn up which would conclusively refute them, then his allegiance to truth becomes incompatible with his unconditional acceptance of those beliefs.
For his owing allegiance to truth is his being prepared now, if

necessary, to reject beliefs found to be false, and this means any of his religious beliefs, should they turn out to be false. But, if he accepts his religious beliefs, only so long as they do not turn out to be false, he fails, it would seem, to accept them unconditionally. Since unconditional belief is what is demanded, this can only be reconciled with the requirements of truth if the propositions believed in are such that they are logically immune from refutation (and, of course, from confirmation also).

It is clear that there is something very odd about the notion of "unconditional belief" as we are being invited to construe it. To believe something unconditionally, it is being suggested, is to believe it in such a way as to refuse in advance to reject it even if it should be shown to be false. The religious believer, as it were, erects madness into a principle. The madman does not *in fact* reject a belief even when it is shown to be false; the believer makes it a *rule* not to do so. If this is what unconditional belief must be, if the propositions believed in are to be open to argument, it is easy to see how MacIntyre is driven to his conclusion that religious assertions are immune from all rational test.

However, if this latter view makes some sense of "unconditional," it does so at the cost of making nonsense of "belief." Where a man believes that *p*, it is a logical possibility to know that *p* or to doubt whether *p*; and all these "propositional attitudes" presuppose that there are or could be considerations which justify them. There would be something very odd indeed about a man's saying "I believe that *p*" and then denying that he had, or needed, any reasons at all for his belief. I am not sure whether we should regard his attitude as intelligible, but irrational, or simply as unintelligible: I rather think the latter. If he said he had forgotten the reasons, or could not put them into words, or could not make *us* understand them, we could make sense of it, but if he just said "there are none," I doubt if we could.

But must "unconditional adherence to God" mean either of these things? Professor Flew in a passage now justly familiar asks: "Just what would have to happen not merely (morally and wrongly) to tempt us but also (logically and rightly) to entitle

us to say 'God does not love us' or even 'God does not exist'?"
I suggest that this makes the distinction we need. The unconditional adherence which the Christian owes to God requires that
he should resist temptation to deny Him, not that he should reject considerations which ought to convince him that he is mistaken. The distinction is, in principle, clear enough. The difficulty is, in practice, that the temptation which an individual
ought to resist will often take the form of his being aware of
considerations which count against his belief, and which tempt
him to give it up. He cannot be sure, as it seems to me, that
there might not be considerations (and therefore, perhaps, the
ones before him) in the face of which he ought to give it up.
Since yielding to temptation, in this connection, *means* being
persuaded to reject a religious belief when he ought not to be
so persuaded, he may find it hard to determine whether what is
happening to him is temptation or not.

This sort of perplexity is not, however, peculiar to the religious
case. Anyone who has experience of navigation on the high seas
will remember occasions when he has taken his sights and fixed
the ship's position and set his course accordingly, only to be
overtaken by prolonged fog or foul weather, which can quickly
induce in him a state verging on panic, in which he feels he no
longer knows where he is and has no longer any confidence in
his previous calculations. He feels sick and has lost sleep; clouds
take on the shape of familiar landmarks, his soundings are ambiguous. Glimpses caught of other vessels seem to show them
pointed in divergent and unexpected directions. This he recognizes to be a situation of temptation, in which the impulse is
strong to yield to doubt and, perhaps, panic. Faith is needed,
though in this case it is only faith in himself and in his own
skill. If, whenever this situation arises, he loses his nerve and
alters his course in response to every changing sign, he is useless
as a navigator. But, and here is the rub, he may be wrong and
he knows it. It is unlikely that he misread his sextant, but not
impossible; the seeming landmark could be genuine, the other
vessels rightly pointed. How is he to know? At some point, to

alter course may become no longer a temptation to be resisted, but the right decision, but at *what* point? This is a matter for judgment.

A still closer analogy, and one that is often pressed by advocates of the view I am criticizing, is that of faith in a person. It would, it is urged, imply lack of faith in one's wife to *argue* her fidelity. But this does not mean, and no one supposes it to mean, that whether a woman is faithful to her husband is not the *sort* of question that admits of argument. The husband who loves his wife does not deny the logical possibility, or indeed the empirical possibility of her infidelity; he discounts it and must do so if any deep relationship is to be achieved. Nevertheless, here too there is a point at which faith may turn to folly.

I do not want to assert without qualification that religious beliefs are "hypotheses" or to make too much of the analogy of personal relationships. *Any* analogy with religious belief is bound to have serious limitations, and to call Christianity (or any world view, for that matter), a hypothesis, is to be insensitive to its sheer scale and range and complexity. I simply argue that even if these conceptions *were* adequate to the case, it would still not follow that commitment precludes justification.

The second main consideration to which MacIntyre attaches weight is this: "Every chain of reasons must have an ending. Religious beliefs can in no sense be translated into and cannot be derived from non-religious beliefs. To ask for a justification of a particular religious belief can only be to ask that it be placed in the total context of belief. To ask for a justification of religious belief as a whole is to ask for a something more ultimate than a fundamental conviction. If religious belief was not fundamental, it would not be religion" (p. 208).

It seems to me that in this passage and others like it MacIntyre betrays certain assumptions about what a justification would have to be which guide and, I should say, misdirect his whole discussion. These are:

(1) A justification starts from certain premisses and moves in a straight line, like a chain, to an ending.

(2) If a conclusion is to be derived from certain premisses, any concepts which appear in it must be translatable in terms of concepts which occur in the premisses.

(3) Where a conclusion is justifiable in terms of certain premisses there must be logical principles or rules, to which one can appeal. Thus, he asserts, ". . . there is no logical transition which will take one from unbelief to belief . . . there are no logical principles which will make the transition for one. There are no reasons to which one can appeal to evade the burden of decision" (p. 209).

I see no reason for recognizing any of these three requirements. It will be easier to deal with (1) which, as I have formulated it, lacks precision, if we first consider (2) and (3). It is not difficult to find counter-examples to (2). Thus I may justify a statement about a material object by reference to sense-data, although it is not possible to translate statements about material objects into statements about sense-data. I may justify the judgment that I ought to do x by reference to the consequences of my doing x, although moral judgements cannot be translated into statements of empirical fact. I may justify my suspicion that a man is jealous by pointing to his behaviour, although the assertion that he is jealous cannot be reduced to any set of assertions about his behaviour.

The third assumption, that thinking is always the application of rules, may seem, at first sight, unobjectionable, but it is, I suggest, either trivial or false. It does not hold, except trivially, with respect to the sort of thinking which requires the exercise of judgement, the sort of thinking which is characteristic of the humanities. Consider, for example, history. Here the case has been made out, to my mind convincingly, by W. H. Dray in his *Laws and Explanation in History*. The historian's typical problem involves the weighing of a set of miscellaneous factors so as to judge of their effect in a particular situation. To insist, as logicians have often done, that this activity *must* be according to some rule, if not a precise one, then a vague one, is the product, Dray believes, of "a certain guiding prejudice; a desire to represent reasoning of all kinds in simple, formal terms" (p. 56). Of course, if the logician insists, a rule of inference can always be invented, but it cannot be specified otherwise than as *the* rule, according to which it can reasonably be inferred that *p*, where *p* is whatever in the particular instance the historian judges it reasonable to infer. The rule of inference thus provided is not a tool which the historian uses when he is on the job; it is simply a garment to make him look logically respectable.

What is true of history is true, perhaps even more evidently, of philosophy. There are in philosophy very few formal proofs or inescapable inferences, yet it would be self-stultifying scepticism for philosophers to conclude that theirs is not a rational discipline. It is a characteristic philosophical procedure to compare a given case with analogous ones, and the philosopher has to *judge* how far these analogies hold. Here again we can, if we like, say that in judging as he does the philosopher follows a rule of inference; but it would be more apt to say that the rule follows him, in that it can only be formulated in terms of the way he judges.

In the light of this discussion it is possible to see what might be meant by talking, in the way MacIntyre does, of justification as starting from premises and moving in a straight line, like a chain, to an ending (assumption (1)), and why there are types of justification which this description does not fit. This is the analogy in terms of which philosophers, from Plato onwards, have naturally thought of deductive reasoning. Scientific thinking can be fitted into the scheme by taking as premises general laws, together with particular observation statements, and predicting further observations whose occurrence can then be experimentally checked. But the thinking of a jury arriving at a verdict, of an art historian working out an attribution, of a scholar interpreting a text, of an historian assessing the causes of a revolution, these can only with distortion be fitted into the scheme. Nevertheless, the compulsion to make them conform to the pattern is immensely strong and we are bound to ask why this is so. The reason is, I suggest, a feeling that arguments which do not go in straight lines can only move in vicious circles. MacIntyre is quite clear that these are the alternatives in the case of religious belief: "Our ground for saying [what we say about God] is that we have the authority of Jesus Christ for saying it; our ground for accepting what he says is what the apostles say about him; our ground for accepting the apostles? Here the argument ends or becomes circular; we either find an ultimate criterion of religious authority, or we refer to the content of what authority says."

What happens if we embrace the alternative that the argument becomes circular and try enlarging the circle a bit by including the content of what authority says? There are some indications that MacIntyre might allow this, and I cannot see why he should not since he seems to be involved in a small circle of his own already. The apostles say "Jesus Christ is authoritative"; but why accept the apostles? Surely because he, who is authoritative, commissioned them. "But why regard him as authoritative?" "Because the apostles . . ." Extend the circle, then, and you may find yourself attaching significance to the life and teaching of Christ as the expression of his divinity, to the re-animation of the apostles as evidence of the Resurrection, to the lives of the Saints as manifesting the Holy Spirit. As Austin Farrer says, "we should not find revelation intrinsically convincing, if everything else made nonsense of it, and it made nonsense of everything else" (Faith and Logic, p. 102).

One may take as an example the effect of the Resurrection appearances upon the apostles. Bishop Gore writes, in a passage of typical Christian apologetic: "The Gospels show us the disciples after the death of Jesus as a dispirited band of men . . . utterly discouraged . . . Then the early chapters of Acts present to us this same body of men confident and courageous—with a courage which no hostility could shake. They had plainly been suddenly driven round a sharp corner by the sort of impact which only some strong external force can exercise" (Knowledge of God, p.

262). It is worth emphasizing that this is, so far at least, a straight historical argument. It conforms strictly to Dray's account of the historian's task: "As historical methodologists have often pointed out," he says, "what the historian has to do is 'think away' the suggested cause in order to judge what difference its non-occurrence would have made in the light of what else he knows about the situation studied." Gore argues that the "strong external force" was the Resurrection. What the Resurrection was is something not to be understood in non-religious terms, something perhaps to be accepted on authority, but it is relevant to the claims of authority if it makes sense of this particular bit of history, and these claims would be sensibly weakened if, for example, the authenticity of Acts were seriously impugned.

MacIntyre comes very close to allowing something of the sort when he says: "The only apologia for a religion is to describe its content in detail: and then either a man will find himself brought to say 'My Lord and my God' or he will not" (p. 205). But his preconceptions about the limits of reasoning inhibit him from recognizing that the process he describes has any *logical* bearing upon the final decision. Instead he begs the question with some characteristic disjunctions: "We point to the state of the world as illustrative of doctrine, but never as evidence for it"; "Belief cannot argue with unbelief; it can only preach to it." The preacher, one might think, must argue with his own unbelief, if no one else's, and if he wants to help his hearers' unbelief, the argument must show in his preaching.

It is clear that preaching does not preclude argument. All the same, it must be admitted that the word "argument" suggests, although it does not require, the rectilinear pattern whose limits I have tried to indicate. "Argument" suggests an orderly progression from point to point: get your opponent to agree to *x* and then move on to *y*; whereas, if what you are putting forward is an interpretation of the whole of a given range of facts, you have to start, as MacIntyre notices, by giving him the full picture as you see it. You do not try initially to argue him into it; the argument starts when he complains that your account fails in some way through inconsistency or inadequacy to fact, whether by ignoring relevant evidence or by misinterpreting it. You then try to meet his objections.

It is worth noticing that rational disagreement about such interpretation need not take the form of the disputants relying on different evidence; they may read the same evidence differently. This is important, because where the comparison is not between divergent interpretations of a limited range of facts, but between competing world-views, there is a sense in which each of the rivals claims to get everything in; so that if judgement between them had to rely on further evidence, there would, *ex hypothesi*, be none available. To avoid the difficulties associated with the notion of a complete description of the universe, the point can be put this way; each interpretation claims to accommodate whatever facts are presented to it.

It is commonly argued today that this rules out the possibility of rational choice. Thus G. J. Warnock, in the chapter on metaphysics which concludes his book, *English Philosophy since 1900*, writes: "We have become familiar enough with the idea that phenomena may be viewed in more than one way, comprehended within more than one theory, interpreted by more than one set of explanatory concepts. It has thus become almost impossible to believe that some *one* way of seeing, some *one* sort of theory, has any exclusive claim to be the *right* way; the notion of 'reality' itself, it would be commonly held, must be given its sense in terms of some particular theory or view, so that the claim that any such theory reveals or corresponds to 'reality' can be given a circular justification which is also open, in just the same way, to quite other views as well" (p. 144).

If Warnock is doing no more than insist that such theories cannot be demonstrated or conclusively refuted, there is no need to quarrel with him, but there is more than a suggestion in this passage that there can be no rational ground for preferring one such explanatory system to another. It is interesting to notice, though hardly surprising, that Warnock does not in practice behave as if this were so. In an earlier chapter he rightly imputes to the Positivists "a particular world-view, a particular ideal of rational acceptability"; and he notes that "they were no more reluctant than, say, Bradley would have been to throw over the plain opinions of the plain man, if these could not be squared with the demands of their peculiar principles." It is clear that Warnock regards this as a serious *objection* to the Positivist world-view.

Professor H. A. Hodges makes the same point as Warnock with respect to philosophical and religious systems. "Such systems are logically watertight; if you take up your position firmly within one of them, you can turn the edge of any objection that may be brought against it. There is a Christian interpretation of any facts or alleged facts which may be brought as evidence against Christianity; just as there are several non-Christian interpretations of those facts or alleged facts which are brought forward as evidence in support of Christianity. To one who is a Christian his own interpretations are bound to seem the obvious and natural ones, and the others will appear forced and unreasonable, while to one who is not a Christian the reverse will appear to be the case" (*Language, Standpoints and Attitudes,* pp. 57–8).

From this point of view a metaphysical system is like a tubeless tyre; try to puncture it and your tin-tack is at once incorporated with it and thereafter shares its circular motion. However, it is far from easy to estimate the force of the argument. It is not surprising that a man finds obvious and natural the interpretation he has come to adopt and forced and unnatural those he has rejected; he accepted the one *because* it seemed reasonable and rejected the others *because* they seemed forced. Nothing at all follows from this as to the soundness or otherwise of his judgement in deciding as he did. Even if we admit that, as a matter of fact, philosophers and theologians are peculiarly liable to prejudice; this has no tendency to show that there can (logically) be no reasons for or against their theories. Indeed, there are plenty of cases of such people actually yielding to argument.

This Hodges concedes, but explains as follows: "On those occasions when a man does yield to arguments against his system or in support of another, it is because he has already, perhaps unconsciously, begun to take up a standpoint outside his system. From that outside standpoint he is able to see the point of arguments which would mean little to him so long as he remained inside; and the result may be that a rival interpretation of experience gradually builds itself up in his mind, until he is compelled to choose between it and his older view. It is in this way that transitions from system to system take place" (p. 58). This is a recognizable description of a familiar process which we may call "conversion." It appears that Hodges wants to interpret as incipient conversion any recognition of the force of arguments against one's own system. Here he comes very close to tautology. Any argument against my own system is, no doubt, to some extent an argument *for* some alternative system; so to recognize the force of the argument is, to that extent, to be ready to adopt an alternative system (not a particular system, but some system or other to which this objection could not be made). If more than this is meant, as that I must to some limited extent, if only subconsciously, be in fact formulating and on the way to adopting an alternative system (a particular one), it clearly will not do. There is more than one possibility open to me, if my system begins to fail me, if it no longer appears to me to "account for" or "do justice to" some type of experience. I may modify my system or reinterpret it in such a way that it *does* take care of the recalcitrant experience; or I may admit its inadequacy on this point and look for some way of justifying or excusing its failure. I may take either of these courses, and doubtless others, without in any degree (except in the trivial sense) adopting, or even envisaging, any alternative system. No doubt it was, abstractly considered, a point in favour of the Babylonian deities, when Yahweh permitted his chosen people to be led into exile. The prophets' response to this experience was not to ignore its challenge to the faith of Israel, still less to veer in any degree towards the surrounding cults, but to deepen their understanding of God's covenant with his people.

The considerations which, to my mind, tell most strongly

against the thesis that in matters of religion we can only plump, are considerations of analogy and of continuity. There is, first, the *analogy* between world-views and other more restricted pieces of interpretation. The arguments advanced to show that there can be no rational justification of a religious or philosophical system can, so far as I can see, be applied with equal force to, let us say, the interpretation of Plato. Here the evidence is limited, and interpretations differ, and supporters of one interpretation find the alternatives to it unconvincing and sometimes almost perversely wrongheaded; yet no one supposes that, when it comes to interpreting Plato, no question of justification can arise. And there is, secondly, the *continuity*, in the same field, between world-views whose rational basis is obviously slight, and others which cannot be so readily faulted. Anyone who consults that fascinating work, *The Dictionary of Sects, Heresies and Schools of Thought*, will find in it plenty of philosophical and religious systems which any intelligent and reasonable man will unhesitatingly reject. Yet all of them possess the logical invulnerability which makes philosophers deny that between world-views there can be any rational choice.

X

Assertion and Analogy

THOMAS MC PHERSON

I am concerned here with whether religious belief is expressible in a set of meaningful assertions. This has been a rather familiar inquiry among philosophers since the publication of Professor Wisdom's "Gods." I do not know that I have a new answer to it, but I hope at least to bring out some of the problems that this kind of inquiry throws up. The short answer to the question is: Yes. (One is inclined to say: *Obviously*, yes.) But it is the necessary qualifications to this answer that will constitute anything of interest in what I have to say.

By "religion" throughout I mean Christianity, and by "religious beliefs" I mean Christian religious beliefs.

I

Before I come to tackle the question I want to indicate the terminological apparatus that I shall use.

I want to make use of a distinction between "literal" meaning, "semiotic" meaning, and "symbolical" meaning. The literal meaning of an utterance is its "ordinary," its "surface" meaning. "Three white leopards sat under a juniper-tree" literally means neither more nor less than that three white leopards sat under a juniper-tree. Perhaps in a poem "Three white leopards sat under a juniper-tree" might also have symbolical meaning. Where criticism is too revealing and provides reasonably adequate "translations" of obscure poetic passages, saying what they mean in "plain English," then those passages do *not* have symbolical meaning. An utterance with symbolical meaning, as this expression will be used here, is one that cannot be "explained" without its point being lost. (I do not suggest that this is what the expression means in ordinary speech.) If the meaning of an utterance is not its "ordinary," "surface" meaning, but if it can nevertheless be explained without losing its point, then its meaning is not symbolical meaning but another kind of meaning, semiotic meaning. This kind of meaning is the kind possessed by, in general, analogies and metaphors.

My use of "symbolical" may be thought to need some defence. A symbol is something that stands for something else, and one expects it to be possible to say *what* a given symbol stands for; but the point about "symbolical meaning," as I have chosen to use the expression here, is that you cannot say what it is symbolical of. Why, then, call it symbolical? Because by contrast with "literal meaning" the expression "symbolical meaning" suggests distance from the object, obscurity; and it is these overtones that I have in mind in using the expression as I do. When we have a straightforward case of standing-for-something-else I use "semiotic." I do not say that utterances with symbolical meaning in my sense do *not* "stand for" anything—for this would indeed make it pointless to use the term "symbolical"—but rather that while sure they stand for something, we are sure also that we cannot explain in other words what it is that they do stand for.

This distinction is pretty rough. It recognises no difference between metaphors and codes. The notion of "ordinary, surface meaning" needs tightening up; for the ordinary surface meaning of a metaphorical utterance could be said to be its meaning *as* a metaphor rather than what that set of words on a literal, non-metaphorical interpretation would mean. So does the notion of

"standing for" need clarification. Again, the dividing line between semiotic meaning and symbolical meaning is liable to van-
ish if looked at too closely: the distinction may arise simply from
differences in our familiarity with the subject matter, so that the
line would not always be in the same place. But, in spite of all
this, I hope the distinction is clear enough. In any case, what I
am interested in is seeing what can be done if it is assumed as a
starting point.[1]

I am writing about three different *kinds* of meaning. The
phrase "different kinds of meaning" is, however, a misleading
one; and I want to make plain what I intend by it. This might,
I think, almost as well be expressed by saying that I am writing
about different kinds of utterance—in the sense that a literal utterance is a different kind of utterance from a metaphorical utterance (or an empirical proposition from an *a priori* one, etc.); this
I choose to express by saying that one has literal meaning and
the other semiotic meaning. To say that they have different kinds
of meaning indicates that the meaning is in one case "on the surface," and that the utterance is in need of no explanation, and in
the other that it is being expressed by words used in an odd context, or in strained senses, and thus that the utterance is capable
of explanation (though in practice not needing it). The point is
that I do not mean something different by "meaning" in each
of the expressions "literal meaning," "semiotic meaning," and
"symbolical meaning": what difference in kind of meaning there
is between utterances of the three types lies not in their "quality
of meaningfulness" but in what I can only call the methods by
which their meaning is expressed.[2]

1. The use of "semiotic" and "symbolical" here derives from Jung. (*Cf. Psychological Types,* pp. 601-2.)
2. Sometimes, I think, "meaning" *is* qualified with the intention of indicating
a different quality of meaningfulness. Compare the parallel case of "true."
People say "psychologically true," "dramatically true," etc., etc. Suppose
someone asks, "Is it true that Christ fed the five thousand?" To reply, "Well,
it's spiritually (or, etc.) true," may well strike the questioner as no more than
a confusing way of saying that it *isn't* true. The multiplication of different
kinds of meaning and truth, in *this* sense, provides too easy an "answer" to
difficulties about the meaningfulness or truth of religious utterances.

In religion there are utterances of all these kinds. (*a*) "Jesus was born in Bethlehem" would, on the whole, be said to have literal meaning. (*b*) "God is our Father" has semiotic meaning. It is a metaphor; or, it states or implies an analogy; or, it is an *as if* statement; or, it uses a familiar relation to stand for a much more difficult one that could only be otherwise expressed at length. (*c*) "God is One Person in Three Persons," and "God was incarnate in Jesus Christ," perhaps have symbolical meaning; these, one might say, cannot be explained in simple, literal terms —or perhaps in any terms—and attempts so to explain them result only in their real point vanishing.[3] They are Christian "mysteries."

These three kinds of meaning are not mutually exclusive; I have suggested this already: the same utterance on one occasion could be meant literally, on another semiotically or symbolically. Also, this classification is not meant to be exhaustive. We need to note, further, that there might be (and indeed are) differences of opinion among religious believers about the status of a given utterance: clearly, there is not the same agreement among Christians about the status of, say, "Christ walked on the water," or "He shall come to judge the quick and the dead," as there is about that of, say, "Jesus was born in Bethlehem."

II

So much for the apparatus. Now for the question.

Any view which says that religious people, when they talk about God, do not intend to make assertions, would undoubtedly be rejected by the ordinary believer. If he has occasion to talk about God he undoubtedly means to make assertions; he is not likely to say, unprompted, that he is expressing his feelings, or uttering sounds because he thinks them pleasant, or, etc. A missionary, in his attempts to convert the heathen, will spend a fair amount of his time in trying to impart information. There is one

3. The Athanasian Creed, for instance, is not an explanation of the doctrine of the Trinity but an extended statement of it.

God, he will say, if that needs to be said; and Jesus Christ is the Son of God. The Son of God lived on earth in human form for a period of years, and during those years, among other things, he taught. And these are some of his teachings . . . . God is our Father and we are his children. God loves us and watches over us. God wants us to love him and also our fellow men . . . . But more important than his teachings was himself, and what he did for us in his death, which took place in a particularly horrible way, and was followed by a miraculous resurrection . . . . What precisely the missionary will say will depend on the missionary himself and on the Christian body that is responsible for him. But much of what he says will consist in assertions, or putative assertions. There is no doubt that he *intends* many of his utterances as assertions. But the question is: are they?

What has become the standard argument on this is Professor Flew's.[4] Flew's point is this: To assert is always also to deny. The person who asserts *p* must intend to deny *not-p*, and if he is not denying anything then he is not asserting anything either. Now the religious believer, who says "God exists," or "God has a plan," or "God loves us as a father loves his children," seems unwilling to admit evidence as telling against his belief. The belief that God is love, for instance, does not seem to be affected by evidence of any amount or any kind of suffering. All that happens is that the original assertion is qualified and qualified (God's love is "not a merely human love"; or it is "an inscrutable love" . . .) until, as Flew puts it, it "dies the death of a thousand qualifications."

Let us call this argument "the Falsification Argument"; *viz.,* the putative assertions of the religious believer are not really assertions because they are incapable of falsification. (The argument is directed, I take it, against utterances with semiotic or symbolical meaning, and can be crudely represented as a complaint that these are not meant literally.)

This Argument is not as straightforward as it looks. If we are

4. "Theology and Falsification," in *New Essays in Philosophical Theology* (ed. Flew and MacIntyre).

in doubt as to whether someone is really asserting anything, says Flew, "one way of trying to understand (or perhaps it will be to expose) his utterance is to attempt to find what he would regard as counting against, or as being incompatible with, its truth." [5] It is not altogether clear what this means. "Trying to understand (or perhaps it will be to expose)" an utterance looks like trying to find out what it *means,* or whether it means anything; attempting to find out what the utterer would regard as counting against its truth looks more like (a roundabout way of) trying to find out what makes him say it, or, on what grounds he wants to *assert* it as true. There seems to be a confusion here. Of course, an utterance must be meaningful if it is to be judged either true or false; but it does not follow from our being unable to judge it either true or false that it is meaning*less.*

There is an ambiguity in the notion of not-being-a-real-assertion as Flew uses it. It is not clear whether his objection to religious putative assertions is that what they say cannot be either verified or falsified, or that they are meaningless, *i.e.,* don't really say *anything.* He seems to want to make both these objections, and the second, illegitimately, on the basis of the first. But these two things ought to be kept distinct. We need to ask: Are religious putative assertions meaningful? and, Are they really assertions (*i.e.,* are they true-or-false)? However, let us leave this for the moment and consider the Falsification Argument as it stands.

There are two natural counters to the Falsification Argument. To the suggestion that the apparent assertions of the religious believer are not really assertions at all the believer may find it natural to reply either: (*a*) Yes, they are, but they are assertions of a special kind which escape the Falsification Argument; or (*b*) They are not meant to be assertions, anyway, but something else. But neither of these counters will do—not, anyway, without considerable refinement.

(*a*) Assertions are assertions. What can be called different kinds of assertion do not differ from each other in the respect that they are assertions but in respect of some other, attached, properties.

5. *Op. cit.,* p. 98.

This I have already indicated. Thus, one can say that metaphorical (semiotic) assertions are a different kind of assertion from straightforward (literal) assertions: but the difference does not lie in their having different qualities of assertiveness; the difference is the difference between being a metaphor and not being a metaphor. Whatever "kind" religious putative assertions be said to belong to, in so far as they are alleged to be assertions the Falsification Argument stands. So long as religious assertions are considered to have semiotic meaning they seem to be in danger of dying the death of a thousand qualifications. They do, perhaps, escape the danger if they are interpreted as having only symbolical meaning: but to regard *all* religious assertions as having only symbolical meaning will not do; it is perverse to regard "God loves us" or "God is our Father" as anything other than analogical statements—that is, it is natural to class them as having semiotic meaning.[6]

(*b*) The second counter takes, crudely, the form of "the attitude view":—The man who talks about God—says that he exists and that he loves his creatures—is not asserting something so much as "worshipping," or "expressing his attitude to the universe" (two very different things, incidentally), etc. But this is no good. Certainly, the religious man has an attitude, or one of several attitudes; but there is more to religion than that. This may sound merely dogmatic; and perhaps it is: but it does seem to me that it is implausible to suggest that, in effect, "God exists" or "God loves us," has only an emotive and not a descriptive use.[7] Any counter to the Falsification Argument that depends on such division of linguistic function will not do. I shall not discuss the attitude view in any detail in what follows.

6. Actually, symbolical utterances, though meaningful, may well not be *assertions*. See Section IV.

7. *Worshipping* is not best described as "emotive"; but I am not attempting to distinguish among the views that can conveniently be put together under the heading "the attitude view."

III

There is a problem created by the Falsification Argument for those who wish to maintain the rational character of religion. The Thomist, for example, seems bound to say that the assertions of religion are genuine assertions—though perhaps not "ordinary" assertions but "assertions of a special kind." The impressive structure of the Doctrine of Analogy is intended to explain, on the assumption that talk about God is meaningful assertion, just what sort of assertions assertions about God are. But, according to the Falsification Argument, what appear to be assertions in religion may not be meaningful assertions at all.

In this Section and the next I want to say more about the first of the natural counters to the Falsification Argument—the reply, that is, that religious assertions are assertions, but assertions which escape the Argument through being assertions *of a special kind*. I shall consider this line of escape in so far as it takes one, or both, of the forms: (i) the assertions of religion have not literal but semiotic meaning, or (ii) they have not literal but symbolical meaning. I shall discuss (i) here, and (ii) in the next Section. My hope is to illuminate some central problems about religious discourse. I shall limit myself mainly to utterances about God. It is arguable that all religious utterances are "in the end" about God; but certainly only some are so explicitly, and these need to be marked off from the others.

The view of religious utterances as having semiotic meaning is widely held. Indeed, the view that in general when we talk about God we talk metaphorically or analogically is, I suppose, that most usually subscribed to. It is just because the most important things that we want to say about God can only be said by means of metaphors, analogies, parables, that we are in danger of failing to say anything at all. For, to put it bluntly, we never mean just what we say; and when pressed to say what we do mean we tend to utter more metaphors, and when we are pressed for the meaning of *those* we may, as Flew suggests, qualify, and qualify, and qualify . . . .

Now the Christian wants to say of his analogies and metaphors that they are "true." On what grounds does he say this?

As a matter of fact, we do not use "true" and "false" of analogies and metaphors as frequently as we use, say, "apt" or "good," or "bad." (For instance, on the occasions when we say "How true!" of a metaphorical or analogical statement we more often than not might equally as well have said, "What a good way of putting it!" And this is certainly not what we usually intend when we say "How true!" of a statement meant literally: "This film is going on just a bit too long."—"How true!") This, of course, is far from settling any difficulties about what is meant by calling a semiotic statement true, but it at least indicates that some light may be thrown on this by following up "apt" or "good" in these contexts rather than "true."

"Good" analogies are those that make their point simply and clearly; and they are those that are fruitful—those that suggest naturally the possibility of development in more than one direction, those that help to bring out connexions that we might have overlooked. In religion, the analogies that strike people as the best are those used by Jesus, or Biblical analogies generally.[8] There is simplicity, fruitfulness, "timelessness," about the analogy of Fatherhood used of God. Some of the Biblical analogies, like that of Shepherd, may mean less to us than to people in other times or places, but they are still simple, "elemental."

It seems hardly relevant to ask: Is it *true* that God's relation to us is that of the father in the parable of the Prodigal Son to (chiefly) his younger son? It seems even less relevant to ask: Is God *really* a shepherd? The point is that analogies are often tendered in explanation of things that cannot be expressed in any but analogical, metaphorical, indirect, ways. We are not reduced to analogy when we want to say that a film has gone on too long, but we are when we want to talk about God. There is often no alternative statement—no simple, non-analogical, literal, statement—that will do the job we want done. If there were such a simple, non-analogical, literal, statement available we should

8. Of course, these also strike us as the best because they are the *authorized* analogies.

not have been reduced in the first place to using analogies and metaphors in order to say what we want to say.[9]

A view which may suggest itself is that the utterances of religion are all semiotic and can only be explained in terms of each other. Perhaps they constitute a kind of semiotic system. To put this in more practical terms: it is as if the religious believer had confined himself within a circle of meaning. If a man stands outside the circle, waiting for some one religious belief to become clear to him before he will commit himself to a religious way of life, he will wait for ever. No religious belief, it might be said, can be explained except in terms of other religious beliefs. The circle is closed. Once it is entered (by Kierkegaard's "leap of faith," perhaps) the system, though not necessarily immediately or in all its parts, becomes plain. One analogy, metaphor, or parable throws light on another, and that on another, and so on. But it is not possible to take any one of them out of the system and explain it in terms other than those proper to the system.

But there is a difficulty in this view. If we are to be able to say that statements are analogical, metaphorical, or parabolic, some at least of their terms must in the literal sense be understood by us. You can only know that "The lion is the king of the beasts" is a metaphor if you know something (though it need not be much)[10] about lions, or beasts, or kingship. So, we may say, you can only know that "God is our Father" is an analogy if you understand certain things about God or fatherhood— that is, certain non-analogical things.[11] We can, in general, only

9. Sometimes we *choose* to talk metaphorically for literary or similar reasons, but most talk about God is *essentially* metaphorical or analogical.

10. You need, in fact, to know only enough to be able to see that the statement is not literal; *i.e.*, you need merely to know that kingship is *literally* a relation that holds between human beings and it then follows that "X is the king of the *beasts*" must be a metaphor. (Or false!) You need to know more than this, of course, to know that it is a *good* metaphor.

11. On the view that God is incomprehensible to human minds, it would be fatherhood that we should need to know something about rather than God; again, simply that it is *literally* a relation between human beings would be enough. Then, granted that "God" is not the name of a human being, it follows that "God is our Father" must be a metaphor.

see that a statement about *A* is a metaphorical or analogical statement if we are able to look at it alongside other statements about *A* that are *not* metaphorical or analogical statements.[12] Accordingly, it does not make sense to say that *all* religious statements have semiotic meaning; it would be pointless to say of some that they had semiotic meaning unless we were also prepared to say of others that they had literal meaning.

A similar point can be made about the *truth* of religious assertions. There is merit in the naïve and literal-minded approach to religious belief seen in, say, Freud (especially when contrasted with Jung): religion must be either true or false, and in no fancy senses of "true" and "false" either. This kind of view does at least help to make plain that *something* in religion must be literally true if anything in it is to be "semiotically true" (if I may use this expression). This, we may note, brings out the importance of the claim that Christianity is an "historical religion"; for the characterization of it as "historical" reminds us that propositions like "Jesus was born in Bethlehem" are part of it as well as propositions like "God is our Father." Christianity is not simply a kind of timeless mythology. But the inclination to treat it as a timeless mythology is a strong one; for it is clear that what really matters in Christianity is not its rockbottom historical basis but the superstructure erected upon it. To say "Jesus was born in Bethlehem" is not to have said anything that would be judged a really important religious belief; only if this is taken to mean "The Son of God was born in Bethlehem" does it do this; and this latter statement, though certainly it can be called an historical statement, is an interpretation of what we may call the bare historical facts and not a statement of them. And when we come to other important items of religious belief—like the Trinity—we are even further away from what is historical in any simple sense. The inclination to discount the historical element in Christianity is, then, strong. But to be reminded that Christianity is an historical religion is at least to be reminded that the more important

12. In the case of God, negative statements (denying certain empirical qualities to him) would fit the bill.

of the expressions of Christian belief are anchored to some straightforward literal statements of the kind that historians must begin from. I shall say more about this anchoring in the final Section.

IV

In the preceding Section I have been writing about religious assertions from the point of view which regards them as statements with semiotic meaning. But suppose someone is prepared to maintain the position that all, or at least all the really important, religious beliefs have purely symbolical meaning—a meaning quite inexplicable and irreducible. The view of religious utterances as having merely symbolical meaning may seem hardly distinguishable from the view of them as having *no* meaning—in the sense that the believer will be no more able to say to himself what his symbols mean than he is able to say this to anyone else. He *has* the symbols and they *do something for* him and he *feels* he understands something in and through them. The use of the term "meaning" may well seem objectionable. I should agree that "meaning" is being used here not in its commonest way. Yet it is sometimes used in this way. For instance, a man is not altogether talking nonsense who says: "I now understand the meaning of human existence, but I cannot possibly explain it."

Let us look more closely at the notion of symbolical meaning. It will help us if we follow up a fairly familiar parallel.

A parallel has quite frequently been drawn between the religious man and the artist. And it has sometimes been said that the religious man, like the artist, is a person who has a kind of special insight into the nature of things; only that where one sees beauty the other sees God. As a description of "the" artist this will hardly do; but it is perhaps a useful way of thinking of at least some of the people who are called artists. And it seems reasonable to say that there may be some insights that cannot be expressed in words, but only in music, painting, etc.; or, if in words, not in matter-of-fact literal statements, but in indirect, roundabout ways—in "poetic language." The well-known "un-translatability" of art forms is significant here. You cannot "translate" a piece of music into a poem, or a poem adequately into prose. You can come near to it, but you will not completely hit it off. Such "translations" miss the point of the original work of art.

There are insights, then, that are conveyed best without words, and insights that are conveyed best when words are used in some ways and not in others. It seems natural to say that the non-verbal symbols of religion (*e.g.,* the placing of lighted candles on an altar) are like the symbols of the non-literary artist. They perhaps express some things that words cannot express as well—and perhaps some of them express things that words cannot express at all. And the verbal symbols of religion are reminiscent of the uses of language by some literary artists. This links with the attitude view of religion. The attitude to the world of the religious man is the attitude appropriate towards something that is both concealing and revealing something else—something else that he thinks of great importance. In this he is like the artist; but the difference between them in this respect lies in the fact that although they both have attitudes they do not have the same attitude;—though this is not to deny either that some artists are religious men as well, and that their art is suffused with their religious attitude to the world.

Creative art combines expression and communication. The artist perhaps is saying: I have found something that I cannot tell you about in words—and yet that I cannot keep silent about: I want you to find it, too. (Though admittedly not all artists have strongly the desire to "communicate" with the world at large.) Something like this can also be said of at least some religious men. Artists are people who create works of art; and what this obvious truth implies is that the artist is not someone who simply goes through mysterious inner experiences which may never show themselves outwardly. An artist is not usefully thought of as someone who first has an inner experience and then expresses it. His having an experience and his expressing it are better thought of as one. You cannot be a great painter and yet never have painted anything; a great writer and never have written anything. In this sense, art is expression. And this artistic creation or expression is generally said to be by means of "symbols," and although no doubt a symbol must be symbolic *of* something (or there would be no point in calling it a symbol), this does not mean that it must be possible to express what it is symbolic of in any other way (in particular, in any non-symbolic way).

Being an item in religious worship, whether a linguistic or a non-linguistic item, can itself be a heading in the classification of kinds of human behaviour. The view that finds symbolic meaning in religious utterances is perhaps saying something like this: What the linguistic and non-linguistic symbols of religion have in common is more important than what they differ in. Neither, say, the Athanasian Creed, when recited in a context of worship, nor the cross on a church's altar, asserts anything about God in a way that lends itself to simple or complete explanation. There will always be mystery. It would sound strange, in fact, to say of the cross that it *asserted* anything. The view we are considering invites us to agree that the fact that a recitation of the Athanasian Creed involves the uttering of sentences in the indicative mood does not imply that in reciting it we are asserting anything either. Symbolic religious utterances are meaningful but are not assertions.

I should not want to recommend the view that *all* religious utterances have merely symbolical meaning. Some religious utterances are clearly best thought of as semiotic, and others as literal. But *some* religious utterances can usefully be thought of as having symbolical meaning: and this helps to preserve the element of mystery which, it seems, is essential to religion.

V

Let us return to our question.

Is religious belief expressible in a set of meaningful assertions?

This question, as we noted, has two halves—are expressions of religious belief meaningful, and are they assertions?

There are among religious beliefs some intended to have literal meaning. These certainly are meaningful. They are also certainly assertions;—the Christian cannot dispute that the belief, say, that Jesus of Nazareth was born in Bethlehem in 4 B.C. is one that could be supported or refuted by evidence.

But utterances with literal meaning are not of central importance for religion; and, in any case, as I said above, the Falsification Argument is directed not against them but against what I am calling utterances with semiotic and symbolical meaning. What are we to say about these?

I may seem to have already begged one half of the question by talking in this paper of semiotic "meaning" and symbolical "meaning." If I now simply repeat that semiotic and symbolical utterances are meaningful this may seem like altogether too short a way with the dissenters. Yet this is the right thing to say. We show what a semiotic utterance means by explaining the metaphor or analogy. "God is our Father" means "God's relation to us is in respects $a, b, c, \ldots$ like that of a father to his children"; just as "The lion is the king of the beasts" means "The lion's relation to other beasts is in respects $a, b, c, \ldots$ like that of a king to his subjects." The case of symbolical utterances is less clear. We *might* say that "God is One Person in Three Persons" means what, for instance, the Athanasian Creed says it means, but this does not really help; for, as I suggested earlier, the Athanasian Creed is not really an explanation but an extended statement of the Doctrine of the Trinity. I prefer to say, rather, that "God is One Person in Three Persons" is meaningful but *not* explainable. This, as I have said earlier, is not a common sense of "meaningful"; but I have also already mentioned my motive in wanting to use it in this way—my desire to preserve a place in this account of religious discourse for the element of mystery.

Are semiotic and symbolical religious utterances assertions? In the case of symbolical utterances, probably not. In the case of semiotic utterances, yes—in the sense that they are anchored to assertions with literal meaning. This anchoring is what makes them true-or-false (and hence assertions). But what precisely is to be understood here by the metaphor of anchoring?

We have three things to consider in the case of a semiotic utterance.

(1) The utterance itself. "God is our Father," say, or, "God loves us as a father loves his children."

(2) Its meaning. "God is our Father" means "God's relation to us is in respects $a, b, c, \ldots$ like that of a father to his children." ($a, b, c, \ldots$ might be cashed as follows: all men are brothers; God will punish the wicked and reward the virtuous; God watches with deep interest and concern all our doings . . . . The metaphors here themselves call for further explanation, of course.)

(3) Its anchoring. To give the anchor of "God is our Father" is to state the reasons that make us want to assert it. Or, if you like, to say how it is anchored is to answer the question: What makes you say that? It is a defect in the Falsification Argument that it does not distinguish meaning from anchoring (that is, it does not distinguish meaning from truth). The anchor may take, for example, the following form: "I completely recovered from my serious illness last year." Now this, of course, does not mention *God*, and there is no logical step from "I completely recovered from my serious illness last year" to "God is our Father." Nevertheless, "I completely recovered from my serious illness last year" is, I think, the kind of thing a man might say in giving his reasons for wanting to assert "God is our Father." Recoveries from illness constitute grounds for asserting "God is our Father"; as "undeserved" suffering constitutes grounds for denying it. In other words, *evidence* is relevant as tending to confirm or disconfirm semiotic religious assertions (though not relevant to symbolical religious utterances—which is why they are not assertions).[13]

---

13. A parallel can be found in ethics. (1) "Stealing is wrong" may be said to *mean* (2) "Stealing causes unhappiness"; and the grounds for asserting it may be stated as (3) "Mary stole sixpence from old Mrs. Smith and her mother and father were made very unhappy," etc. Of course, there is no

In conclusion. The anchoring of semiotic religious assertions may be of another kind. They may be anchored in *authority*. This kind of anchoring, in some ways, causes fewer difficulties for the religious believer; in some ways, more. But this is another story.

logical path from (3) to (1); but it is presumably on the basis of (3) that a Utilitarian feels justified in asserting (1). For an Intuitionist, steps (2) and (3) would be different in content but not in form.

XI

A Neglected Use of Theological Language

ROBERT C. COBURN

In recent years a number of analyses of theological discourse have been suggested and, in some instances, elaborated. Carnap's theological emotivism,[1] Braithwaite's "intentional" analysis,[2] and Hare's "quasi-attitudinal" account[3] are obvious cases in point. However, by virtue in the main of their crude and/or simplistic character, none of these analyses has won very wide-spread approval among philosophers, whether "believers" or not. This metatheological situation would seem to me to be best remedied if philosophers concerned with understanding theological discourse were to adopt the following three measures. First, to keep ever in mind Bishop Butler's remark that "everything is what it is, and not another thing"; second, to assume the applicability to theological discourse of the principle—recently labelled the Janus-principle—that linguistic expressions often can and char-

1. See R. Carnap, *Philosophy and Logical Syntax* (London, 1935) ch. 1. Carnap does not explicitly discuss theology, but what he says of metaphysics clearly indicates what he would say about theological discourse.
2. See R. B. Braithwaite, *An Empiricist's View of the Nature of Religious Belief* (Cambridge, 1953).
3. See R. M. Hare, "Religion and Morals," in *Faith and Logic*, B. Mitchell (ed.) (Boston, 1957), ch. VII.

acteristically do perform two or more jobs at once;[4] and third, to attempt more piecemeal examinations of the jobs done by theological language. At any rate, adoption of the first two measures would tend, I think, to protect philosophers against the temptation to accept or advance palpably reductionistic and/or single-track views such as the above. The third measure would seem appropriate simply by dint of the fact that often when a problem appears difficult to deal with directly and as a whole, attention to the hoary adage "divide and conquer" proves fruitful.

Accordingly, in the present paper I shall confine myself to a consideration of one use of theological language; a use, furthermore, which seems to me to be unique to this mode of discourse and which I shall assume to be neither the only nor even the essential use which this kind of language has. However, as the title of this paper indicates, I do think the use I shall consider is one which has thus far been neglected by philosophers interested in understanding theological discourse; and as the length of this paper suggests, I do think it is a use which is sufficiently important to deserve attention.

The discussion will fall into two parts. In the first I shall be concerned mainly to provide an account of the use in question. In the second I shall try to indicate the way in which the assumption that the use I have articulated is a genuine and significant one sheds light upon certain metatheological problems which arise out of reflection upon the Western theological tradition. Before proceeding to the first section of the paper, however, I want to draw attention to an important distinction in order to stifle at the outset a possible source of confusion and misunderstanding.

This is a distinction—first drawn, I believe, by Austin—concerning the notion of the use(s) of, or the job(s) done by, a piece of language—such as a sentence. Stated most simply the distinction is between (a) what one does in using a piece of language (in e.g. uttering a certain sentence), and (b) what one is trying to do in using it (that is, in, e.g. uttering the sentence in

4. Cf. P. H. Nowell-Smith, Ethics (London, 1954), p. 100.

question). Put more fully it is the distinction between the action normally or characteristically performed in using a piece of language, and the peculiar purpose a given individual tries to accomplish in using this piece of language—and *a fortiori* in performing the action its use characteristically involves. The following examples illustrate this distinction. The characteristic use of a sentence like "I admit that Saltonstall is getting on in years" is to perform the act of admitting something. But the sentence could be used on a given occasion for the purpose of encouraging somebody or reconciling somebody to something or assuaging somebody's anger, etc. Again, a sentence like "I promise to keep quiet" has as its characteristic or normal use the making of a promise of a certain kind. But it could be used on a particular occasion to get somebody to behave in a certain way, to deceive somebody about one's own intentions, to arouse somebody to action, etc.

Now the reason for introducing this distinction is simply to make clear that when, in what follows, I speak of the use(s) of, or job(s) done by, a given piece of theological language, I shall be referring to the action(s) characteristically or normally performed by an utterance[5] of the expression or sentence in question. Accordingly, when I say that such and such is a use of a sentence like "Jesus is the Christ," I shall not mean that such and such is a use to which this sentence could conceivably be put; nor should I be construed as saying that such and such is the only use to which this sentence may be put. Finally, by virtue of my assumption of the applicability of the Janus-principle to theological discourse, I should not be construed as saying that such and such is the only use which the sentence normally or characteristically has either.

I

One way of providing a rough characterization of a type of discourse is by indicating the sorts of questions which utterances

5. For ease of exposition I shall write as though all uses of language involved speaking.

of declarative sentences belonging to this type of discourse typically function to answer. Thus theoretical discourse, so-called, is sometimes characterized as consisting largely of answers to such questions as: "What sort of a bug is this?", "What are the laws of thermodynamics?", "Do blue-eyed catfish exist?", "Why do men sometimes lose control of their limbs?"; and practical discourse, so-called, similarly is characterized as consisting in the main of answers to practical questions, central among which are the questions, "What shall I (he) do?" and "What ought I (he) to do?" Now I do not know if theological discourse can be characterized in any helpful way—even roughly—by referring simply to some single type of question. But the use of theological sentences I want to consider can, I think, best be described by indicating a certain kind of question which utterances of theological sentences normally function to answer. Questions of this kind I shall call—borrowing a phrase from Toulmin—*religious limiting questions,* and preliminary to stating what a religious limiting question is it will be necessary first to explain the notion of a limiting question as I shall use it.

By a limiting question I shall mean a form of words[6] which has the grammatical structure of a question, but which is such that a typical utterance of the form of words does not amount to asking a straightforward question of either a theoretical or a practical sort. Rather, such an utterance characteristically constitutes a piece of linguistic behaviour which simply expresses and which constitutes a criterion for the presence of some state or condition of the soul, so to speak.

That there should be linguistic performances of this sort is a very natural hypothesis given the variety of considerations which render attractive the doctrines that (a) the grammatical form of an expression is often a poor clue to its "logical form," that (b) "inner processes" stand in need of outward criteria, and

6. Like "question" itself, however, I shall also use the expression "limiting question" as having a logic analogous to that of "statement" as well as that of "sentence." It will, I trust, be clear from the context how any particular occurrence of the expression is to be understood.

that (c) linguistic behaviour of certain kinds can count as cri-
teriological evidence for the presence of certain sorts of "inner
processes."

However, natural or not it is evident, I think, that this hypothesis is strongly suggested by the facts. Consider, for example,
the following question: "Why ought I to do what is right?" At
least sometimes when this question is asked by an individual,
either of himself or of another, the *prudence* of being moral is
not being inquired into. Nor, sometimes anyhow, can one make
what would be regarded by the questioner as a relevant response
by saying the kinds of things one could say in response to a
straightforwardly practical question like "Why ought I to tell
John of Mary's infidelity?"—*e.g.* that such and such a moral
principle seems to cover the case in question, or that *x* ought to
have done that last year and *x*'s situation then is clearly analogous to the one in question. Furthermore, it appears also to be
true that on some occasions when this question is raised it is
not functioning in the way such a question as "Why are all
bachelors unmarried?" at least occasionally functions. For on
some occasions anyway the asking of the question under consideration does not provide ground for thinking the person who
asks it has a defective or at least seriously deviant understanding
of such words as "ought" and "right."

What then is being done when this question is raised on occasions like the above? The answer becomes clearer, I think,
when it is recognized that often when this or a very similar question is raised, the individual raising the question is in a situation
of moral conflict, and more specifically, a situation in which the
moral demand stands in opposition to some strong non-moral
interest or desire. For in the light of this fact, the answer which
obviously suggests itself is that the question "Why ought I to do
what is right?" is functioning not as an ordinary practical question at all—as it superficially appears—, but rather, as we might
put it, as a species of learned moral-conflict behaviour.

And quite similar things can be said about at least some utterances of the following questions too: "Why did this have to

happen to me?", "What is the ultimate significance of life?", "What is the explanation of the fact that there is a world at all?" For each of these questions can be asked in such a way as clearly to have some significance, and yet also in such a way that no answer of a kind ordinarily adequate to put down questions of the sort to which each is most readily assimilated either is appropriate or satisfies the asker ("I know that acute nephritis often begins with streptococcal infection of the throat and that Susan had just such an infection several days ago; but why did this all have to happen to *my* daughter?"). Furthermore, each can be raised in such a manner that it is clearly too simple merely to say that the questioner fails fully to grasp the sense of one or more of the words his question involves. Finally when these conditions are satisfied, it appears at least sometimes to be the case that the occasions upon which these questions are raised are occasions in which the questioner is in a "spiritual" condition of some kind, a condition such as grief or despair or what William James somewhere calls *zerrissenheit,* or is engaging in a "spiritual" activity of some kind, an activity such as marvelling or worshipping or blaspheming. Accordingly, the most plausible way of viewing at least some utterances of these questions is, I submit, as limiting questions.

Having thus clarified the notion of a limiting question, it is possible now to characterize what I have called *religious* limiting questions.

There are doubtless many ways of classifying the limiting questions which might with some justice be called religious; and also it seems reasonable to suppose that there is no very clear line to be drawn separating religious limiting questions from non-religious ones. However, one helpful classification of most of the clear cases of what it is natural to speak of as religious limiting questions can be made, it seems to me, by referring to the main types of problems which it has often, and quite plausibly, been maintained are those to which the Christian religion speaks. These are: "moral" problems, problems of *morale,* and problems concerning the ultimate significance or "meaning" of things.

Problems of the first type include conflicts between duty and interest, conflicts between opposing moral outlooks, the problem of determining a proper hierarchical ordering of the various goods of life, and the problem of handling guilt. By "problems of *morale*," I mean those which arise out of our inability to reconcile ourselves to the various ills that flesh is heir to—sickness, failure, missed opportunities, and the final, ineluctable frustration of death—death of friends and family, and ultimately our own death. Under the third heading are those problems felt by all who yearn to see things whole, to find an intelligible pattern in experience, to sense the presence in the world of some "underlying unity" or "overarching purpose" which will provide the diverse works and loves of men with "coherence" and "enduring worth." By separating these problems into three groups, I do not mean to suggest, of course, that they do not overlap or merge into one another. Indeed quite the contrary is the case. An individual who finds himself facing a personal tragedy of some kind may very well begin to wonder about the "intelligibility" of the world as a whole and in consequence about the most appropriate way of life. Still, these groups of problems do seem in some cases anyhow to be more or less distinguishable; and unclean distinctions, like unclean spark plugs, seem generally to be better than none at all.

With these distinctions in mind, religious limiting questions can be characterized as that class of limiting questions the asking of which constitutes behaviour which expresses and is criteriologically connected with the condition of having or feeling a problem of one or more of the kinds just noted.

A typical religious limiting question might thus be: "What is the meaning of life?" For this is a question the asking of which on a particular occasion might be most plausibly construed as an expression of, and as non-inductive evidence of, the asker's sensing the integrity of his world to be dissolving. The other questions noted above as examples of questions the use of which on particular occasions might count as the asking of limiting questions, however, also would qualify as questions which could be used to raise religious limiting questions, and this for reasons which should now be obvious without further comment.

We are now in position to characterize the use of theological sentences to which I wish to draw attention. That use is to provide answers of a certain kind of religious limiting questions. It remains at this point but to explain the *kind* of answer which it is my claim that theological language sometimes functions to provide to these "questions," and to justify this claim.

It may very well be, of course, that theological discourse functions to answer religious limiting questions in many different ways. It may be, for example, that certain theological "statements," like "Jesus is the Christ," carry in some complicated way empirical import, and that by virtue of this semantic feature occasionally "answer" religious limiting questions as a result of drawing the questioner's attention to certain facts he has overlooked and thereby altering his "spiritual" condition so that he is no longer inclined to raise some particular limiting question. Or again, it may be that certain theological sentences carry what might be called "pictorial" import, *i.e.* tend to catalyze in those who hear these sentences uttered a certain perspective or way of looking at things, much as good metaphors do; and that by virtue of this feature also "answer" religious limiting questions by once more removing the disquietude, say, which has erupted in the asking of such a question. However, I shall not here explore these possibilities. Rather, I shall concentrate on only one kind of answer which it seems to me theological language normally functions to provide for religious limiting questions, *viz.* answers which I shall refer to as "logically complete."

By a *logically complete answer* to a question I mean an answer the acceptance of which by the person raising the question is logically incompatible with his continuing to ask the question; that is to say, incompatible in the sense that his continuing to ask the question in some form or other would normally be taken as showing either that he had not understood the answer which had previously been provided, or that he had not accepted it.

I say "normally" to bring out the fact that in special circumstances it may well be that the incompatibility of which I speak may not obtain, but that such incompatibility may nonetheless be presumed to obtain apart from any anomalies which provide reason to suppose the contrary. By making use of Nowell-Smith's notion of a logically odd question, *i.e.* a question which in a given context cannot sensibly be raised because it has already been answered, an alternative and considerably briefer account can be given as follows: an answer to a question is a logically complete one provided it renders any subsequent utterance of the question it answers logically odd.

The following pieces of dialogue illustrate this type of answer.

(1) A: Why are you listening to *that* record?
(2) B: I enjoy Mozart.
(3) A: I see; but why listen to it? (Meaning: "Why is the fact that you enjoy Mozart a good reason for listening to him?")
(4) A: Does she beileve he said it?
(5) B: She says she remembers quite distinctly his using those very words.
(6) A: I didn't ask you about her memories; what I asked is if she *believes* he said it—now does she?

In the first case, B's answer to A, (2), is clearly a logically complete one, and A's reiteration of his question, (3), is *a fortiori* logically odd, because, apart from any reason to suppose that A is trying B's patience or the like, we would take A's saying (3) as indication either that he failed to understand or to accept B's reply, or that he simply does not have an adequate grasp of the sense of the verb "to enjoy." Exactly similar remarks are *à propos* in the second case, though of course *here* we should say that A's response, (6), to B's reply to his initial query would provide reason to suppose, again apart from anomalies countering the normal presumption, that A does not fully understand that "remember" normally carries the implication of a certain degree of conviction as regards what it is that is claimed to have been remembered.

Now in contending that one important, though completely

neglected, use of theological language is that of providing logically complete answers to religious limiting questions what I am asserting is that the acceptance by a person A of theological "statements" like

S: The ways of the Almighty and all-wise God are righteous, though beyond our understanding

however "acceptance" of theological "statements" is properly understood, is logically incompatible with A's raising such a limiting question as

P: But why was *my* child crippled by polio?

That is to say, the asking of P would normally be taken to count against A's acceptance of S, the sincerity with which he uttered S, if he uttered S, or his understanding of S; and also whatever would count in favour of A's understanding of S and his genuine acceptance of S would, again normally, count against interpreting his subsequent utterance of P as the raising of a limiting question.

I should point out, however, that I do not wish to be construed as maintaining that there is any simple one-to-one correspondence between theological sentences and the sentences which can be used to put religious limiting questions. Quite to the contrary, I should say that a given theological sentence might very well be used to answer a large variety of religious limiting questions by virtue of the way in which theological discourse as a whole hangs together. Thus the assertion of a sentence like "Jesus is the Christ," because of the logical connections of the notion of the Christ with the entire Judeo-Christian framework of ideas concerning God, Creation, the Fall, etc., might very well be an appropriate "answer" to such ostensibly different limiting questions as: (*a*) "Why ought I to do what is right?", (*b*) "Why do men have such hard hearts?", (*c*) "What is the ultimate end of life?", and (*d*) "Why is there anything at all?" Though, of course, such questions might also have more directly relevant answers of a theological sort. The following would be cases in point: (*a'*) "It is God's will that we do our duty," (*b'*) "In Adam's fall all men fell from grace," (c') "The end of life is the glorification of God," and (d') "God freely chose to create the world out of nothing."

In justification of the claim that theological language does this sort of job (at least) two procedures are appropriate. One could, in the first place, try to describe actual or hypothetical situations by reference to which modes of speech come plainly into view which are clearly relevant to this claim. And, secondly, one could try to show how the hypothesis that this claim is true explains certain phenomena which otherwise seem quite baffling. In the next section of this paper I shall explore the latter approach at some length. However, by way at least of illustration of the former I should like to conclude the present section with the following brief remarks.

In *The Brothers Karamazov*, two characters appear—one a leading figure in the novel, and the other the alleged imaginative creation of this figure—each of which is extraordinary in ways which shed considerable light upon the claims under consideration. I refer to Ivan and the Grand Inquisitor.

Ivan, it will be recalled, at one point during his conversation with Alyosha in pt. II, bk. V, says

> I accept God and am glad to, and what's more I accept His wisdom, His purpose—which are utterly beyond our ken; I believe in the underlying order and the meaning of life; I believe in the eternal harmony in which they say we shall one day be blended. I believe in the Word to Which the universe is striving and Which Itself was "with God," and Which Itself is God and so on, and so on . . .

Then, shortly after this seeming confession of faith, Ivan raises the question why innocent children should suffer. "Can you understand," he says,

> why a little creature, who cannot even understand what's done to her, should beat her little aching heart with her tiny fist in the dark and cold, and weep her meek unresentful tears to dear, kind God to protect her?

And later:

> If all must suffer to pay for the eternal harmony, what have chil-
> dren to do with it, tell me, please? . . . Why should they, too,
> furnish material to enrich the soil for the harmony of the future?

The Grand Inquisitor, Ivan's creation, is similarly paradoxical.
For, on the one hand, he is described as accepting the figure
before him as the Christ, as identical with the figure who walked
the earth 1,900 years before and who came to constitute the
cynosure of the Christian faith. He asks "What use is it for me
to hide anything from Thee? Don't I know to Whom I am
speaking? All that I can say is known to Thee already." Yet,
on the other, he asks, "Why art Thou come to hinder us?", and
we are given to understand by everything that he says that he
can see no reason whatever for following Christ's example, for
accepting the Christ-like way of life as he understands it.

In short, both Ivan and the Grand Inquisitor speak of themselves as religious believers; yet each, implicitly or explicitly,
raises a certain religious limiting question.

Now the obvious question which these cases raise is: If we
accept their questions as religious limiting questions—as I think
it is clear we must—, can we also accept these people as genuine
believers? The answer which strikes me as evident is that we
cannot, and this answer, I submit, supports my contention that
theological language has the use I have suggested. It might be
said in criticism of this point, of course, that we have other
evidence in the novel that Ivan and the Grand Inquisitor are
non-believers and this is why it seems so obvious that their
ostensible claims to believe are suspect. Now I should not wish
to deny the former point; but I would quarrel with the implication drawn on the ground that even were there no such evidence, even were Ivan and the Grand Inquisitor in other respects
the spiritual twins of Alyosha and Zossima respectively, it would
still be obvious that the genuineness of their limiting questions
would count against the genuineness of their faith and/or the
depth of their understanding of theological concepts. To see

this one need but imagine Alyosha at the end of the novel alone, grieving Ilusha's death, and asking: "Why, why Ilusha; why couldn't it have been I, rather than poor little Ilusha?"; or Zossima deciding that Christ intended men to take responsibility only for their own conduct, and asking, "Then why should we live as Christ intended that we should?"

II

I turn now to the task of exhibiting the explanatory power which results when the feature of theological language I have described in the preceding section is assumed to be genuine and significant. The procedure I shall follow is to consider seriatim six matters of a primarily conceptual or metatheological nature which seem to me both to require explanation and to receive at least partial explanation when reference is made to this feature. For convenience of reference I shall at times speak of this feature in virtue of which theological language allegedly functions to provide what I have called logically complete answers to religious limiting questions as the "religious" dimension of its "meaning," or more briefly, as its "religious meaning" or "import."

If we understand the notion of "responding to life, or the world, religiously," or simply "being religious," by reference to such things as the disposition to live agapistically, to exhibit hope in times of tragedy, to take the deep things of life seriously, to engage in worshipful practices of a formal and/or an informal sort, and periodically to entertain or have in mind various of the pictures, sayings, parables, doctrines, etc., of some religious tradition, then it can be argued, I believe, that responding to life religiously is a criterion for saying of a person that he has religious belief. However, even without the argument, it should be obvious that many religious thinkers have felt a strong tendency to connect religiosity and belief in a very intimate way. St. Paul is a patent case in point: faith without love, he seems often to want to say, simply fails to be the genuine article.

Calvin is another, as comes out in the remark he somewhere makes to the effect that he who claims to believe in God but does not worship, does not respond to Him in praise and contrition, believes in an idol and not in the true God. In more recent times, one thinks of course in the present connection of Professor Tillich, for whom believing in God and having or "being grasped by" what he calls "ultimate concern" are either the same or anyhow very nearly the same thing. Now one of the matters of which any analysis of theological discourse must provide some account is just this tendency for religiosity and religious belief to coalesce.

I do not think that reference to the religious meaning of theological language enables us to provide a wholly satisfactory explanation of this phenomenon; but the following point would seem at least to contribute to what may one day qualify as such. It is clear, I believe, that satisfaction of some of the conditions which we should want to include in any analysis of religiosity— such as *e.g.* the disposition to act and feel agapistically, and to show courage and hope in times of distress—tends to be incompatible with being in those "spiritual" states which normally erupt in the asking of (at least certain) religious limiting questions. That this is also true of the other conditions we should want to include is perhaps less obvious, but nonetheless, I think, arguable. In any case, if these points can be made out, it follows from the assumption that theological "statements" possess religious meaning, that acceptance of such "statements" by an individual necessarily tends to show itself in behaviour which is either religious in character, or at least not irreligious, in as much as being in a condition which does not erupt in the asking of religious limiting questions is an essential feature of such acceptance. In other words, if it is true that theological language carries what I have called religious import, a person could not be said to have sincerely accepted such a "statement" as "God wills that we do our duty" if he continued to ask such a limiting question as "But why should I do my duty?" because of their logical incompatibility; but this means that acceptance of such theological "statements" tends to be incompatible logically with non-religiosity, by virtue of the intimate connections between religiosity and the absence of dispositions to ask religious limiting questions. Hence, the tendency for religiosity and belief to be associated in the way the Western theological tradition indicates.

A closely related problem upon which the use of theological language I have described bears in what is, I think, an illuminating way is the problem of why the man of faith, according to the tradition, is continually subject to the threat of what is sometimes referred to as "unfaith"; or, to put the matter more dramatically, why the believer is traditionally counselled ever to have on his lips the classical prayer: "O Lord, I believe; help Thou my unbelief." After all, if theological "statements" did the job simply of stating certain facts or putative facts, as seems to have been, and to be, the usual assumption, it is at least perplexing that acceptance of such "statements" should be as unstable a phenomenon as the tradition suggests. One would think that once a person had overcome whatever difficulties he might feel concerning the acceptance of some statement, his assent to it would—anyhow usually—remain relatively settled. Yet apparently it is not so for the paradigm believer; and explanations which invoke the Devil and/or Original Sin are hardly of the right sort to satisfy.

Now the explanation, or anyhow the part of the explanation, of this fact which reference to the religious dimension of the meaning of theological language yields is this. By virtue of this semantic feature of theological language, it may be said, whenever a person asks a religious limiting question he *eo ipso* rejects theological doctrine—either in part or, what is more likely because of the integrity of theological language as a whole, *in toto*. Moreover, the conditions of which the asking of religious limiting questions are more or less essential ingredients are conditions which are virtually unavoidable for normal human beings. Tragedy in some form is always with us; so also are *zerrissenheit* and moral perplexity—at least in some degree. But this is just to say that unfaith, understood as involving the rejection of theological affirmations, is virtually unavoidable—indeed almost inevitably a recurrent feature of the spiritual pilgrimage of the "believer."

A third matter which requires explanation is the agnostic strain within the theological tradition, *i.e.* the persistent tendency to understand God as an essentially mysterious entity, as a being of such a nature that all our words, not simply in fact but necessarily, fail adequately to describe or characterize Him—except, of course, insofar as they are used to say what He is not.

Doubtless as in the previous cases, this agnostic strain is "overdetermined" in the sense that many factors cooperate in moving theologians to insist upon God's essential elusiveness. But once again consideration of the use of theological discourse I have tried to bring into relief suggests what at least one of these factors may be.

Suppose the word "God" did function primarily to refer to or name an entity which logically could be described in the way ordinary persons can be described, *i.e.* not exhaustively, but nonetheless literally and as precisely and extensively as anyone might wish. Suppose further that, as a matter of fact, some definite description which is finite in length, constructible in English, and non-theological in character, *i.e.* devoid of such specifically theological words as "infinite," "holy," and the like, applies to God. On these suppositions, one could say exactly the same thing about exactly the same object by uttering the sentence "God knows our inmost thoughts" and by uttering the sentence which results when "God" in the mentioned sentence is replaced by the definite description in question. That is, the statement made by uttering the first sentence would carry the same import as that made by uttering the second—assuming anyway that the definite description in the second is used referentially rather than attributively.[7] But, in fact, if it is true that statements made by the use of sentences like "God knows our inmost thoughts"

7. This terminology is Kieth Donnellan's. See his paper "Reference and Definite Descriptions," *The Philosophical Review*, LXXV (1966).

possess religious meaning, then statements made by the use of sentences which contain a definite description of the kind in question in the place of "God" in sentences like "God knows our inmost thoughts" would not possess the same logical power as the former, the power, namely, to provide logically complete answers to religious limiting questions.

Now given these background considerations, the explanation of the theological agnosticism of the tradition which reference to the religious meaning of theological language yields would be as follows. Many theologians, it could be urged, have seen the above point concerning the irreplaceability of "God" by non-theological definite descriptions—though, to be sure, at best only through a glass darkly. But, the argument would continue, because of their uncritical acceptance of a descriptivist understanding of the use of theological sentences, and *a fortiori* their assumption that "God" functions as an ordinary proper name like "John" or "Towzer," they quite naturally have taken this fact about "God" as a clue to the nature of the peculiar being named by "God"; more specifically they have taken this fact as indicating that God is the kind of thing to which no positive, literal, non-theological descriptive phrase is truly applicable *simpliciter.*

To this account it might, of course, be replied that the reference to the religious meaning of theological "statements" which it involves is unnecessary. After all, it might be said, all this account requires is that there should be some difference in the import of a "statement" made in the utterance of a sentence like "God is love" and the statement results when "God" is replaced in the above sentence by the hypothetical, non-theological definite description; not that there should be the specific difference to which I have pointed. Clearly, there is a difference just by virtue of the fact that proper names and definite descriptions do not "mean" in the same way. A proper name in grammatical subject-position, for example, can be used only to refer, whereas a definite description in grammatical subject-position can be used either referentially or attributively. Thus, the reply might conclude, why could not the theological agnosticism of the tradition be explained by saying simply that many theologians have recognized this logical difference between proper names and definite descriptions and mistakenly expressed this insight as one concerning the nature of God?

This objection to the above account, however, is easily answered. For if the semantic difference upon which the account I have offered turns were merely a difference concerning the logical roles of proper names and definite descriptions, then it becomes difficult to see why theologians have spoken of God in ways which are different from the ways in which they have spoken of ordinary human beings. After all, human beings have proper names too; but this has led no one to say of human beings that they are essentially mysterious and unfathomable in the way God has been thought to possess these traits. To be sure, human beings can never be exhaustively described; and in this sense they too are essentially mysterious, if you like. But when it is maintained that God is mysterious, a good deal more is being maintained than this. As we have seen, what is being held is not just that no finite description expresses *all* of God's characteristics, but rather that no non-theological descriptions can be constructed which adequately express *any* of God's characteristics.

In sum, then, what I am suggesting is that if we suppose that one significant role of theological "statements" is to answer limiting questions of a certain kind in a certain way, then we enable ourselves to understand the agnostic tendency of theologians in close analogy to the way that recent analysts of moral language have suggested we understand G. E. Moore's talk about goodness as a very peculiar, "non-natural" quality. Namely, as the logical outcome of, primarily, (a) his view that "good" is not definable in or reducible to so-called "naturalistic" terms, in conjunction with (b) his assumption that the meaning of a word is the "thing" for which it "stands," or which it "denotes."

Moreover, a parallel account can be given of still a fourth matter which requires explanation, *viz.* the persistent tendency of thinkers in the Western theological tradition to reject as somehow inadequate metaphysical explications of theological concepts —and especially the concept of God. That is, the "God of the Philosopher" has traditionally been viewed as a religious monstrosity, we may say, because, in part, metaphysical translations of theological "statements" fail to answer religious limiting questions in the way the translated statements do, and this by virtue of failing to carry the same religious import as the language of the philosophically uncorrupted theologian. Though here again, the "in part" needs to be stressed. I do not, of course, wish to be construed as contending that this logical consideration is the only one which has been determinative of the anti-speculative diatribes of some of the more auspicious theologians of the tradition.

A problem closely related to this last one is the problem of why it is that the word "God" can properly—at least, I think we feel, properly in some sense—be used in the way it is by metaphysicians advancing doctrines as diverse as those of, say, Aquinas, Spinoza, Hegel, and Whitehead; or, to put the matter in an alternative way, how it is that "God" can be given these quite different meanings and yet somehow, in some sense, still express the same concept.

The answer to this question which is obviously suggested is one which closely parallels the analogous problem in moral philosophy concerning "good." It can be said that "God" expresses the same concept even when its "metaphysical" sense is quite different in one system from what it is in another because its religious meaning remains or tends to remain constant in all of its uses. That is, even though a "statement" like "God willed it" evokes quite different pictures, etc., in the systems of, say, Spinoza and Whitehead, the "statement" might very well still constitute a logically complete answer to one or more religious limiting questions despite the particular context, linguistic or otherwise, in which it is made. This fact in itself is at least a partial basis for saying, as we seem to want to, and *a fortiori* explaining how it is, that in some sense Spinoza and Whitehead are "talking about the same thing" when they use the word "God."

As a last example of the explanatory power of the feature of theological language I have articulated, let us consider the question why it has traditionally been maintained that God is a person—a supreme person, to be sure, and thus different from ordinary persons, but nonetheless in some important sense(s) still a person in just the way we are persons. Once again, however, I should like to stress at the outset that the account to follow should not be viewed as anything like a complete answer to this extremely complex question.

According to the thesis which I have advanced concerning theological discourse, one of the jobs theological "statements" do is to answer religious limiting questions in a logically complete way. Among the limiting questions which are thus answered by theological "statements" are at least some utterances of such questions as these: "Why does anything exist?", "Why is the world the way it is?", "Why is it my duty to keep promises?", "Why is life often so hard and cruel?" Now, to say that a theological "statement" like "God made the world to be as it is" answers the limiting question "Why is the world the way it is?" in a logically complete way is, it will be recalled, to say that any further inquiry as to why the world is as it is is out of place, logically inappropriate. But if "God" is thought of as referring to something, as has traditionally been the case, and if further this something is conceived of as non-personal, such further inquiry does *not* seem to be out of place. For after all, if x, something other than the deliberate action of a person, is the cause or explanation of y, there seems to be nothing peculiar in asking after the cause or explanation of x by way of gaining a "deeper" understanding of the cause of y. On the other hand, if again "God" is construed as the name of something, and this something is conceived of as personal, then it does become odd to inquire why the world is as it is once one has accepted the view that God made it to be as it is. The reason is that, as H. L. A. Hart and A. M. Honoré have recently pointed out, "in the common-sense notion of causation a deliberate human action has a special status as a cause and is not regarded in its turn as something which is caused." [8] Thus it seems not implausible to suggest that it is—at least in part—because (a) "God" has traditionally been viewed as naming something, because (b) it is a fact that if x, which is the cause (or explanation) of y, is the deliberate action of a person, then further inquiry concerning the cause or explanation of x is often inappropriate, and because (c) theological language functions to provide logically complete answers to religious limiting questions, that there has been a powerful tendency in the Western theological tradition to think of God in personal terms.

POSTSCRIPT, 1968: This essay has been reprinted with only minor changes. If I were to write afresh on this topic, I would not say many of the things written here or would say them differently. However, I still think that there is a kernel of truth, perhaps, in the central idea.

8. H. L. A. Hart and A. M. Honoré, "Causation in the Law," *Law Quarterly Review,* 72 (1956), 77.

Notes on the Contributors

Dallas M. High (editor of the present volume) is Associate Professor of Philosophy and Religion at Hiram College; effective Fall 1969, Associate Professor of Philosophy and Chairman of the Department, University of Kentucky. He is the author of *Language, Persons, and Belief,* published in 1967.

Erich Heller is Professor of German at Northwestern University. His writings include many essays, articles, and books. Among his books are *The Hazard of Modern Poetry* (1953); *The Disinherited Mind* (1957); *Thomas Mann: The Ironic German* (1961); and *The Artist's Journey into the Interior* (1965).

Paul L. Holmer is Professor of Theology at Yale University Divinity School. He is the author of *Theology and the Scientific Study of Religion* (1961) and *Youth Considers Doubt and Frustration* (1967). His articles and essays have appeared in numerous journals.

I. T. Ramsey is Bishop of Durham (England) and former Nolloth Professor of the Philosophy of the Christian Religion, University of Oxford. Among his widely influential writings are *Religious Language* (1957); *Freedom and Immortality* (1960); *On Being*

Sure in Religion (1963); *Models and Mystery* (1964); *Christian Discourse* (1965).

Frederick Ferré is Professor of Philosophy at Dickinson College. In addition to essays and articles in journals he has authored *Language, Logic and God* (1961); *Basic Modern Philosophy of Religion* (1967); and co-authored *Exploring the Logic of Faith* (1962).

C. B. Daly is Bishop of Ardagh and Clonmacnois (Ireland) and former Lecturer in Scholastic Philosophy at The Queen's University of Belfast. He has written many essays and articles on philosophy and religion for learned journals.

William H. Poteat is Professor of Christianity and Culture at Duke University. He is co-editor and contributor to *Intellect and Hope: Essays in the Thought of Michael Polanyi* (1968) and has published numerous articles on the meaning of religious language.

Basil Mitchell is Nolloth Professor of the Philosophy of the Christian Religion, University of Oxford. As well as a regular contributor to philosophical journals, he is the author of *Law, Morality and Religion in a Secular Society* (1967).

Thomas McPherson is Senior Lecturer in Philosophy at the University College of South Wales and Monmouthshire. He has written on philosophical and religious subjects for many journals and is the author of a book, *Philosophy of Religion* (1965).

Robert C. Coburn is Associate Professor of Philosophy at the University of Chicago. He has published articles and essays on philosophy and religion.

Index of Names

238